Dinner a Day

People with Diabetes Cookbook

Creative and Healthy Recipes for Every Night of the Year

∾

PAMELA RICE HAHN
with BRIERLEY E. WRIGHT, R.D.

A adamsmedia

Avon, Massachusetts

Published by
Adams Media, an F+W Publications Company
57 Littlefield Street, Avon, MA 02322. U.S.A.
www.adamsmedia.com

ISBN 10: 1-59869-833-8
ISBN 13: 978-1-59869-833-6

Printed in China.

J I H G F E D C B A

Library of Congress Cataloging-in-Publication Data
is available from the publisher.

This publication is designed to provide accurate and authoritative information
with regard to the subject matter covered. It is sold with the understanding that
the publisher is not engaged in rendering legal, accounting, or other professional advice. If legal advice or other expert assistance is required, the services
of a competent professional person should be sought.
　　　—From a *Declaration of Principles* jointly adopted by a Committee of the
American Bar Association and a Committee of Publishers and Associations

Many of the designations used by manufacturers and sellers to distinguish their
product are claimed as trademarks. Where those designations appear in this
book and Adams Media was aware of a trademark claim, the designations have
been printed with initial capital letters.

Contains material adapted and abridged from *The Everything® Diabetes Cookbook*
by Pamela Rice Hahn, copyright © 2002 by F+W Publications, Inc.; and *The
Everything® Sugar-Free Cookbook* by Nancy T. Maar, copyright © 2008 by F+W Publications, Inc.

Dinner a Day: for People with Diabetes Cookbook is intended as a reference volume
only, not as a medical manual. In light of the complex, individual, and specific
nature of health problems, this book is not intended to replace professional
medical advice. The ideas, procedures, recipes, and suggestions in this book
are intended to supplement, not replace, the advice of a trained medical professional. Consult your physician before adopting the suggestions in this book,
as well as about any condition that may require diagnosis or medical attention.
The authors and publisher disclaim any liability arising directly or indirectly
from the use of this book.

This book is available at quantity discounts for bulk purchases.
For information, please call 1-800-289-0963.

Contents

Introduction

❧**Making** dietary changes to manage your (or a family member's) diabetes may seem intimidating at first, especially when you consider that what you eat is just one component of diabetes management. However, the eating habits that control your diabetes are really just the same as any other plan for a better diet, and when viewed as healthy choices and realistic goals—as opposed to rigid rules and regulations—you'll find the diet component of diabetes simple to manage, and hopefully even a fun learning experience for you and your family. Before you know it, it will be easier to maintain near-normal blood glucose levels. Talk with your dietitian and medical provider to set guidelines and goals for delicious meals and healthful living first; then dive into this cookbook for quick and easy diabetic-friendly dinner solutions that are in line with your diet goals. You'll find with *Dinner a Day: for People with Diabetes Cookbook* your entire family—diabetic or not—will enjoy dinner. Even better, monotonous dinners stop here! This cookbook boasts a year's worth of dinner for you and your family. You'll find it chock full of variety—from appetizers and small meals to breakfast for dinner, meat and meatless options, and sweet treats. If family dinner is a staple in your house, you've come to the right place! Bon appétit!

1

Appetizers and Small Meals

~**Pita** and bread are great to pair with these dips, but remember to account for their carbohydrate content. Check the nutrition facts label for grams of carbohydrate per serving.

Cucumber Slices with Smoked Salmon Cream

Yields: about ½ cup
Serving size: 1 teaspoon

stats **Per serving:**

Calories:..............27.39
Protein:...............1.18 g
Carbohydrates: ....0.53 g
Fat:....................2.32 g
Sat. Fat:...............1.40 g

2–3 cucumbers
1 ounce Ducktrap River smoked
    salmon
8 ounces Neufchâtel cheese, room
    temperature
½ tablespoon lemon juice
½ teaspoon freshly ground pepper
Dried dill (optional)

1. Cut the cucumbers into slices about ¼-inch thick. Place the slices on paper towels to drain while you prepare the salmon cream.

2. Combine the smoked salmon, Neufchâtel cheese, lemon juice, and pepper in a food processor; blend until smooth.

3. Fit a pastry bag with your choice of tip; spoon the salmon cream into the bag. Pipe 1 teaspoon of the salmon cream atop each cucumber slice. Garnish with dried dill, if desired.

Comparative Analysis

If you choose to use cream cheese instead of Neufchâtel, the Nutritional Analysis will be: Calories: 35.48; Protein: 0.96 g; Carbohydrate: 0.50 g; Fat: 3.36 g; Sat. Fat: 2.05 g; Cholesterol: 10.15 mg; Sodium: 40.81 mg.

Flaxseed Oil–Fortified Salsa Dip

Yields:: about 1 cup
Serving size: 1 tablespoon

stats **Per serving:**

Calories:.............18.12
Protein:..............0.21 g
Carbohydrates: ......0.75 g
Fat:.................1.50 g
Sat. Fat:..............0.13 g

⅛ cup flaxseed oil
½ cup mild salsa
1 teaspoon freeze-dried chives
1 teaspoon dried basil
Pinch of sea salt
¼ cup chopped onion

Blend all the ingredients together in food processor or blender for a smooth dip; otherwise, mix thoroughly with a fork.

Preventative Measures

Whole-ground flaxseed is rich in phytoestrogens (the plant substances that mimic the female sex hormone estrogen) in even greater quantities than in soy, so it's now also considered another possible way to help prevent breast cancer in postmenopausal women. Flaxseed also has omega-3 and -6 essential fatty acids, both of which are known for their health benefits. (Source: *WebMDHealth, http://my.webmd.com*)

Lemon Tahini Vegetable Dip

Yields: about 5 cups
Serving size: 1 tablespoon

stats **Per serving:**

Calories:.............26.27
Protein:..............1.15 g
Carbohydrates: ......0.76 g
Fat:.................2.32 g
Sat. Fat:..............0.31 g

1 cup sesame seeds
¼ cup lemon juice
1 cup water
2 tablespoons ground flaxseed
1 teaspoon garlic powder
⅛ teaspoon cider vinegar
1 teaspoon sea salt

Put all the ingredients in a food processor; blend until smooth.

3

Garlic and Feta Cheese Dip

Yields: 1½ cups
Serving size: 1 tablespoon

stats **Per serving:**

Calories: 11.48
Protein: . . . . .0.28 g
Carbohydrates: . . . . . .0.29 g
Fat: . . . . .1.04 g
Sat. Fat: . . . . .0.54 g

½ cup feta cheese, crumbled
4 ounces softened cream cheese
¼ cup Hellmann's or Best Foods Real
    Mayonnaise
1 clove dry-roasted garlic (see Dry
    Roasted Garlic, below)
¼ teaspoon dried basil
¼ teaspoon dried cilantro or oregano
⅛ teaspoon dried dill
⅛ teaspoon dried thyme

In a food processor, combine all the ingredients and process until thoroughly mixed. Cover and chill until ready to serve with assorted vegetables.

tip

This dip is somewhat high in fat if you use regular cream cheese, whereas nonfat cream cheese would lower the total fat in this recipe by 38 grams. People on a salt-restricted diet need to check with their dietitians about using nonfat cream cheese because it's much higher in sodium.

Dry-Roasted Garlic

Roasted garlic is delicious spread on toasted baguette slices, but is also flavorful in some of the salad dressings and other recipes in this book. The traditional method calls for roasting a full head of garlic in olive oil. Dry roasting works just as well and doesn't add fat.

Preheat oven to 350°F and lightly spray a small, covered baking dish with nonstick spray. Slice off ½ inch from the top of each garlic head and rub off any loose skins, being careful not to separate the cloves. Place the garlic in a baking dish, cut-side up (if roasting more than 1 head of garlic, arrange them in the dish so that they don't touch). Cover and bake until the garlic cloves are very tender when pierced, about 30–45 minutes. Roasted garlic heads will keep in the refrigerator for 2 to 3 days.

Spicy Almond Dip

Yields: about ½ cup
Serving size: 1 tablespoon

stats **Per serving:**

Calories: 22.57
Protein: . . . . .0.73 g
Carbohydrates: . . . . . .1.47 g
Fat: . . . . .1.69 g
Sat. Fat: . . . . .0.14 g

¼ cup ground, raw almonds
2 teaspoons Worcestershire sauce
½ teaspoon honey
½ teaspoon chili powder
1 teaspoon poppy seeds
½ teaspoon onion powder
⅛ cup water
Pinch of black pepper

Put all the ingredients in a food processor; blend until smooth.

Cinnamon Nut Butter

Yields: ¾ cup
Serving size: 1 teaspoon

 Per serving:

Calories: 17.10
Protein: . . . . .0.55 g
Carbohydrates: . . . . . .1.06 g
Fat: . . . . .1.33 g
Sat. Fat: . . . . .0.15 g

¼ cup sesame seeds
¼ cup ground almonds
¼ cup sunflower seeds
1 tablespoon honey
½ teaspoon cinnamon
Pinch of cocoa (optional)
Pinch of sea salt (optional)

Put all the ingredients in a food processor; blend to desired consistency, scraping down the sides of the bowl as necessary. Serve with toast points, crackers, or celery sticks. Refrigerate any leftovers.

6

Onion Dip

Yields: 1½ cups
Serving size: 1 tablespoon

 Per serving, without salt:

Calories: 12.07
Protein: . . . . 0.60 g
Carbohydrates: . . . . . . 1.15 g
Fat: . . . . 0.59 g
Sat. Fat: . . . . 0.09 g

1 cup nonfat yogurt
1 tablespoon olive oil
½ cup water
1 teaspoon lemon juice
1 teaspoon cider vinegar
1 medium-sized sweet onion,
     chopped
Sea salt to taste (optional)
Lemon pepper to taste (optional)

Combine all the ingredients in a food processor; pulse to desired consistency. Refrigerate for 1 hour before serving to allow the flavors to merge.

Quick Thickener

If your dip or spread is too runny, stir in ¼ teaspoon of potato flour. Let it set for 1 to 2 minutes, then add more flour if necessary. The addition of potato flour won't make a significant change to the flavor or Exchange Approximations.

French Onion Soup Dip

Yields: about 1¾ cups
Serving size: 1 tablespoon

stats **Per serving:**

Calories:............6.92
Protein:............1.04 g
Carbohydrates: ......0.48 g
Fat:................0.08 g
Sat. Fat:............0.05 g

1 cup chopped sweet onion
2 tablespoons reduced (double-
    strength) beef broth
1 tablespoon Parmesan cheese
1 cup nonfat cottage cheese

1. Put the onion and beef broth in a micro-wave-safe dish. Cover and microwave on high for 1 minute; stir. Continue to microwave on high for 30-second intervals until the onion is transparent. Stir in Parmesan cheese. Set aside and allow to cool.

2. In a blender, process the cottage cheese until smooth. Mix the cottage cheese into the onion mixture. Serve warm or refrigerate until needed and serve cold.

Guilt-Free Flavors

Adjust the flavor of dips or spreads without adding calories by adding onion or garlic powder or your choice of herbs.

Horseradish Dip

Yields: 1¾ cups
Serving size: 1 tablespoon

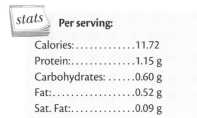 **Per serving:**

Calories: 11.72
Protein: . . . . 1.15 g
Carbohydrates: . . . . . . 0.60 g
Fat: . . . . 0.52 g
Sat. Fat: . . . . 0.09 g

1 cup nonfat cottage cheese
1 tablespoon olive oil
½ cup nonfat plain yogurt
3 tablespoons prepared horseradish
1 teaspoon lemon juice
Optional seasonings to taste:
Onion powder to taste
Pinch of cumin
Sea salt
Pinch of ginger

Combine all the ingredients in a blender or food processor; process until smooth.

Bean Dip

Yields: about 2 cups
Serving size: 1 tablespoon

stats **Per serving:**

Calories:............6.76
Protein:.............0.39 g
Carbohydrates: ......1.36 g
Fat:.................0.03 g
Sat. Fat:.............0.01 g

½ cup cooked pinto (or other) beans
1 tablespoon Bragg's Liquid Aminos
3 tablespoons cider vinegar
1 teaspoon honey
¼ teaspoon dried basil
¼ teaspoon dried parsley
1 stalk celery, diced
¼ cup chopped green onion
½ cup alfalfa sprouts, lightly chopped
1 medium tomato, diced

Add the beans, Liquid Aminos, cider vinegar, honey, and dried herbs to a blender; process until smooth. Stir in remaining ingredients.

Low-Sodium Substitutions

Bragg's Liquid Aminos is a lower-sodium substitution for soy sauce. Because Bragg's isn't a fermented product, many people who can't tolerate soy can use it.

Garbanzo Dip

Yields: about 2 cups
Serving size: 1 tablespoon

 Per serving:

Calories: 25.44
Protein: . . . . .1.64 g
Carbohydrates: . . . . . .4.79 g
Fat: . . . . .0.06 g
Sat. Fat: . . . . .0.02 g

3 cups cooked garbanzo (or other)
    white beans
½ teaspoon ground cumin
1 tablespoon lemon juice
1 tablespoon parsley flakes
¼ teaspoon dried basil
1 teaspoon onion powder
¼ teaspoon garlic powder
1 tablespoon honey

Combine all the ingredients in a food processor or blender; process until smooth. Add 1 teaspoon of water or bean broth if you need to thin the dip.

Herbed Cheese Spread

Yields: about 1 cup
Serving size: 1 tablespoon

stats **Per serving:**

Calories: 20.06
Protein: . . . . .1.34 g
Carbohydrates: . . . . . .0.32 g
Fat: . . . . .1.50 g
Sat. Fat: . . . . .0.94 g

2 teaspoons chopped fresh parsley
  leaves
2 teaspoons chopped fresh chives
1 teaspoon chopped fresh thyme
½ cup nonfat cottage cheese
½ teaspoon freshly ground black
  pepper
4 ounces Neufchâtel cheese, room
  temperature

Place the herbs in a food processor; pulse until chopped. Add the cheeses; process until smooth.

Toasted Nut Garnish

Herbed Cheese Spread is good on Garlic Toast (see page 279) sprinkled with a few toasted pine nuts, sunflower or sesame seeds, or other chopped nuts. Toast the nuts in a small skillet in a single layer. Over low heat, toast until lightly golden, stirring often to prevent burning. This takes 3 to 4 minutes. Cool on paper towels.

Smoked Mussel Spread

Yields: 4¼ cup
Serving size: 1 tablespoon

 stats **Per serving:**

Calories:...........20.51
Protein:............1.21 g
Carbohydrates: ......0.78 g
Fat:................1.40 g
Sat. Fat:............0.77 g

4 ounces cream cheese
1 cup nonfat plain yogurt
½ cup nonfat cottage cheese
2 ounces Ducktrap River smoked
    mussels
¼ cup chopped onion or scallion
1 teaspoon dried dill
1 teaspoon dried parsley

Place all the ingredients in a food processor or blender; process until smooth. Chill for at least 2 hours or overnight before serving.

 tip

This spread also works well made with smoked oysters, shrimp, or turkey.
Serve on crackers or cracker-sized bread rounds.

Conservative Exchanges

Keep in mind that whenever Exchange Approximations are given in this book, it's always with an "err on the side of caution" philosophy, so the numbers are rounded up.

Zesty Almond Spread

Yields: about ¼ cup
Serving size: 1 tablespoon

stats **Per serving, without salt:**

Calories:.............50.13
Protein:..............1.54 g
Carbohydrates: ......3.73 g
Fat:..................3.65 g
Sat. Fat:.............0.28 g

30 unsalted almonds
2 teaspoons honey
1 teaspoon chili powder
¼ teaspoon garlic powder
Pinch of sea salt (optional)

Place all the ingredients in a food processor or blender; process to desired consistency.

Easy Olive Spread

Yields: about 3 cups
Serving size: 1 tablespoon

stats **Per serving:**

Calories: 15.01
Protein: . . . . .0.67 g
Carbohydrates: . . . . . .0.74 g
Fat: . . . . .1.11 g
Sat. Fat: . . . . .0.30 g

1 cup black olives
3 cloves garlic
1 tablespoon fresh Italian flat-leaf parsley
1 tablespoon fresh basil
2 teaspoons minced lemon zest
Freshly ground black pepper to taste
½ cup nonfat cottage cheese
2 tablespoons cream cheese
1 tablespoon Hellmann's or Best Foods Real Mayonnaise

1. Combine the olives, garlic, herbs, and spices in a food processor; pulse until chopped. Transfer to a bowl and set aside.

2. Add the cottage cheese, cream cheese, and mayonnaise to the blender or food processor; process until smooth. Fold the cheese mixture into the chopped olive mixture.

Delicious Substitutions

Substitute marinated mushrooms or artichoke hearts for the olives in the Easy Olive Spread recipe.

Mushroom Caviar

Yields: about 3 cups
Serving size: 1 tablespoon

stats **Per serving:**

Calories: 8.77
Protein: . . . . .0.25 g
Carbohydrates: . . . . . .0.77 g
Fat: . . . . .0.61 g
Sat. Fat: . . . . .0.08 g

1½ cups portobello mushrooms
1½ cups white button mushrooms
¼ cup chopped scallions
4 cloves dry-roasted garlic (see Dry-
     Roasted Garlic on page 4)
1 teaspoon fresh lemon juice
½ teaspoon balsamic vinegar
1 tablespoon extra-virgin olive oil
½ teaspoon fresh, chopped thyme
     (optional)
Sea salt and freshly ground black
     pepper to taste (optional)

1. Cut the portobello mushrooms into ¼-inch cubes. Cut the white button mushrooms into halves or quarters. The mushroom pieces should be roughly uniform in size. Place the mushrooms and chopped scallion in a microwave-safe bowl; cover, and microwave on high for 1 minute. Rotate the bowl. Microwave for 30-second intervals until tender.

2. Transfer scallions and mushrooms to a food processor. Reserve any liquid to use for thinning the caviar, if necessary. Pulse food processor several times to chop the mixture, scraping down sides of the bowl as needed. Add remaining ingredients; pulse until mixed. Place in a small crock or serving bowl. Serve warm.

tip

Refrigerated leftovers will last a few days. Spread on toasted bread and pop under the broiler for 1–2 minutes for tasty mushroom-garlic toast.

Pseudo-Sauté

When onions and scallions are sautéed in butter or oil, they go through a caramelization process that doesn't occur when they're steamed. To create this flavor without increasing the fat in a recipe, transfer steamed vegetables to a nonstick wok or skillet (coated with nonstick spray, or a small portion of the oil called for in the recipe) and sauté until the extra moisture evaporates.

Gluten-Free Sesame Seed Crackers

Yields: 36 crackers
Serving size: 1 cracker

 Per serving:

Calories: 49.85
Protein: . . . . .1.98 g
Carbohydrates: . . . . . .5.01 g
Fat: . . . . .2.71 g
Sat. Fat: . . . . .0.37 g

1½ cups spelt flour
1 cup sesame seeds
¼ cup arrowroot
1 tablespoon olive or vegetable oil
3 tablespoons nonfat yogurt
¼ cup nonfat dry milk
½ teaspoon Ener-G nonaluminum
    baking powder
½ cup water
⅔ teaspoon sea salt (optional)

1. Preheat oven to 400°F. Mix together all ingredients; add water a little at a time to form a soft dough-like consistency. Be careful not to work the dough too much; you do not want to knead spelt flour.

2. On a floured surface, use a rolling pin to roll the dough until it's ⅛-inch thick. Use a cookie cutter to cut it into shapes (or use a pizza cutter to crosscut the dough into square- or rectangular-shaped crackers); place them on a cookie sheet treated with nonstick spray. Prick each cracker with a fork. Bake for about 12 minutes, or until golden brown. Store cooled crackers in an airtight container.

Almond Honey Mustard

Yields: about ½ cup
Serving size: 1 teaspoon

stats **Per serving, without salt:**

Calories: 20.53
Protein: . . . . 0.47 g
Carbohydrates: . . . . . . 1.07 g
Fat: . . . . 1.77 g
Sat. Fat: . . . . 0.17 g

¼ cup unsalted almond butter
2 teaspoons mustard
1 teaspoon honey
2 tablespoons lemon juice
½ teaspoon garlic powder
Pinch of cumin (optional)
Pinch of sea salt (optional)

Add all the ingredients to a food processor or blender; process until smooth.

CHAPTER

2

Breakfast and Brunch Foods for Dinner

Egg-White Pancakes

Serves 2

 stats **Per serving:**

Calories:............197.11
Protein:..............13.62 g
Carbohydrates: ......30.53 g
Fat:.................2.69 g
Sat. Fat:.............0.47 g

4 egg whites
½ cup oatmeal
4 teaspoons reduced-calorie or low-
*   sugar strawberry jam*
1 teaspoon powdered sugar

1. Put all the ingredients in a blender; process until smooth.

2. Preheat a nonstick pan treated with cooking spray over medium heat. Pour half of the mixture into the pan; cook 4–5 minutes. Flip the pancake and cook until the inside of the cake is cooked. Repeat, using remaining batter for second pancake.

3. Dust each pancake with the powdered sugar, if using.

Creative Toppings

Experiment with toast and pancake toppings. Try a tablespoon of raisins, almonds, apples, bananas, berries, nut butters (limit these to 1 teaspoon per serving), peanuts, pears, walnuts, or wheat germ.

Buckwheat Pancakes

Serves 2

 stats **Per serving:**

Calories: 220.00
Protein:. . . . . .11.00 g
Carbohydrates: . . . . . .44.00 g
Fat:. . . . . .1.00 g
Sat. Fat:. . . . . .0.00 g

1 cup whole-wheat flour
½ cup buckwheat flour
1½ teaspoons baking powder
2 egg whites
¼ cup apple juice concentrate
1¼–1½ cups skim milk

1. Sift the flours and baking powder together. Combine the egg whites, apple juice concentrate, and 1¼ cups of the skim milk. Add the milk mixture to the dry ingredients; mix well, but do not overmix. Add the remaining milk if necessary to reach the desired consistency.

2. Cook the pancakes over medium heat in a nonstick skillet or on a griddle treated with nonstick spray.

Eggs Benedict Redux

Serves 1

 stats **Per serving:**

Calories: 317.66
Protein:. . . . . .18.26 g
Carbohydrates: . . . . . .36.75 g
Fat:. . . . . .11.20 g
Sat. Fat:. . . . . .3.33 g

1 (2-ounce) slice reduced-calorie oat-
    bran bread
1 egg
1 ounce Ducktrap River smoked
    salmon
1 teaspoon fresh lemon juice
2 tablespoons nonfat plain yogurt

1. Toast the bread and poach the egg. Place the salmon over the top of the toasted bread. Top the salmon with the poached egg.

2. Stir the lemon juice into the yogurt and spoon that mixture over the top of the egg; serve immediately.

21

Berry Puff Pancakes

Serves 6

 stats **Per serving:**

Calories: 110
Protein: . . . . .5 g
Carbohydrates: . . . . . .36.75 g
Fat: . . . . .2 g
Sat. Fat: . . . . .1 g

2 large whole eggs
1 large egg white
½ cup skim milk
½ cup all-purpose flour
1 tablespoon granulated sugar
⅛ teaspoon sea salt
2 cups of fresh berries, such as
  raspberries, blackberries,
  boysenberries, blueberries,
  strawberries, or a combination
1 tablespoon powdered sugar

1. Preheat oven to 450°F. Treat a 10-inch ovenproof skillet or deep pie pan with non-stick spray. Once the oven is heated, place the pan in the oven for a few minutes to get hot.

2. Add the eggs and egg white to a medium bowl; beat until mixed. Whisk in the milk. Slowly whisk in the flour, sugar, and salt.

3. Remove the preheated pan from the oven; pour the batter into it. Bake for 15 minutes. Reduce the heat to 350°F and bake for an additional 10 minutes, or until the batter is puffed and brown. Remove from the oven; slide the puffed pancake onto a serving plate. Cover the pancake with the fruit and sift the powdered sugar over the top. Cut into 6 equal wedges and serve.

Syrup Substitutes

Spreading 2 teaspoons of your favorite Smucker's Low Sugar jam or jelly on a waffle or pancake not only gives you a sweet topping, it can be one of your Free Exchange List choices for the day.

Buttermilk Pancakes

Serves 2

stats **Per serving:**

Calories: 143.32
Protein: . . . . .5.72 g
Carbohydrates: . . . . . .25.87 g
Fat: . . . . .1.60 g
Sat. Fat: . . . . .0.51 g

1 cup all-purpose flour
2 tablespoons nonfat buttermilk
*   powder*
¼ teaspoon baking soda
½ teaspoon low-salt baking powder
1 cup water

1. Blend together all the ingredients; add more water if necessary to get batter consistency you desire.

2. Pour a quarter of the batter into a nonstick skillet or a skillet treated with nonstick cooking spray. Cook over medium heat until bubbles appear on the top half of the pancake. Flip and continue cooking until the center of pancake is done. Repeat process with remaining batter.

Nut-Butter Batter

For a change of pace, try adding 1 Exchange amount per serving of nut butter to pancake batter, and then use jelly or jam instead of syrup.

Sweet-Potato Flour Crêpes

Yields: 10 crepes
Serving size: 1 crepe

 Per serving:

Calories: 67
Protein: . . . . .2.79 g
Carbohydrates: . . . . . .11 g
Fat: . . . . .1.1 g
Sat. Fat: . . . . .0.35 G

2 eggs
¾ cup Ener-G sweet-potato flour
½ teaspoon vanilla
1 cup skim milk
1 tablespoon nonfat dry milk
Pinch of sea salt

1. Put all the ingredients in a blender or food processor; process until the mixture is the consistency of cream.

2. To prepare the crêpes, treat an 8-inch non-stick skillet heated over medium heat with nonstick spray. Pour about 2 tablespoons of the crêpe batter into the hot pan, tilting in a circular motion until the batter spreads evenly over the pan. Cook the crêpe until the outer edges just begin to brown and loosen from the pan. Flip the crêpe to the other side and cook about 30 seconds. Using a thin spatula, lift the crêpe from the pan and place on warm plate. Continue until all the crêpes are done.

Fruit Smoothie

Serves 1

 stats **Per serving:**

The Nutritional Analysis and Fruit Exchange for this recipe will depend on your choice of fruit. Otherwise, allow ½ Skim Milk Exchange and ½ Misc. Food Exchange. The wheat germ adds fiber, but at less than 20 calories a serving, it can count as 1 Free Exchange.

1 cup skim milk
2 Exchange servings of any diced fruit
1 tablespoon honey
4 teaspoons toasted wheat germ
6 large ice cubes

Put all the ingredients into a blender or food processor; process until thick and smooth!

Batch 'Em

Make large batches of smoothies so you can keep single servings in the freezer. Get out a serving as you begin to get ready for your day. This should give the smoothie time to thaw enough for you to stir it when you're ready to have breakfast.

Tofu Smoothie

Serves 1

 stats **Per serving:**

Calories: 287.79
Protein: . . . . .19.83 g
Carbohydrates: . . . . . .35.01 g
Fat: . . . . .10.96 g
Sat. Fat: . . . . .1.60 g

1⅓ cups frozen unsweetened
*   strawberries*
½ of a banana
½ cup (4 ounces) silken tofu

In a food processor or blender, process all the ingredients until smooth. Add a little chilled water for thinner smoothies if desired.

Overnight Oatmeal

Serves 4

stats **Per serving:**

Calories: 220.76
Protein: . . . . .8.77 g
Carbohydrates: . . . . . .42.19 g
Fat: . . . . .2.88 g
Sat. Fat: . . . . .0.53 g

1 cup steel-cut oats
14 dried apricot halves
1 dried fig
2 tablespoons golden raisins
4 cups water
½ cup mock cream

Add all the ingredients to a slow cooker with a ceramic interior; set to low heat. Cover and cook overnight (for 8–9 hours).

Baked Grapefruit

Yields: 2 servings
Serving size: ½ grapefruit

stats **Per serving:**

Calories: 92.5
Protein: . . . . .1.2 g
Carbohydrates: . . . . . .17.7 g
Sugar: . . . . .12.45 g
Fat: . . . . .4 g

1 large grapefruit, halved and
    sectioned
2 tablespoons Splenda Brown
2 teaspoons buttery spread
Whole strawberries for garnish

Preheat oven to 400°F. Place the grapefruit halves on a pan. Sprinkle with Splenda Brown, dot with buttery spread, and bake 10 minutes. Garnish with strawberries.

Grilled, Baked, and Broiled Fruit

You can create excellent side dishes by cooking fruit in either a sweet or a savory manner. Add green grapes to your poached chicken or pears to your duckling. Aside from being delicious, fruit is good for you!

Egg Clouds on Toast

Serves 1

 stats **Per serving:**

Calories: 56.68
Protein: . . . . .4.42 g
Carbohydrates: . . . . . .9.28 g
Fat: . . . . .0.43 g
Sat. Fat: . . . . .0.07 g

2 egg whites
½ teaspoon sugar
1 cup water
*1 tablespoon frozen apple juice
   concentrate*
*1 slice reduced-calorie oat-bran
   bread, lightly toasted*

1. In a copper bowl, beat the egg whites until they thicken. Add the sugar; continue to beat until stiff peaks form.

2. In a small saucepan, heat the water and apple juice over medium heat until it just begins to boil; reduce heat and allow mixture to simmer. Drop the egg whites by the teaspoonful into the simmering water. Simmer for 3 minutes; turn the egg-white "clouds" over and simmer an additional 3 minutes.

3. Ladle the "clouds" over the bread and serve immediately.

tip

Additional serving suggestions:
Spread 1 teaspoon of low-sugar or all-fruit spread on the toast (½ Fruit Exchange) before you ladle on the "clouds." Or, for cinnamon French-style toast, sprinkle ¼ teaspoon cinnamon and ½ teaspoon powdered sugar (less than 10 calories) over the top of the clouds.

Smoked Bacon Breakfast Sandwiches

Yields: 2 servings
Serving size: 1 sandwich

stats **Per serving:**

Calories: 456.68
Protein: . . . . .15.31 g
Carbohydrates: . . . . . .32.28 g
Sugar: . . . . .4.28 g
Fat: . . . . .31.2 g

4 slices smoked bacon
4 slices sugar-free whole-wheat bread
2 teaspoons mayonnaise
Dijon mustard to taste
2 medium-sized tomatoes, sliced
8 fresh basil leaves
2 ounces sharp Cheddar cheese,
    grated
Freshly ground black pepper to taste
2 tablespoons butter or cholesterol-
    free margarine

1. Wrap bacon in paper towels and micro-wave until crisp.

2. Spread half of the bread slices with mayonnaise and mustard. Add the bacon, tomato, basil, and cheese. Sprinkle with pepper. Top with remaining bread slices.

3. Melt the butter over medium heat in a large frying pan. Pan-grill the sandwiches until cheese melts and they are brown on both sides.

tip

You'll soon become very educated in the art of reading labels if you're on a sugar-free diet. You'll also start making sugar substitutions in your own recipes.

Breakfast Sausage

Yields: 6 servings
Serving size: 4½ ounces each
patty

 Per serving:

Calories: 273
Protein: . . . . .20.42 g
Carbohydrates: . . . . . .0.65 g
Sugar: . . . . .0 g
Fat: . . . . .20.6 g

1 pound lean ground pork
½ pound ground veal
¼ pound ground sirloin or chuck
2 tablespoons fresh shredded sage
    leaves or 1 tablespoon dried sage
¼ teaspoon ground nutmeg
¼ teaspoon ground cloves
1 teaspoon Splenda Brown
1 teaspoon Worcestershire sauce
1 teaspoon fine sea salt
1 teaspoon coarsely ground black
    pepper
2 tablespoons canola or peanut oil

Thoroughly mix all of the ingredients except
for the canola oil. Form the meat and seasonings into patties. Heat the oil over medium
heat; fry the sausages for about 4 minutes
per side.

Homemade Sausage

You can vary the meats you use to make your
sausage, but pork is a traditional staple. You can
change the spices, using more or less cloves or
nutmeg or adding a pinch of cinnamon. You can
also make the sausage even more savory by adding some onion and fresh garlic.

Salt-and-Sugar-Cured Salmon

Yields: 12 servings
Serving size: ¼ pound

stats **Per serving:**

Calories: 216
Protein: . . . . .30 g
Carbohydrates: . . . . . .3 g
Sugar: . . . . .0 g
Fat: . . . . .9.6 g

*3-pound filet of salmon, skin on,
    scaled, and halved laterally*
⅓ cup kosher salt
½ cup Splenda
1 large bunch dill weed
*1 teaspoon freshly ground or coarsely
    crushed black pepper*
*1 inch gingerroot, peeled and
    chopped*

1. Place the salmon in a glass baking dish. Combine remaining ingredients in a separate bowl. Spread over the salmon.

2. Cover with foil or plastic wrap. Refrigerate for 6 hours. Turn the fish and refrigerate for 6 hours. Repeat process for 48 hours. Scrape off the salt mixture. Slice thinly. Serve on rye toast or crackers.

Picnic Breakfast Stuffed Hardboiled Eggs

Yields: 6 servings
Serving size: 1 egg

stats **Per serving:**

Calories: 93
Protein: . . . . .7.8 g
Carbohydrates: . . . . . .1.7 g
Sugar: . . . . .0.5 g
Fat: . . . . .5.8 g

¼ pound crabmeat
¼ cup homemade mayonnaise
Juice of ½ lemon
½ teaspoon Old Bay seasonings or
    chili powder
6 hardboiled eggs, halved, yolks
    removed from whites
1 teaspoon Worcestershire sauce
½ teaspoon dried dill weed
Freshly ground black pepper to taste

1. Mix the crabmeat, mayonnaise, lemon juice, and Old Bay seasoning or chili powder.

2. Set cooked egg-white halves on a serving platter. Mash the egg yolks together. Using a fork, mix them with the crabmeat salad; add Worcestershire sauce. Sprinkle with dill weed and pepper. Pile on the egg whites.

3. Wrap stuffed eggs individually with foil if packing for picnic. Or serve on a platter, with cucumber slices separating stuffed eggs to keep them from rolling around.

tip

These stuffed eggs travel beautifully and make any picnic special. Enjoy them anywhere—at the beach, on a mountaintop, or in the car.

Perfect Hardboiled Eggs

Start with very fresh eggs. Using a pin, make a very small hole in the larger end of each egg. Place the eggs in cold water. Start them over high flame. When they come to a boil, reduce heat to very low. Let cook for 5 minutes. Turn off heat. Let eggs sit for another 4–5 minutes. Run pan of eggs under cold water. Crack and peel as soon as possible.

High-Flying Poached Eggs in Tomato Sauce

Yields: 2 servings
Serving size: 2 eggs

stats **Per serving:**

Calories: 446.2
Protein: . . . . .18.6 g
Carbohydrates: . . . . . .38.8 g
Sugar: . . . . .5.8 g
Fat: . . . . .25.62 g

2 tablespoons olive oil
½ cup onion, minced
1 clove garlic, chopped
1 teaspoon Splenda
2 cups crushed tomatoes
1 tablespoon fresh rosemary,
    chopped
4 fresh basil leaves, torn
Salt and pepper to taste
4 slices toast
4 eggs

1. Heat the olive oil in a large frying pan. Sauté the onion and garlic. Add the Splenda, tomatoes, rosemary, basil, salt, and pepper.

2. Bring the sauce to a simmer and cover; cook 10 minutes. Make the toast and place on warm plates.

3. Break the eggs into the simmering sauce; poach 2–3 minutes. Spoon eggs and sauce over toast.

tip

Poaching the eggs directly in the tomato sauce not only adds great flavor, it makes cleanup a snap. Use hearty artisan-style country bread to soak up the sauce.

Hot and Cold

If you are serving a hot meal, whether it's poached eggs or anything else, warm the plates before serving. Similarly, you should warm the soup bowls and cups for hot soups. The oven makes a handy plate warmer after you've taken the food out and turned it off, or you can use a hot plate.

Egg-and-Cheese Wraps

Yields: 2 servings
Serving size: 2 wraps

stats **Per serving:**

Calories:............485.29
Protein:.............21.75 g
Carbohydrates: ......42.14 g
Sugar: ....3.2 g
Fat:................25.16 g

1 tablespoon butter or buttery
    spread
4, 6-inch flour or corn tortillas
4 eggs
4 tablespoons salsa
4 tablespoons grated Monterey Jack
    or Pepper Jack cheese

1. Melt the butter in a nonstick frying pan. Set the broiler to 350°F. Put the tortillas on a cookie sheet and run them under the broiler until toasted on one side.

2. While the tortillas are toasting, break eggs into frying pan and fry. Drizzle the untoasted side of tortillas with salsa. Place an egg on each tortilla.

3. Spoon the cheese on top of the eggs. Fold each wrap and serve. If you'd like, you can also warm wraps in a 350°F oven 4–5 minutes.

tip

This dish is easy and very popular with kids. It also makes a nice weekend treat, one that's tasty while leaving you a little extra time to relax.

Wrap and Roll

You can serve wraps whole or halved at mealtime, or you can slice them into pretty little discs to serve as snacks or appetizers. Try stuffing your wraps with all kinds of goodies. You can mix various kinds of cheeses, meats, and fruits into spreads to make nutritious little surprises.

Smoked-Ham-and-Peach Omelet

Yields: 2 servings
Serving size: 1 omelet

stats **Per serving:**

Calories: 271
Protein: . . . . .18 g
Carbohydrates: . . . . . .16 g
Sugar: . . . . .11.5 g
Fat: . . . . .15.72 g

2 ripe peaches, blanched, peeled, and sliced, or ½ cup frozen sliced peaches
1 tablespoon lemon juice
1 tablespoon Splenda
¼ teaspoon ground cloves
1 tablespoon buttery spread or margarine
4 eggs, well beaten
¼ cup lowfat milk
Salt and pepper to taste
½ cup smoked ham, chopped

1. Sprinkle the sliced peaches with lemon juice; toss to coat. Combine Splenda and cloves; mix with peaches. Let macerate for 10 minutes.

2. Heat margarine in a skillet over medium heat.

3. Whisk eggs and milk together; pour into the skillet. Sprinkle with salt and pepper. Drain the juice from the peaches into a bowl. Spread the ham and peaches over one side of the omelet.

4. Flip the omelet when the bottom is browned.

5. Finish cooking and cut in half. Slide onto plates. Heat the reserved peach juice in skillet and pour over the omelet.

tip

Ham and fruit are excellent together. You can also make this omelet with fresh or frozen nectarines, apricots, or raspberries. For an added variation, try making this omelet with different spices, such as cinnamon or nutmeg.

Family Frittata with Onions, Potatoes, and Sausage

Yields: 4 servings
Serving size: ¼ fritata

stats **Per serving:**

Calories: 525.5
Protein: . . . . .23.25 g
Carbohydrates: . . . . . .26.58 g
Sugar: . . . . .8 g
Fat: . . . . .37.4 g

2 Breakfast Sausage patties (page 29)
1 cup sweet onion, peeled and sliced
*   into thin rings*
4 large or 8 small new potatoes,
*   parboiled and sliced thin*
8 eggs, well beaten
½ cup milk
2 tablespoons buttery spread or
*   olive oil*
Salt and pepper to taste
1 tablespoon fresh thyme or 1
*   teaspoon dried thyme*

1. Line up the sausage, onion, and potatoes next to the stove.

2. Beat the eggs and add the milk; continuing to whisk until well combined. Set aside.

3. Melt the butter or heat the olive oil in a large 12" frying pan over medium-high heat. Brown the potatoes. Add the onions; cook until they caramelize.

4. Pour in the egg-milk combination. Sprinkle with sausage, salt, pepper, and thyme. Reduce heat, cover, and let cook about 10 minutes, or until the eggs are set.

tip

This is an excellent breakfast or light supper dish. As with most egg dishes, the quantities of sausage and other fillings can be adjusted according to your taste. You can substitute other herbs and have fun with the variations.

Mixed Berry-Filled Omelet

Yields: 2 servings
Serving size: ½ omelet

stats **Per serving:**

Calories: 185.5
Protein: . . . . .12.3 g
Carbohydrates: . . . . . .8.6 g
Sugar: . . . . .5.3 g
Fat: . . . . .12 g

¼ cup fresh blueberries
¼ cup fresh raspberries
1 tablespoon Splenda
1 teaspoon grated orange zest
1 teaspoon buttery spread or
    margarine
4 eggs
¼ cup milk
Salt and freshly ground black pepper

1. Mix the berries, Splenda, and orange zest; let macerate 30 minutes. Heat the buttery spread or margarine in a nonstick pan over medium flame.

2. Whisk the eggs and milk together. Pour into the hot pan and cook until the mixture just begins to set.

3. Spoon the berries in a strip down the middle of the omelet and flip the sides over the berries. Let cook until set. Split the omelet in half and serve, using the berry juice as a sauce.

tip

You can vary the berries you choose by season and availability in the market. Blackberries make a nice change.

Macerating Fruits

Macerating is the act of softening an object by soaking it in liquid. The principle is similar to marinating meats.

Tomato-Basil Omelet

Yields: 2 servings
Serving size: ½ omelet

stats **Per serving:**

Calories: . . . . .272.3 g
Protein: . . . . .20.4 g
Carbohydrates: . . . . . .7.1 g
Sugar: . . . . .5.26 g
Fat: . . . . .17.76 g

1 medium tomato, cored and thinly
    sliced
8 fresh basil leaves, shredded or 1
    teaspoon dried basil
2 teaspoons olive oil
4 eggs, beaten
¼ cup low-fat milk
¼ cup Parmesan cheese, grated
Salt and pepper to taste
2 slices white American cheese

1. Set the tomato slices and basil leaves next to the stove. Heat the olive oil in a nonstick pan over medium heat.

2. Mix the egg, milk, and Parmesan cheese; pour into the pan. Arrange the tomatoes and basil down the center. Sprinkle with salt and pepper.

3. Fold over the sides of the omelet. Place the cheese on top; run the omelet under the broiler until the cheese melts. Cut in half and serve.

Salsa-and-Cheddar Omelet

Yields: 2 servings
Serving size: ½ omelet

 stats **Per serving:**

Calories: 351.69
Protein: . . . . .20.4 g
Carbohydrates: . . . . . .12.17 g
Sugar: . . . . .6 g
Fat: . . . . .24.86 g

½ cup Tomato Salsa (below), warmed
½ cup sharp white Cheddar cheese, coarsely grated
2 teaspoons buttery spread or olive oil
½ cup sweet onion, chopped
4 eggs, well beaten
¼ cup low-fat milk
Low-fat sour cream for garnish
Fresh cilantro or parsley for garnish

1. Set the warmed salsa and grated cheese next to the stove. Heat the oil or margarine over medium heat; sauté the onion.

2. Whisk the egg and milk together and pour over the onion. When the omelet just begins to set, spread half with the salsa and cheese. Flip the other side up and over to cover.

3. Cook until the omelet reaches the desired level of firmness. Garnish with a dollop of sour cream and a sprig of cilantro or parsley.

tip

This is a delectable omelet, especially when served with a pile of black bean salad on the side. Be sure to make your own condiments if you are on a sugar-free diet.

Tomato Salsa

Salsa is a great appetizer or condiment! To make, heat 2 tablespoons of oil in a large saucepan over medium heat. Add ½ cup chopped white onions, minced garlic cloves, and 2 Poblano or Serrano chiles. Sauté until soft, about 5 minutes.

Then stir in 8 ounces of fresh plum tomatoes, coarsely chopped, juice from 1 fresh lime, ¼ teaspoon of ground coriander, 1 teaspoon salt, ½ teaspoon splenda, 1 teaspoon cumin powder, and ¼ cup fresh cilantro or Italian parsley. Reduce heat and cover. Cook for 15 minutes. Serve chilled or at room temperature. The analysis is: Calories: 10.38, Protein: 0.13 g, Carbohydrates: 0.76 g, Sugar: 0.36 g, Fat: 0.82 g. Yields 1½ cups; serving size 2 teaspoons.

Muesli

Yields: 1 serving
Serving size: ½ cup

 Per serving:

Calories: 153.27
Protein:. . . . . .4 g
Carbohydrates: . . . . . .31.95 g
Sugar: . . . . .19.34 g
Fat:. . . . . .3 g

2 tablespoons rolled oats
3 tablespoons warm water
1 apple, peeled and grated
2 teaspoons Splenda Brown
¼ cup yogurt
1 tablespoon lemon juice

Soak the rolled oats in warm water 15 minutes. Add the apple, Splenda Brown, yogurt, and lemon juice. Microwave 4 minutes to serve hot, or store in the refrigerator to serve cold at your convenience.

Prosciutto with Melon

Yields: 4 servings
Serving size: ¼ melon

stats **Per serving:**

Calories: 69
Protein:. . . . . .6 g
Carbohydrates: . . . . . .8.5 g
Sugar: . . . . .5.6 g
Fat:. . . . . .1.4 g

½ cantaloupe or ¼ honeydew melon,
*   skinned and cut into 4 slices*
Juice of ½ lime
4 paper-thin slices prosciutto
4 slices fresh lime
Coarsely ground black pepper

Arrange the melon on a platter. Sprinkle with lime juice, wrap with prosciutto, and serve with extra lime slices and plenty of pepper.

The Breakfast Rut

It's easy to keep serving the same old things for breakfast in the morning when you're usually short on time, because you don't have to think about what to cook. However, introducing some variety to your diet is more healthful than staying in a rut.

Lime-Banana Smoothie

Yields: 2 servings
Serving size: 1 cup

stats **Per serving:**

Calories: 173
Protein: . . . . 7 g
Carbohydrates: . . . . . . 26 g
Sugar: . . . . 19.7 g
Fat: . . . . 6 g

Juice of 1 lime
1½ cups plain yogurt
1 cup cracked ice
1 banana
1 tablespoon Splenda
½ teaspoon lime zest
Fresh mint for garnish

Add all ingredients but the mint to blender; blend until smooth. Pour into frosty glasses. Garnish each smoothie with a sprig of fresh mint.

tip

Smoothies are a wonderfully refreshing way to start any day, but they're particularly good on a hot and sultry night as well, especially after a big meal for lunch.

Peach Melba Smoothie

Yields: 2 servings
Serving size: 1 foaming cup

stats **Per serving:**

Calories: 130.5
Protein: . . . . .5 g
Carbohydrates: . . . . . .20 g
Sugar: . . . . .14.78 g
Fat: . . . . .4.12 g

2 fresh, ripe peaches, peeled and
    sliced or 1 cup frozen peaches
1 teaspoon lemon juice
1 cup plain yogurt
2 tablespoons sugar-free raspberry
    jam or jelly
2 teaspoons Splenda
1 teaspoon pure vanilla extract
1 cup crushed ice or ice chips
Fresh raspberries for garnish

Add all ingredients but the raspberries to blender; blend until smooth. Pour into frosty glasses and garnish each smoothie with a few raspberries.

Grilled Peaches with Cream Cheese

Yields: 4 servings
Serving size: 1 peach

stats **Per serving:**

Calories:............107.59
Protein:.............1.95 g
Carbohydrates: ......1.91 g
Sugar: ....14.20 g
Fat:................3.94 g

4 large peaches, halved and pitted
4 teaspoons lemon juice
3 tablespoons cream cheese, room
    temperature
1 tablespoon Splenda
4 pinches cinnamon

1. Sprinkle the peaches with lemon juice.

2. Place the peaches cut-side down on grill over medium flame.

3. Grill peach halves about 4 minutes. Meanwhile, combine cream cheese and Splenda. Turn the peaches and divide the cheese between the halves.

4. Let grill another 2–3 minutes. Sprinkle with cinnamon and serve hot.

CHAPTER

3

A Bounty of Breads and Muffins

Basic White Bread

Yields: 2 large loaves
Serving size: 1 slice

stats **Per serving:**

Calories: 76.86
Protein: . . . . .2.00 g
Carbohydrates: . . . . . .15.00 g
Fat: . . . . .0.83 g
Sat. Fat: . . . . .0.21 g

5½–6 cups flour
1 package (2½ teaspoons) active dry
    yeast
¼ cup warm water
2 tablespoons sugar
1¾ cups warm potato water or plain
    water
2 tablespoons shortening
1 tablespoon sea salt

1. Place about ⅓ the flour in a large bowl and set aside. Mix the yeast with ¼ cup warm water in another bowl; stir well. Add the sugar and potato water to the yeast; add that mixture to the flour in the bowl; stir well. Set aside 5 minutes to allow the yeast to "proof."

2. Stir the mixture and cut in the shortening using a pastry blender or your hands. Stir in the salt and as much of the remaining flour as possible. The dough has enough flour when it's still somewhat sticky to the touch, yet pulls away from the side of the bowl as it's stirred. Turn the dough onto a lightly floured work surface. Knead for 8–10 minutes, until smooth and elastic; add flour as necessary. The dough will take on an almost "glossy" appearance once it's been kneaded sufficiently.

Basic White Bread

(continued)

3. Transfer the dough to a bowl treated with nonstick spray. Cover with a damp cloth; place in a warm, draft-free area. Allow to rise until double in volume, about 1–1½ hours.

4. Punch the dough down and let it rise a second time, until almost doubled in bulk.

5. Treat two 9" × 5" bread pans with nonstick spray. Punch the dough down again; divide into 2 loaves. Shape the loaves; place in the prepared bread pans. Cover and let rise until almost doubled.

6. Preheat oven to 350°F. Bake 20–30 minutes, or until golden brown. Remove bread from pans and allow to cool on a rack.

Bread Basics

Always place bread pans and muffin tins in the center of the oven to allow proper heat circulation.

Cinnamon-Raisin Bread

Yields: 2 large loaves
Serving size: 1 slice

 Per serving:

Calories: 94.56
Protein: . . . . .2.13 g
Carbohydrates: . . . . . .19.65 g
Fat: . . . . .0.85 g
Sat. Fat: . . . . .0.22 g

1 cup raisins
2½ teaspoons cinnamon
Basic White Bread recipe
    (pages 44-45)

1. Toss the raisins with 1 tablespoon of flour to coat them; shake off excess. When stirring in the bulk of the flour, add the raisins (Step 2 of Basic White Bread).

2. While following steps 3–4 for Basic White Bread, mix together ⅓ cup sugar and 2½ teaspoons cinnamon in a separate bowl. Divide the dough in half (Step 5 of Basic White Bread). Using a rolling pin, roll each half into a rectangular shape about ½-inch thick. Use a pastry brush to brush each rectangle with enough water to dampen the dough. Divide the cinnamon-sugar mixture into 2 equal portions; sprinkle across the dampened surface of the dough.

3. Starting at a long end of the rectangle, use your fingers to roll the dough. Place it in a 9" × 5" loaf pan, tucking under the ends of the dough. Repeat with the second rectangle of dough. Allow to rise until doubled in bulk; bake according to the instructions for Basic White Bread.

Any Way You Slice It . . .

It's usually easier to slice a loaf of homemade bread into 10 thicker slices than into 20 thinner ones. To arrive at 1 serving, either cut each thick slice in half or remove the crusts. (Be sure to reserve the crusts for use in other recipes.)

Whole-Wheat Bread

Yields: 2 loaves
Serving size: 1 slice

stats **Per serving:**

Calories: 86.42
Protein:. . . . . .2.27 g
Carbohydrates: . . . . . .17.06 g
Fat:. . . . . .1.23 g
Sat. Fat:. . . . . .0.32 g

*1 package (2½ teaspoons) active dry
    yeast*
2 cups warm water
*3 cups unbleached all-purpose or
    bread flour*
2 tablespoons sugar
½ cup hot water
2 teaspoons salt
½ cup brown sugar
3 tablespoons shortening
3 cups whole-wheat flour

1. Add the yeast to the 2 cups warm water. Stir in the all-purpose flour and sugar. Beat the mixture until smooth, either by hand or with a mixer. Set the mixture in a warm place to "proof" until it becomes foamy and bubbly (up to 1 hour).

2. Combine ½ cup hot water, salt, brown sugar, and shortening; stir. Allow to cool to lukewarm. (Stirring the sugar until it's dissolved should be sufficient to cool the water; test to be sure, as adding liquid that's too warm can "kill" the yeast.) Add to the bubbly flour mixture (the "sponge"). Stir in the whole-wheat flour; beat until smooth, but do not knead.

3. Divide the dough into 2 lightly greased pans, cover, and set in a warm place until doubled in size. Preheat oven to 350°F and bake for 50 minutes.

History Lesson

The sponge process of making bread was more popular years ago, when foodstuffs were less processed and the quality of yeast was less reliable. The yeast works in a batter and the dough rises only once. The sponge process produces a loaf that is lighter but coarser grained.

Bread-Machine White Bread

Yields: 1 large loaf
Serving size: 1 slice

stats **Per serving:**

Calories: 89.44
Protein: . . . . 2.82 g
Carbohydrates: . . . . . . 17.34 g
Fat: . . . . 0.81 g
Sat. Fat: . . . . 0.13 g

1¼ cups skim milk
2 tablespoons nonfat milk powder
1 tablespoon olive or canola oil
1 teaspoon sea salt
1 tablespoon granulated sugar
4 cups unbleached all-purpose or
   bread flour
1 package (2½ teaspoons) active dry
   yeast

Add the ingredients to your bread machine in the order recommended by the manufacturer, being careful that the yeast doesn't come in contact with the salt.

48

Honey-Oat Bran Bread

Yields: 1 large loaf
Serving size: 1 slice

stats **Per serving:**

Calories: 85.78
Protein: . . . . .3.22 g
Carbohydrates: . . . . . .15.59 g
Fat: . . . . .1.25 g
Sat. Fat: . . . . .0.24 g

1¼ cups skim milk
2 tablespoons nonfat buttermilk
    powder
1 tablespoon olive or canola oil
1 medium egg
1 cup oat bran
1 teaspoon sea salt
½ cup whole-wheat flour
2½ cups unbleached all-purpose or
    bread flour
1 tablespoon honey
1 package (2½ teaspoons) active dry
    yeast

Add the ingredients to your bread machine in the order recommended by the manufacturer, being careful that the yeast doesn't come in contact with the salt. Use the light-crust setting.

7-Grain Bread

Yield: 1 large loaf
Serving size: 1 slice

stats **Per serving:**

Calories: 82.47
Protein: . . . . 3.02 g
Carbohydrates: . . . . . . 15.30 g
Fat: . . . . 1.14 g
Sat. Fat: . . . . 0.21 g

1¼ cups skim milk
2 tablespoons nonfat milk powder
1 tablespoon olive or canola oil
¾ cup dry 7-grain cereal
½ cup oat bran
1 teaspoon sea salt
2¼ cups unbleached all-purpose or
    bread flour
½ cup whole-wheat flour
1 tablespoon honey
1 package (2½ teaspoons) dry yeast

Add the ingredients to your bread machine in the order recommended by the manufacturer, being careful that the yeast doesn't come in contact with the salt. Bake on whole-wheat bread setting.

Lactose-Free Bread

When cooking for someone who is lactose intolerant, substitute equal amounts of water or soy milk for any milk called for in bread recipes.

Cheddar Corn Bread

Yields: 1 large loaf
Serving size: 1 slice

stats **Per serving:**

Calories:............101.84
Protein:.............3.20 g
Carbohydrates: ......15.93 g
Fat:.................2.72 g
Sat. Fat:.............1.60 g

1¼ cups water
1 tablespoon honey
3 tablespoons butter
¼ cup nonfat milk powder
1 package (2½ teaspoons) active dry
    yeast
2½ cups unbleached all-purpose or
    bread flour
1 cup yellow cornmeal
1½ teaspoons sea salt
⅔ cup grated Cheddar cheese

Add all the ingredients except the cheese in the order suggested by your bread machine manual. Process on the basic bread cycle, light crust according to the manufacturer's directions. At the beeper (or at the end of the first kneading), add the cheese.

Cottage Cheese Bread

Yields: 1 large loaf
Serving size: 1 slice

 Per serving:

Calories: 76.09
Protein: . . . . .3.01 g
Carbohydrates: . . . . . .12.69 g
Fat: . . . . .1.33 g
Sat. Fat: . . . . .0.70 g

¼ cup water
1 cup nonfat cottage cheese
2 tablespoons butter
1 egg
1 tablespoon sugar
¼ teaspoon baking soda
1 teaspoon salt
3 cups unbleached all-purpose or
    bread flour
1 package (2½ teaspoons) active dry
    yeast

Add the ingredients to your bread machine in the order recommended by the manufacturer, being careful that the yeast doesn't come in contact with the salt. Check the bread machine at the "beep" to make sure the dough is pulling away from the sides of the pan and forming a ball. Add water or flour, if needed. (Note: You do not want the dough to be overly dry.) Bake at the white bread setting, light crust.

Why Breads Need Salt

Salt is only used in bread to enhance the flavor. If salt comes directly in contact with the yeast before the yeast has had a chance to begin to work, it can hinder the action of the yeast. Keep that in mind when you add ingredients to your bread machine.

Hawaiian-Style Bread

Yields: 1 large loaf, 24 slices
Serving size: 1 slice

stats **Per serving:**

Calories: 89.15
Protein: . . . . .2.41 g
Carbohydrates: . . . . . .16.64 g
Fat: . . . . .1.33 g
Sat. Fat: . . . . .0.69 g

1 egg
½ cup pineapple juice (or ⅛
    cup frozen pineapple juice
    concentrate and ⅜ cup water)
¾ cup water
2 tablespoons butter
1 teaspoon vanilla
½ teaspoon dried ginger
1 teaspoon salt
1½ cups unbleached bread flour
2⅛ cups unbleached all-purpose
    flour
¼ cup sugar
2 tablespoons nonfat milk powder
1 package (2½ teaspoons) active dry
    yeast

Unless the instructions for your bread machine differ, add the ingredients in the order listed here. Use the light-crust setting.

Tools of the Trade

Nonstick pans with a dark surface absorb too much heat, which causes breads to burn. Chicago Metallic makes muffin, mini-muffin, and other bread pans with a lighter-colored, Silverstone nonstick coating that are much better suited for baking.

Milk Biscuits

Yields: 24 biscuits
Serving size: 1 biscuit

stats **Per serving:**

Calories:............98.47
Protein:.............2.19 g
Carbohydrates:......12.96 g
Fat:.................4.15 g
Sat. Fat:.............2.51 g

3 cups unbleached all-purpose flour
1 teaspoon salt
1½ teaspoons baking soda
1 tablespoon cream of tartar
1 teaspoon baking powder
½ cup butter
1⅓ cups milk

1. Preheat oven to 400°F. For quick mixing, use a food processor. Add all of the ingredients at once; pulse until just blended. Be careful not to overprocess, as the rolls won't be as light.

2. To mix by hand, sift together the dry ingredients. Cut in the butter using a pastry blender or fork until the mixture resembles coarse crumbs. Add the milk and stir until the mixture pulls away from the sides of the bowl.

3. Use 1 heaping tablespoon for each biscuit, dropping the dough onto greased baking sheets. (You can also try pan liners, such as parchment.) Bake until golden brown, about 20–30 minutes.

tip

Despite the downside of all the butter, the upside to all the butter is that these biscuits are so rich you won't even notice that they don't contain any sugar. Consult your dietitian, however, if you are on a diet to control your cholesterol.

Healthy Substitutions

You can substitute ¼ cup nonfat yogurt for half of the butter in this recipe.

Angelic Buttermilk-Batter Biscuits

Yields: 24 biscuits
Serving size: 1 biscuit

 Per serving:

Calories:............74.45
Protein:.............1.97 g
Carbohydrates: ......11.81 g
Fat:.................2.12 g
Sat Fat: ....1.25 g

3 tablespoons nonfat buttermilk
   powder
2 tablespoons granulated sugar
¾ cup warm water
1 tablespoon active dry yeast
2½ cups unbleached all-purpose
   flour
½ teaspoon sea salt
½ teaspoon baking powder
¼ cup unsalted butter
¼ cup nonfat plain yogurt

1. Put the buttermilk powder, sugar, and warm water in food processor; process until mixed. Sprinkle the yeast over the buttermilk-sugar mixture; pulse once or twice to mix. Allow the mixture to sit at room temperature about 5 minutes, or until the yeast begins to bubble. Add all the remaining ingredients to the food processor; pulse until mixed, being careful not to overprocess the dough.

2. Preheat oven to 400°F; drop 1 heaping teaspoon per biscuit onto a baking sheet treated with nonstick spray. Set the tray in a warm place; allow the biscuits to rise about 15 minutes. Bake the biscuits 12–15 minutes.

Why Breads Need Sugar

Bread recipes need sugar or sweetener, like honey, to "feed" the yeast. This helps the yeast work, which in turn helps the bread rise.

Zucchini Bread

Yields: 2 large loaves
Serving size: 1 slice

stats **Per serving:**

Calories: 130.61
Protein: . . . . 3.38 g
Carbohydrates: . . . . . . 23.15 g
Fat: . . . . 2.89 g
Sat. Fat: . . . . 0.42 g

3 eggs
1½ cups sugar
1 cup nonfat plain yogurt
1 tablespoon vanilla
2 cups loosely packed, grated,
    unpeeled zucchini
2 cups unbleached all-purpose flour
2 teaspoons baking soda
½ teaspoon baking powder
1 teaspoon sea salt
1½ teaspoons cinnamon
1 cup chopped walnuts

1. Preheat oven to 350°F. Treat two 9" loaf pans with nonstick spray. In a large bowl, beat the eggs until frothy. Beat in the sugar, yogurt, and vanilla until thick and lemon-colored; stir in the zucchini.

2. Sift together the flour, baking soda, baking powder, salt, and cinnamon. Stir dry ingredients into the zucchini batter; fold in the nuts.

3. Pour the mixture into the prepared pans. Bake 40 minutes, or until the center springs back when lightly touched. Allow to cool 10 minutes before turning out onto a wire rack.

Are Your Eyes Bigger than Your Stomach?

Use mini-loaf pans; it's much easier to arrive at the number of servings in the form of a full slice when you use smaller loaf pans. There's a psychological advantage to getting a full, rather than a half, slice.

Orange-Date Bread

Yields: 2 large loaves
Serving size: 1 slice

stats **Per serving:**

Calories:............79.03
Protein:.............1.92 g
Carbohydrates: ......16.33 g
Fat:.................0.95 g
Sat. Fat:.............0.14 g

2 tablespoons frozen orange juice
    concentrate
2 tablespoons orange zest
¾ cup pitted, chopped dates
½ cup brown sugar
¼ cup granulated sugar
1 cup plain nonfat yogurt
1 egg
1¼ cups all-purpose flour
¾ cup whole-wheat flour
1 teaspoon baking soda
1 teaspoon baking powder
½ teaspoon salt
1 tablespoon vegetable oil
1 teaspoon vanilla extract

1. Preheat oven to 350°F. Spray 4 mini-loaf pans with nonfat cooking spray. In a food processor, process the orange juice concentrate, orange zest, dates, sugars, yogurt, and egg until mixed. (This will cut the dates into smaller pieces, too.) Add the remaining ingredients; pulse until mixed, scraping down the side of the bowl if necessary.

2. Divide the mixture between the 4 pans. Spread the mixture so each pan has an even layer. Bake until a toothpick inserted into the center of a loaf comes out clean, about 15–20 minutes. Cool the bread in the pans on a wire rack 10 minutes. Remove the bread to the rack and cool to room temperature.

Caramelized Onion-and-Gorgonzola Bread

Yields: one loaf
Serving size: 1 slice

 Per serving:

Calories:............91.57
Protein:.............3.94 g
Carbohydrates: ......12.32 g
Sugar: ....1.21 g
Fat:.................3.66 g

2 tablespoons olive oil
1 Vidalia or other sweet onion, thinly
    sliced
2 eggs
⅔ cup skim milk
¼ cup Splenda
2 cups all-purpose or whole-wheat
    flour
1 teaspoon salt
1 teaspoon baking powder
½ teaspoon baking soda
1 teaspoon dried oregano
⅔ cup Gorgonzola cheese, crumbled

1. Preheat oven to 350°F. Prepare a standard loaf pan with nonstick spray.

2. Heat the oil in a nonstick pan. Add onions; cook over very low heat until caramelized. Set aside.

3. In a large bowl, beat the eggs, milk, and Splenda until smooth. Add the onions, flour, salt, baking powder, baking soda, oregano, and cheese; mix well; pour into the loaf pan.

4. Bake 60 minutes on a rack in the middle of oven. Remove the bread from oven and set on a cooling rack. Slice and serve warm or at room temperature.

Serve as a side with soup, salad, or with your dinner entrée.

Savory Summer-Squash Bread

Yields: one loaf
Serving size: 1 slice

 Per serving:

Calories: 60.62
Protein: . . . . .2.25 g
Carbohydrates: . . . . . .9.48 g
Sugar: . . . . .0.90 g
Fat: . . . . .1.60 g

2 eggs
½ cup milk
1 cup zucchini or yellow summer
    squash, trimmed and grated
2 green onions, finely chopped
1 tablespoon melted unsalted butter
1 teaspoon celery salt
½ teaspoon freshly ground black
    pepper
1 teaspoon Splenda
¼ cup Italian flat-leaf parsley,
    minced
2 teaspoons fresh savory, chopped or
    1 teaspoon dried savory
1 teaspoon baking powder
1 teaspoon baking soda
1 cup all-purpose flour
½ cup whole-wheat flour

1. Preheat oven to 350°F. Prepare a standard loaf pan with nonstick spray. Whisk the eggs and milk together in a blender. Add the grated squash, green onions, and unsalted butter; blend till combined.

2. Combine celery salt, pepper, Splenda, parsley, savory, baking powder, baking soda, and flours in a separate bowl. Add to moist ingredients; mix thoroughly.

3. Pour into the loaf pan and bake 60 minutes. Remove the pan from oven and cool loaf on a rack.

 tip

This recipe is excellent with whipped cream cheese. You can make several batches and freeze them to enjoy that fresh, summery taste any season.

Herbs Make Food Savory

You can do a lot with herbs to make even the plainest dishes more appealing. For added zing, mix sweet and savory flavors. Most supermarkets carry a good selection of fresh herbs. You can also grow your own on a sunny windowsill or in your backyard and pick them as you need them.

Swedish Coffee Bread

Yields: one loaf
Serving size: 1 slice

 Per serving:

Calories: 47.4
Protein: . . . . .1.18 g
Carbohydrates: . . . . . .6.51 g
Sugar: . . . . .1.33 g
Fat: . . . . .2.20 g

1 ounce live yeast, crumbled
½ cup warm milk
½ cup unsalted butter
1 cup Splenda, divided
1 teaspoon salt
3 eggs, divided
½ cup cold milk
2 cups all-purpose flour
2 cups whole-wheat flour, plus extra
    for sprinkling
1 tablespoon ground cardamom
1 tablespoon ground cinnamon
1 cup raisins without added sugar
1 cup chopped pecans or walnuts

1. In a small bowl, mix the yeast and warm milk; set aside. In a large bowl, mix the unsalted butter, ½ cup Splenda, and salt. Beat in two of the eggs and cold milk. Add the yeast; set aside 10 minutes. Stir in the flour; mix well, cover, and let rise in a warm place 60 minutes.

2. Sprinkle a flat surface with flour; roll the dough out onto it. Knead the dough until it is smooth and elastic. Roll into a long rope, about 18" long and ⅓" thick.

3. Mix ½ cup Splenda, cardamom, and cinnamon in a small bowl. Sprinkle the dough with the Splenda and spice mixture; spread the raisins and nuts on top. Spray a cookie sheet with nonstick spray.

4. Cut the dough in three 6" pieces. Braid the pieces together; place on the cookie sheet.

5. Cover and let rise 60 minutes. When the dough has doubled in size, heat oven to 350°F. Beat the remaining egg; brush the dough with egg and bake 25–30 minutes.

Hot Corn Bread with Cherry Peppers

Yields: one loaf
Serving size: 1 slice

stats **Per serving:**

Calories: 76.03
Protein:. . . . . .2.80 g
Carbohydrates: . . . . . .12.98 g
Sugar: . . . . .0.91 g
Fat:. . . . . .1.68 g

1 tablespoon cooking oil
2 cherry or jalapeño peppers,
 stemmed, seeded, deveined, and
 minced
1 tablespoon fresh chives, snipped
 with kitchen scissors
2 eggs, lightly beaten
1 cup buttermilk
1 teaspoon dried oregano
1 teaspoon baking powder
1 teaspoon baking soda
1 cup cornmeal
1 cup all-purpose or whole-wheat
 flour
2 tablespoons Splenda

1. In a small saucepan, heat the oil; sauté the peppers and chives over medium heat about 5 minutes. Set aside. The oil will serve as shortening for your bread.

2. Preheat oven to 350°F and prepare a standard loaf pan with nonstick spray. In a bowl, whisk the eggs and buttermilk together. Slowly beat in the rest of the ingredients; fold in the peppers, chives, and oil mixture.

3. Pour into the loaf pan and bake 60 minutes in the middle of oven. Let cool slightly before turning out and cutting. Serve with sugar-free jalapeño jelly.

tip

Cherry peppers are mild to moderately hot, jalapeños tend to be hotter; try different varieties of hot peppers to see what your palate prefers. The seeds and veins have a great deal of added heat, so you may want to clean away these elements.

Too Hot Is Dangerous!

Every time you burn your mouth on hot peppers, you kill some of your taste buds. That's why people who get used to hot food want it progressively hotter. Most—but not all—taste buds will regenerate in time.

Oatmeal-Walnut Bread

Yields: one loaf
Serving size: 1 slice

stats **Per serving:**

Calories: 111.5
Protein:. . . . . .3.31 g
Carbohydrates: . . . . . .9.08 g
Sugar: . . . . .1.04 g
Fat:. . . . . .7.39 g

2 eggs
1 cup milk
2 tablespoons melted unsalted butter
2 tablespoons Splenda
1 teaspoon salt
1 teaspoon vanilla extract
1 teaspoon baking soda
1 teaspoon baking powder
1 teaspoon cinnamon
½ cup rice or tapioca flour
1 cup uncooked old-fashioned or
   Irish oatmeal
1 cup walnut pieces, toasted

1. Preheat oven to 350°F. Prepare a standard bread loaf pan with nonstick spray. In a large bowl, beat the eggs, milk, butter, Splenda, salt, and vanilla extract together.

2. Stir in the rest of the ingredients; mix thoroughly.

3. Bake 60 minutes on a rack in the middle of the oven. Remove the bread from oven and set on a cooling rack. Slice and serve warm or at room temperature.

tip

This quick and easy breakfast bread is excellent with eggs—why not have breakfast for dinner? The bread leftovers also make for a great snack.

Chestnut Bread

Yields: one loaf
Serving size: 1 slice

stats **Per serving:**

Calories: 57.49
Protein: . . . . .2.54 g
Carbohydrates: . . . . . .8.92 g
Sugar: . . . . .1.93 g
Fat: . . . . .1.48 g

1 egg
⅔ cup milk
1 cup canned chestnuts, drained,
    rinsed, and dried
1 tablespoon unsalted butter, melted
2 tablespoons Splenda
2¼ cups chestnut flour
1 teaspoon salt
1 teaspoon baking powder
1 teaspoon baking soda
2 egg whites, beaten stiff

1. Preheat oven to 350°F. Prepare a loaf pan with nonstick spray.

2. Combine the egg, milk, chestnuts, butter, and Splenda in a blender; puree.

3. Pour the pureed mixture into a large bowl. Stir in the flour, salt, baking powder, and baking soda; fold in the egg whites.

4. Bake 60 minutes on a rack in the middle of oven. Remove bread from oven and set on a cooling rack. Slice and serve warm or at room temperature.

tip

You can use imported French chestnuts in cans or jars; be sure not to get sugared chestnuts or those packed in sugar syrup.

Cheese-and-Herb Bread

Yields: one loaf
Serving size: 1 slice

stats **Per serving:**

Calories: 112.60
Protein: . . . . 3.95 g
Carbohydrates: . . . . . . 14.83 g
Sugar: . . . . 0.92 g
Fat: . . . . 4.07 g

2 eggs
1 cup skim milk
1 tablespoon walnut oil
2 cups rice or corn flour
1 tablespoon baking powder
1 teaspoon salt
2 teaspoons dried oregano
1 tablespoon dried rosemary
1 cup Cheddar cheese, grated

1. Preheat oven to 350°F. Prepare a standard loaf pan with nonstick spray.

2. Whisk the eggs, milk, and oil together in a large bowl.

3. Beat in the flour, baking powder, salt, oregano, and rosemary. Spread half of the batter in the loaf pan. Sprinkle with cheese and spread the rest of the batter on top.

4. Bake for 4–50 minutes. Serve hot so that cheese is still melted inside.

tip

This easy and excellent bread is delicious when served hot with soup for a light supper.

64

Banana-and-Tart Apple Bread

Yields: one loaf
Serving size: 1 slice

 Per serving:

Calories: 97.35
Protein: . . . . .2.6 g
Carbohydrates: . . . . . .16.25 g
Sugar: . . . . .53.87 g
Fat: . . . . .3.11 g

1 ripe banana, peeled and sliced
1 tart green apple, peeled, cored, and
    quartered
2 eggs
⅔ cup milk
3 tablespoons unsalted butter,
    melted
½ cup Splenda
2 cups all-purpose or whole-wheat
    flour
1 teaspoon salt
1 teaspoon baking powder
½ teaspoon baking soda
1 teaspoon ground mace

1. Preheat oven to 350°F. Prepare a standard loaf pan with nonstick spray.

2. Combine the banana, apple, eggs, milk, and butter in a food processor; add ingredients one at a time until smooth. Mix the Splenda, flour, salt, baking powder, baking soda, and mace in a large bowl. Add the liquids; blend well. Pour into the loaf pan.

3. Bake 60 minutes on a rack in the middle of oven. Remove the bread from the oven and cool on rack. Slice and serve warm or at room temperature.

Bran Muffins

Yields: 12 muffins
Serving size: 1 muffin

stats **Per serving:**

Calories: 86
Protein: . . . . .4 g
Carbohydrates: . . . . . .15 g
Sugar: . . . . .1.35 g
Fat: . . . . .3.2 g

2 eggs, beaten
1 teaspoon salt
1 cup milk
1 tablespoon unsalted butter, melted
½ cup rice or corn flour
½ cup whole-wheat flour
1 cup oat or wheat bran
¼ cup Splenda
1 tablespoon baking powder

1. Preheat oven to 350°F. In a large bowl, beat together the eggs, salt, milk, and butter.

2. Mix in the flours, bran, Splenda, and baking powder. Prepare muffin tin with nonstick spray. Fill each cup halfway.

3. Bake 20 minutes. Cool, remove from tin, and serve with unsalted butter or sugar-free jam.

tip

Enhance the recipe by adding a handful of nuts, dried currants, or raisins.

The Versatile Muffin

You can add many different things to muffins and quick breads. Besides different kinds of nuts, you can also add sugar-free dried fruits, such as apples and apricots, either soaked until soft in water or left chewy. These make great afternoon snacks and can be frozen for a fast breakfast.

Blueberry Muffins

Yields: 12 muffins

Serving size: 1 muffin

stats **Per serving:**

Calories: 128.83
Protein: . . . . .4.56 g
Carbohydrates: . . . . . .24 g
Sugar: . . . . .2.73 g
Fat: . . . . .3.06 g

2 eggs
1 teaspoon salt
1 cup milk
1 tablespoon unsalted butter, melted
1½ cups whole-wheat flour
1 cup coarse cornmeal
1 tablespoon baking powder
½ cup Splenda
1 cup fresh or frozen blueberries,
    rinsed and dried

1. Preheat oven to 350°F.

2. Whisk the eggs, salt, milk, and butter together until light and fluffy. Stir in the flour, cornmeal, baking powder, and Splenda; gently fold in the berries.

3. Prepare a muffin tin with nonstick spray. Fill each cup halfway with batter. Bake 15–20 minutes.

tip

These muffins freeze beautifully, so make a double batch and reheat leftovers for a quick breakfast treat. Make extras when blueberries are in season, plentiful, and inexpensive.

Fresh Berries

Make sure you dry fresh berries before you add them to muffin batter. If they are wet, the added moisture will throw off your recipe. If the berries are super juicy, you can always add more flour.

Autumn Muffins

Yields: 12 muffins
Serving size: 1 muffin

stats **Per serving:**

Calories: 131.06
Protein: . . . . 3.66 g
Carbohydrates: . . . . . . 22.73 g
Sugar: . . . . 5.52 g
Fat: . . . . 2.59 g

1 tablespoon unsalted butter
¼ cup onion, minced
½ cup celery, finely minced
2 eggs
1 cup milk
1 teaspoon baking soda
1 teaspoon baking powder
1 tablespoon Splenda
1 teaspoon dried thyme
1 teaspoon dried sage
1 cup flour
1 cup cornmeal
⅔ cup sugar-free dried cranberries

1. Preheat oven to 350°F. Prepare a muffin tin with nonstick spray. Melt the butter in a pan. Sauté the onions and celery over medium heat until softened. Set aside.

2. In a large bowl, beat the eggs and milk together. Stir in remaining ingredients; mix thoroughly. Fill each cup halfway with batter. Bake 20–25 minutes.

Dried Fruits

Dried fruits make an excellent addition to both sweet and savory breads and muffins—try dried cherries and raisins. Before buying, make sure there's no sugar added commercially to the dried fruit.

Muffins with Sun-Dried Tomatoes & Pine Nuts

Yields: 14 muffins
Serving size: 1 muffin

 Per serving:

Calories: 129.94
Protein: . . . . 4.59 g
Carbohydrates: . . . . . . 17.44 g
Sugar: . . . . 1.25 g
Fat: . . . . 4.88 g

2 eggs
1 cup buttermilk
1 tablespoon unsalted butter, melted
1 teaspoon Splenda
1 teaspoon salt
½ cup fresh parsley, minced
1 teaspoon dried oregano
1 cup cornmeal
1 cup unbleached all-purpose flour
1 teaspoon baking powder
1 teaspoon baking soda
½ cup pine nuts, lightly toasted
½ cup sun-dried tomatoes, chopped

1. Preheat oven to 350°F. Prepare muffin tins with nonstick spray.

2. Whisk together the eggs, buttermilk, butter, Splenda, salt, parsley, and oregano. Slowly beat in the remaining ingredients one at a time. Fill the cups halfway with batter.

3. Bake 20 minutes in the middle of the oven. Cool, turn out, and serve.

Corn-and-Ham Muffins

Yields: 12 muffins
Serving size: 1 muffin

 Per serving:

Calories: 116
Protein:. . . . . .5.97 g
Carbohydrates: . . . . . .16.73 g
Sugar: . . . . .1.45 g
Fat:. . . . . .3.37 g

2 eggs
1 cup buttermilk
1 tablespoon unsalted butter, melted
4 ounces smoked Virginia ham, finely
    chopped
1 teaspoon baking soda
1 teaspoon baking powder
2 tablespoons Splenda
¼ teaspoon ground cloves
1 cup whole-wheat flour
1 cup cornmeal or corn flour
4 tablespoons grated sharp Cheddar
    cheese

1. Preheat oven to 350°F. In a large bowl, beat the eggs, buttermilk, butter, and ham together. Stir in the baking soda, baking powder, Splenda, cloves, flour, and cornmeal; blend well.

2. Prepare the muffin tin with nonstick spray. Fill each cup halfway with batter. Bake 20–25 minutes.

3. Place 1 teaspoon of cheese on each muffin and return to oven just long enough to melt.

tip

These hearty and wonderful muffins are the perfect complement to split pea soup.

Zucchini-Spice Muffins

Yields: 16 muffins
Serving size: 1 muffin

 Per serving:

Calories: 94.73
Protein: . . . . .2.7 g
Carbohydrates: . . . . . .17.85 g
Sugar: . . . . .1.03 g
Fat: . . . . .2.07 g

2 eggs
1 teaspoon salt
1 cup milk
1 tablespoon unsalted butter, melted
1½ cups rice flour
½ cup whole-wheat flour
1 tablespoon baking powder
1 teaspoon salt
12 teaspoons ground cloves
1 teaspoon ground cinnamon
½ teaspoon ground allspice
½ cup Splenda
1 cup zucchini, grated

1. Preheat oven to 350°F. Prepare muffin tin with nonstick spray. Whisk the eggs, salt, milk, and butter together. Add the rest of the ingredients one at a time, mixing thoroughly between additions.

2. Fill each cup halfway with batter. Bake 20 minutes, or until nicely brown.

Try mixing zucchini with grated carrots and apples as a base for cakes, breads, and muffins for a different texture and flavor.

Endless Options

The possibilities for sugar-free quick breads and muffins are only limited by your imagination. Go to your market or grocery store and check out fruits and vegetables, and don't be afraid to use different cheeses in your muffin and bread recipes.

Polenta Griddle Cakes

Serves 6
Serving size: 1 cake

 Per serving:

Calories: 147.05
Protein: . . . . .4.43 g
Carbohydrates: . . . . . .17.68 g
Sugar: . . . . .1.47 g
Fat: . . . . .7.01 g

3 cups water
1 teaspoon salt
1 cup coarsely ground cornmeal
1 tablespoon Splenda
2 eggs, beaten
⅔ cup milk
½ teaspoon nutmeg
2 tablespoons unsalted butter or
      canola oil
Sugar-free applesauce, jam, or fresh
      berries

1. In a large pot, bring the water to a boil and add the salt. Slowly add the cornmeal. Reduce heat and let cook until thick, stirring constantly. Allow to cool slightly.

2. Stir in the Splenda. Whisk the eggs, milk, and nutmeg together in a separate bowl; mix them with the polenta, blending well.

3. Heat the unsalted butter or oil on a griddle over medium flame. Drop spoonfuls of batter on the griddle. Cook until well browned. Flip each griddle cake with a spatula and brown the reverse side.

4. Serve hot topped with applesauce or jam or with fresh berries on the side.

Buttermilk Volcano Biscuits

Yields: 12 biscuits
Serving size: 1 biscuit

 Per serving:

Calories: 97.12
Protein: . . . . .3.13 g
Carbohydrates: . . . . . .20.70 g
Sugar: . . . . .1.5 g
Fat: . . . . .0.98 g

2 cups corn or rice flour
4 teaspoons baking powder
1 tablespoon Splenda
1 teaspoon salt
1 cup unsalted buttermilk

1. Preheat oven to 400°F. Prepare a cookie sheet with nonstick spray. Mix the flour, baking powder, Splenda, and salt in a large bowl. Add the buttermilk; mix till stiff.

2. Use a spoon to drop the biscuit dough on the cookie sheet. Twist your spoon as you drop each biscuit to make the volcano shape. If you want lava, make a double biscuit with a dollop of sugar-free jam in the middle.

3. Bake for 15–20 minutes or until golden. To make a wild-looking shortbread, prepare this recipe and serve topped with berries and cream.

Biscuits Are Fun

Biscuit dough makes a fine topping for cobblers and deep-dish pies. Biscuits complete every dinner dish, and they make a good snack or tea-time bite. Because they are so easy to make, they are ideal for children who want to help in the kitchen. Baking biscuits together is a great way to get your children interested in nutrition.

Strawberry-Stuffed French Toast

Yields: 2 servings
Serving size: 2 pieces of toast

stats **Per serving:**

Calories:............313.38
Protein:.............12.60 g
Carbohydrates: ......29.63 g
Sugar: ....6.91 g
Fat:.................18.82 g

⅔ cup strawberries, chopped
1 tablespoon Splenda
2 heaping tablespoons cream cheese,
    room temperature
2 eggs
¼ cup milk
1 teaspoon orange zest
4 slices very thin wheat bread
1 tablespoon buttery spread or
    margarine
Whole strawberries for garnish

1. Combine the strawberries, Splenda, and cream cheese. Set aside.

2. Whisk the eggs, milk, and orange zest together. Soak the bread in the egg mixture.

3. Melt the buttery spread in a large skillet over medium flame. Add all 4 pieces of bread to the skillet.

4. Flip the toast after the first side is browned and brown second side. Remove from pan and spread strawberry mixture on 2 of the slices. Make sandwiches with the strawberries and cheese mixture in the center.

5. Sprinkle the top of sandwiches with extra strawberries.

Soups and Stews

Eggplant-and-Tomato Stew

Serves 4

stats **Per serving:**

Calories:............135.02
Protein:.............4.44 g
Carbohydrates: ......26.23 g
Fat:.................3.28 g
Sat. Fat:............0.47 g

2 eggplants, trimmed but left whole
2 teaspoons olive oil
1 medium-sized Spanish onion,
    chopped
1 teaspoon chopped garlic
2 cups cooked or canned unsalted
    tomatoes, chopped with liquid
Optional seasonings to taste:
1 teaspoon hot pepper sauce
Ketchup
Nonfat plain yogurt
Fresh parsley sprigs

Preheat oven to 400°F. Roast the eggplants on a baking sheet until soft, about 45 minutes. Remove all the meat from the eggplants. In a large sauté pan, heat the oil; sauté the onions and garlic. Add the eggplant and all the other ingredients, except the yogurt and parsley. Remove from heat and transfer the mixture to a food processor; pulse until it becomes creamy. Serve at room temperature, garnished with a dollop of yogurt and parsley, if desired.

Too Salty?

If a soup, sauce, or liquid is too salty, peel and place a raw potato in the pot. Use half of a potato for each quart of liquid. Simmer, and then discard the potato, which will have absorbed some of the salt.

Lentil Soup with Herbs and Lemon

Serves 4

 Per serving:

Calories:............214.01
Protein:.............14.91 g
Carbohydrates: ......34.12 g
Fat:.................2.89 g
Sat. Fat:.............0.40 g

1 cup lentils, soaked overnight in 1
    cup water
6 cups low-fat, reduced-sodium
    chicken broth
1 carrot, sliced
1 stalk celery, sliced
1 yellow onion, thinly sliced
2 teaspoons olive oil
1 tablespoon dried tarragon
½ teaspoon dried oregano
Sea salt and black pepper to taste
    (optional)
1 tablespoon lemon juice
4 thin slices of lemon

1. Drain and rinse the lentils. Add the lentils and broth to a pot over medium heat; bring to a boil. Reduce the heat and simmer until tender, approximately 15 minutes. (If you did not presoak the lentils, increase the cooking time by about 15 more minutes).

2. While the lentils are cooking, sauté the carrot, celery, and onion in oil 8 minutes, or until the onion is golden brown. Remove from heat and set aside.

3. When the lentils are tender, add the vegetables, herbs, and salt and pepper, if using; cook 2 minutes. Stir in the lemon juice and ladle into 4 serving bowls; garnish with lemon slices.

Believe It or Not!

Put a fork at the bottom of the pan when you cook a pot of beans. The beans will cook in half the time.

Lentil-Vegetable Soup

Serves 4

 stats **Per serving, with water:**

Calories:............273.27
Protein:..............16.45 g
Carbohydrates: ......52.69 g
Fat:..................0.95 g
Sat. Fat:.............0.16 g

5 cups water or your choice of broth
1 medium-sized sweet potato, peeled
    and chopped
1 cup uncooked lentils
2 medium onions, chopped
¼ cup barley
2 tablespoons parsley flakes
2 carrots, sliced
1 celery stalk, chopped
2 teaspoons cumin

Combine all the ingredients in a soup pot; simmer until the lentils are soft, about 1 hour.

Quick Lobster Bisque

A combination of lobster broth, tomato paste, and seasonings, Minor's Lobster Base makes this "soup" a rich and satisfying soup course or snack. Microwave ½ cup water and 1 teaspoon lobster base for 1 minute on high. Stir until the base is dissolved. Add in ½ cup milk. If the soup cools too much, microwave at 70 percent power for another 15–30 seconds. Nutritional Analysis (per cup): 57 calories if it's made with skim milk; 68 calories if you use mock cream. Allow ½ Skim Milk and 1 Free Exchange for either version.

Tomato-Vegetable Soup

Serves 6

 stats **Per serving:**

Calories: 157.51
Protein: . . . . 4.99 g
Carbohydrates: . . . . . . 31.21 g
Fat: . . . . 3.14 g
Sat. Fat: . . . . 0.44 g

1 tablespoon olive oil
2 teaspoons minced garlic
⅔ teaspoon cumin
2 carrots, chopped
2 stalks celery, diced
1 medium onion, chopped
⅔ cup unsalted tomato paste
½ teaspoon red pepper flakes
2 cups canned, unsalted peeled
    tomatoes, with juice
⅔ teaspoon chopped fresh oregano
3 cups low-fat, reduced-sodium
    chicken broth
3 cups fat-free beef broth
2 cups diced potatoes
2 cups shredded cabbage
½ cup green beans
½ cup fresh or frozen corn kernels
½ teaspoon freshly cracked black
    pepper
¼ cup lime juice or balsamic vinegar

1. Heat the olive oil in a large stockpot and sauté the garlic, cumin, carrot, and celery for 1 minute; add the onion and cook until transparent.

2. Stir in the tomato paste and sauté until it begins to brown. Add the remaining ingredients except for the lime juice or vinegar.

3. Bring to a boil; reduce heat and simmer 20–30 minutes, adding additional broth or water if needed. Just before serving, add the lime juice or balsamic vinegar.

tip

It isn't necessary to follow the sauté suggestions at the beginning of this recipe, but the soup will taste much richer if you do. (Sodium content will vary depending upon the broths used.)

Easy Measures

Consider freezing broth in an ice-cube tray. Most ice-cube tray sections hold ⅛ cup (2 tablespoons) of liquid. Once the broth is frozen, you can transfer the cubes to a freezer bag or container. This makes it easy to measure out the amount you'll need for recipes.

Baked Beef Stew

Serves 4

 stats **Per serving:**

Calories: 429.81
Protein: . . . . .31.25 g
Carbohydrates: . . . . . .61.28 g
Fat: . . . . .7.33 g
Sat. Fat: . . . . .2.17 g

1 (12-ounce) can unsalted tomatoes,
    undrained
1 cup water
3 tablespoons quick-cooking tapioca
1 teaspoon sugar
1 pound lean beef stew meat,
    trimmed of all fat, cut into 1"
    pieces
4 medium carrots, cut into 1" chunks
4 small potatoes, peeled and
    quartered
4 celery stalks, cut into ¾" chunks
2 medium onions, chopped
2 slices whole-wheat bread, torn into
    cubes

1. Preheat oven to 375°F. In a large bowl, combine the tomatoes, water, tapioca, and sugar.

2. Add all the remaining ingredients; mix well. Pour into a baking dish treated with nonstick spray.

3. Cover and bake 2 hours, or until the meat and vegetables are tender.

Flavor Saver

If you discover that you've scorched a soup, don't stir it or scrape the bottom; stirring is what distributes the burned flavor. Carefully pour the liquid into another pan—you should be able to salvage what remains. If it still tastes slightly burnt, adding a little milk should remove that disagreeable flavor. For acidic soups, add some grape jelly.

Cold Roasted Red-Pepper Soup

Serves 4

 stats **Per serving, without salt:**

Calories:............73.00
Protein:.............5.00 g
Carbohydrates:......9.00 g
Fat:................4.00 g
Sat. Fat:............1.00 g

1 teaspoon olive oil
½ cup chopped onion
3 roasted red bell peppers, seeded
   and chopped
3¼ cups low-fat, reduced-sodium
   chicken broth
½ cup nonfat plain yogurt
½ teaspoon sea salt (optional)
4 sprigs fresh basil (optional)

1. Heat a saucepan over medium-high heat. Add the olive oil and sauté the onion until transparent. Add the peppers and broth. Bring to a boil; reduce the heat and simmer 15 minutes. Remove from heat; purée in a blender or food processor until smooth.

2. Allow the soup to cool; stir in the yogurt and the salt, if using. Chill well in the refrigerator. Garnish the soup with fresh basil sprigs, if desired.

81

Nutty Greek-Snapper Soup

Serves 4

stats **Per serving:**

Calories: 309.00
Protein: . . . . .39.00 g
Carbohydrates: . . . . . .25.00 g
Fat: . . . . .6.00 g
Sat. Fat: . . . . .0.70 g

1-pound (16-ounce) red snapper fillet
2 large cucumbers
4 green onions, chopped
4 cups nonfat plain yogurt
1 cup packed, mixed fresh parsley,
    basil, cilantro, arugula, and
    chives
3 tablespoons lime juice
Salt and pepper to taste (optional)
¼ cup chopped walnuts
Herb sprigs for garnish (optional)

1. Rinse the red snapper fillet and pat dry with paper towels. Broil the fillet until opaque through the thickest part, about 4 minutes on each side, depending on the thickness of the fillet. Let cool. (Alternatives would be to steam or poach the fillets.)

2. Peel and halve the cucumbers; scoop out and discard the seeds; cut into roughly 1" pieces. Put half the cucumber with the green onions in the bowl of a food processor. Use the pulse button to coarsely chop; transfer to a large bowl. Add the remaining cucumber, yogurt, and herb leaves to the food processor; process until smooth and frothy. Stir the lime juice into the soup; season with salt and pepper to taste, if using. Cover and refrigerate for at least 1 hour or up to 8 hours; the longer the soup cools, the more the flavors will mellow.

3. While the soup cools, break the cooled red snapper fillet into large chunks, discarding the skin and any bones. Ladle the chilled soup into shallow bowls and add the red snapper. Sprinkle the chopped walnuts over the soup, garnish with herb sprigs, and serve.

tip

You can make this soup using leftover fish, or substitute halibut, cod, or sea bass for the snapper.

Vegetable-and-Bean Chili

Serves 8

 stats **Per serving:**

Calories: 205.17
Protein: . . . . .11.87 g
Carbohydrates: . . . . . .34.97 g
Fat: . . . . .3.10 g
Sat. Fat: . . . . .0.64 g

4 teaspoons olive oil
2 cups chopped cooking onions
½ cup chopped green bell pepper
3 cloves garlic, chopped
1 small jalapeño pepper, finely
    chopped (Only include the seeds
    if you like the chili extra hot!)
1 tablespoon chili powder
1 teaspoon ground cumin
1 (28-ounce) can unsalted tomatoes,
    undrained
2 zucchini, peeled and chopped
2 (15-ounce) cans unsalted kidney
    beans, rinsed
1 tablespoon chopped semisweet
    chocolate
3 tablespoons chopped fresh cilantro

1. Heat a heavy pot over moderately high heat. Add the olive oil, onions, bell pepper, garlic, and jalapeño; sauté until the vegetables are softened, about 5 minutes. Add the chili powder and cumin; sauté 1 minute, stirring frequently to mix well.

2. Chop the tomatoes and add them with their juice, along with the zucchini. Bring to a boil; lower heat and simmer, partially covered, 15 minutes, stirring occasionally. Stir in the beans and chocolate; simmer, stirring occasionally, an additional 5 minutes, or until the beans are heated through and the chocolate is melted. Stir in the cilantro and serve.

Rich and Creamy Sausage-Potato Soup

Serves 2

 Per serving:

Calories: 326.26
Protein: . . . . .16.53 g
Carbohydrates: . . . . . .52.72 g
Fat: . . . . .5.77 g
Sat. Fat: . . . . .1.91 g

1 teaspoon olive oil
½ teaspoon butter
½ cup chopped onion, steamed
1 clove roasted garlic (see page 4)
1 ounce crumbled, cooked chorizo
¼ teaspoon celery seed
2 Yukon gold potatoes, peeled and
    diced into 1" pieces
½ cup fat-free chicken broth
1½ cups mock cream
1 teaspoon white wine vinegar
1 teaspoon vanilla extract
Optional seasonings to taste:
Fresh parsley
Sea salt and freshly ground black
    pepper to taste

In a saucepan, heat the olive oil and butter over medium heat. Add the onion, roasted garlic, chorizo, celery seed, and potatoes; sauté until the mixture is heated. Add the chicken broth and bring the mixture to a boil. Cover the saucepan, reduce heat, and maintain simmer 10 minutes, or until the potatoes are tender. Add the mock cream and heat. Remove pan from the burner and stir in the vinegar and vanilla.

Skim the Fat

You can remove fat from soups and stews by dropping ice cubes into the pot. The fat will cling to the cubes as you stir. Be sure to take out the cubes before they melt. Fat also clings to lettuce leaves; simply sweep them over the top of the soup. Discard ice cubes or leaves when you're done.

Chicken-Corn Chowder

Serves 10

stats **Per serving:**

Calories:............193
Protein:.............17.39 g
Carbohydrates:......20.74 g
Fat:.................4.8 g
Sat. Fat:............2.86 g

*1 pound boneless, skinless chicken
    breast, cut into chunks
1 medium onion, chopped
1 red bell pepper, diced
1 large potato, diced
2 (16-ounce) cans low-fat, reduced-
    sodium chicken broth
1 (8¾-ounce) can unsalted cream-
    style corn
½ cup all-purpose flour
2 cups skim milk
4 ounces Cheddar cheese, diced
½ teaspoon sea salt
Freshly ground pepper to taste
½ cup processed bacon bits*

1. Spray a large soup pot with nonstick cooking spray and heat on medium setting until hot. Add the chicken, onion, and bell pepper; sauté over medium heat until the chicken is browned and the vegetables are tender. Stir in the potatoes and broth; bring to a boil. Reduce the heat; simmer, covered, 20 minutes. Stir in the corn.

2. Blend the flour and milk in a bowl; gradually stir it into the pot. Increase heat to medium and cook until the mixture comes to a boil; reduce heat and simmer until soup is thickened, stirring constantly. Add the cheese; stir until it's melted and blended into the soup. Add the salt and pepper to taste and sprinkle with bacon bits before serving.

tip

To trim down the fat in this recipe, use a reduced-fat cheese, such as Cabot's 50% Light Cheddar.

Smoked Mussel Chowder

Serves 6

 stats   **Per serving:**

Calories: 272.74
Protein:. . . . . .7.59 g
Carbohydrates: . . . . . .36.67 g
Fat:. . . . . .8.29 g
Sat. Fat:. . . . . .1.57 g

2 tablespoons olive oil
1 medium onion, chopped
2 carrots, diced
2 stalks celery, diced
½ bulb fennel, diced
1 teaspoon chopped garlic
4 red potatoes, cut into ½" cubes
1 cup dry white wine
2½ cups clam juice
1 bay leaf
Pinch of cayenne pepper
½ teaspoon thyme
2 medium-sized white potatoes,
    peeled and quartered (to yield
    2½ cups)
1 cup skim milk
4 ounces Ducktrap River smoked
    mussels
Sea salt and freshly ground black
    pepper to taste (optional)
Fresh parsley sprigs (optional)

1. Heat the olive oil in soup pot. Add the onions, carrots, celery, fennel, and garlic; gently sauté 10 minutes (do not brown vegetables). Add the red potatoes, wine, clam juice, bay leaf, cayenne and thyme. Let the soup simmer until the potatoes are cooked.

2. In a separate pan of boiling water, cook the white potatoes until tender. Mash the potatoes by putting them through a potato ricer or into the bowl of a food processor along with some of the skim milk. Once the red potatoes in the chowder are tender, stir in the mashed potatoes, remaining milk, and mussels. Do not let the soup come to a boil. Salt and pepper to taste and serve garnished with parsley sprigs, if desired.

Salmon Chowder

Serves 4

 Per serving:

Calories:. 363.90
Protein:. . . . . .20.44 g
Carbohydrates: . . . . . .61.27 g
Fat:. . . . . .5.67 g
Sat. Fat:. . . . . .2.20 g

1 (7½-ounce) can unsalted salmon
2 teaspoons butter
1 medium onion, chopped
2 stalks celery, chopped
1 sweet green pepper, seeded and
    chopped
1 clove garlic, minced
4 carrots, peeled and diced
4 small potatoes, peeled and diced
1 cup fat-free chicken broth
1 cup water
½ teaspoon cracked black pepper
½ teaspoon dill seed
1 cup diced zucchini
1 cup mock cream
1 (8¾-ounce) can unsalted cream-
    style corn
Freshly ground black pepper to taste
½ cup chopped fresh parsley
    (optional)

1. Drain and flake the salmon, discarding liquid. In large nonstick saucepan, melt the butter over medium heat; sauté the onion, celery, green pepper, garlic, and carrots, stirring often until the vegetables are tender, about 5 minutes. Add the potatoes, broth, water, pepper, and dill seed; bring to boil. Reduce heat, cover, and simmer 20 minutes, or until the potatoes are tender.

2. Add the zucchini; simmer, covered, another 5 minutes. Add the salmon, Mock Cream, corn, and pepper. Cook over low heat until just heated through. Just before serving, add parsley, if desired.

Spicy Ham-and-Bean Soup

Yields: 10 servings
Serving size: 12 ounces

stats **Per serving:**

Calories:............133.90
Protein:.............6.47 g
Carbohydrates:......14.09 g
Sugar: ....1.20 g
Fat:.................5.96 g

2 smoked ham hocks
2 quarts water
2 tablespoons olive oil
½ large sweet onion, chopped
1 sweet red pepper, stemmed, seeded,
    and chopped
4 cloves garlic, chopped
2 tablespoons Splenda
¼ teaspoon ground cloves
Salt and freshly ground black pepper
    to taste
1 tablespoon red pepper flakes or
    to taste
1½ quarts chicken broth
1 cup canned sugar-free, crushed
    tomatoes
2 (13-ounce) cans white kidney
    beans, drained and rinsed
½ bunch parsley leaves, chopped

1. Boil ham hocks in water (2 quarts, or enough to cover) until meat is falling off the bone. Cool and remove skin, fat, and bone. Chop and save meat. Return broth to a boil and reduce by half (to measure 1 quart). Cool broth and skim fat from top.

2. Heat the oil in a large soup pot over medium heat. Sauté the onion, red pepper, and garlic.

3. Stir in the Splenda, cloves, salt and pepper to taste, and crushed red pepper. Add the chicken broth, tomatoes, beans, ham meat, and reduced ham broth.

4. Bring to a boil; reduce heat to a simmer. Cover and cook 2 hours. Stir in chopped parsley just before serving.

Chicken-and-Wild-Rice Soup with Cranberries

Yields: 12 servings
Serving size: 10 ounces

stats **Per serving:**

Calories: 159.2
Protein: . . . . 12.17 g
Carbohydrates: . . . . . . 10.08 g
Sugar: . . . . 2.37 g
Fat: . . . . 8.12 g

1 cup fresh cranberries
4 cups water, divided
¼ cup Splenda
2 tablespoons olive oil
1 cup red Spanish onion, finely
    chopped
2 stalks celery with leaves, minced
½ cup wild rice
1 quart beef broth
2 quarts chicken broth
2 teaspoons soy sauce
1 teaspoon anchovy paste
1 teaspoon dried thyme leaves
6 fresh sage leaves, torn or 1
    teaspoon dried sage
1 tablespoon unsalted butter
1 pound boneless, skinless chicken
    breasts, cut in slivers
Salt and freshly ground pepper to
    taste

1. Place the cranberries, 2 cups of water, and Splenda in a small saucepan; bring to a boil. Reduce heat; simmer until the berries pop. Remove from heat and set aside.

2. Heat the oil in a large soup pot over medium heat. Add the onion and celery; cook 5 minutes, stirring constantly. Stir in the rice. Add the remaining 2 cups of water, beef and chicken broth, soy sauce, anchovy paste, thyme, and sage. Pour in the cranberries. Cover pot and let simmer.

3. Meanwhile, heat the butter in a saucepan over medium heat. Add the chicken and cook 5 minutes, stirring constantly. Set aside.

4. Keep soup at simmer 2 hours, or until wild-rice grains have bloomed. Add chicken, salt, and pepper. Cover and simmer another 10 minutes. Serve hot.

Quick Italian Sausage

Yields: 10 servings
Serving size: 2 sausages

stats **Per serving:**

Calories:............. 104.32
(with meatballs: ...... 181.2)
Protein:.............. 9.57 g
(with meatballs:...... 10.97 g)
Carbohydrates: .... 1.49 g
(with meatballs:....... 0.57 g)
Sugar: .... 0.57 g
(with meatballs:....... 0.08 g)
Fat:................... 6.66 g
(with meatballs:...... 12.76 g)

Basic recipe:
2 cloves garlic, minced
½ cup onion, minced
1½ teaspoons fennel seeds
1 teaspoon dried oregano
1 egg, lightly beaten
1 teaspoon dried sage
1 pound ground pork
1 pound ground sirloin
Salt and freshly ground black pepper
  to taste
1 teaspoon hot red pepper flakes, or
  to taste
2 teaspoons soy sauce
½ cup finely grated Parmesan or
  Romano cheese

1. Thoroughly combine all ingredients in a bowl. Form into patties and sauté in a non-stick pan with nonstick spray. Brown 4 minutes per side over medium heat.

2. For sausage-ball variation: Form the meat into small balls; roll in bread crumbs.

3. Heat the oil to 350°F in a large frying pan; fry the sausage balls until brown. Drain on paper towels to eliminate as much oil as possible.

Chili-Spiced Beef-and-Black Bean Soup

Yields: 12 servings
Serving size: 8 ounces

stats **Per serving:**

Calories: 196.55
Protein: . . . . 14.42 g
Carbohydrates: . . . . . . 21.58 g
Sugar: . . . . 2.44 g
Fat: . . . . 8.45 g

2 tablespoons olive oil
1 large onion, chopped
4 cloves garlic, chopped
1 sweet red bell pepper, stemmed,
    seeded, deveined, and chopped
1 sweet green bell pepper, stemmed,
    seeded, deveined, and chopped
2 jalapeño peppers, stemmed,
    seeded, deveined, and chopped
½ pound lean ground sirloin
½ pound lean ground pork
2 tablespoons Splenda
2 (13-ounce) cans beef broth
2 tablespoons chili powder
¼ teaspoon ground cloves
¼ teaspoon cinnamon
1 teaspoon unsweetened cocoa
    powder
1 (28-ounce) can crushed Italian
    plum tomatoes
3 (13-ounce) cans black beans,
    drained
Salt and freshly ground black pepper
    to taste
Juice of 1 lime

1. Heat the olive oil in a large kettle over medium heat. Add the onion, garlic, and bell and jalapeño peppers. Cook 5 minutes, stirring constantly.

2. Add the rest of the ingredients, one at a time, stirring constantly. Cover and reduce heat to a simmer. Cook 3 hours, stirring occasionally. Do not let boil.

3. If the liquid cooks down, add water or more broth to keep level consistent.

tip

Use dollops of sour cream or shredded Cheddar cheese to garnish this dish. Leftovers can be frozen.

Lemon and Lime Juice

Even in a jam, do not use the reconstituted or concentrated juice that comes in the little plastic lemons and limes. Buy several lemons and/or limes and squeeze them, straining the juice into plastic bags. Seal and label the bags and freeze them.

Zucchini-and-Sausage Soup

Yields: 6 servings
Serving size: 8 ounces

 Per serving:

Calories:............134.6
Protein:.............4.94 g
Carbohydrates: ......14.08 g
Sugar: ....3.89 g
Fat:.................6.75 g

2 tablespoons olive oil
2 yellow onions, chopped
4 garlic cloves, minced
2 medium zucchini, sliced
2 fresh plum tomatoes, diced
1 teaspoon Splenda
1 teaspoon salt
2 tablespoons white wine vinegar
2 cups water
3 cups chicken broth
½ pound Quick Italian Sausage
    (page 90), sausage-ball variation
1 cup orzo or orchetta, cooked and
    drained
½ cup fresh basil leaves, trimmed
1 teaspoon dried oregano leaves
1 teaspoon dried red pepper flakes
Freshly ground black pepper to taste
1 teaspoon freshly grated Parmesan
    cheese per bowl, for garnish

1. Heat the olive oil in a large soup kettle over medium heat. Sauté the onion, garlic, and zucchini 5 minutes, stirring constantly. Add the tomatoes, Splenda, salt, vinegar, water, and broth. Let come to a boil.

2. Add the meatballs to the boiling soup a few at a time. Add the pasta, basil, oregano, pepper flakes, and pepper. Let cook 15 minutes.

3. Garnish with cheese.

There's Something About Meatballs

Whether they are big and beefy, small and Swedish, or slathered in tomato sauce, people love meatballs. Put out some meatballs for your next party and watch them disappear. Sausage meat is excellent for meatballs, as is a combination of beef, pork, and veal.

Italian Escarole, Sausage, and Bean Soup

Yields: 12 servings
Serving size: 9 ounces

 Per serving:

Calories: 167.54
Protein: . . . . .9.48 g
Carbohydrates: . . . . . .18.14 g
Sugar: . . . . .1.91 g
Fat: . . . . .6.57 g

2 tablespoons olive oil
½ pound Quick Italian Sausage
    (page 90)
1 whole red onion, chopped
8 cloves garlic, slivered
1 fennel bulb, slivered
Juice of 1 lemon
1 head escarole, cored and chopped
2 teaspoons dried rosemary
1 teaspoon dried oregano
2 cups water
2 quarts chicken broth
Salt and freshly ground pepper to
    taste
2 (13-ounce) cans white kidney
    beans, drained and rinsed
1 teaspoon grated Parmesan cheese
    per bowl of soup, for garnish

1. Heat the oil in a large soup pot over medium heat. Add the sausage, breaking up with a wooden spoon. When it starts to brown, add the onion, garlic, and fennel.

2. Continue to cook and stir until the vegetables soften, but do not brown. Add the rest of the ingredients, with the exception of the garnish.

3. Cover and reduce heat to a slow simmer. Cook 60 minutes. Ladle into bowls. Sprinkle each bowl with Parmesan cheese.

Spanish Garlic-and-Sausage Soup

Yields: 8 servings
Serving size: 8 ounces

 **Per serving:**

Calories: 199.13
Protein: . . . . 8.62 g
Carbohydrates: . . . . . . 7.2 g
Sugar: . . . . 3.03 g
Fat: . . . . 14.96 g

2 tablespoons olive oil
1 head roasted garlic
½ cup red onion
½ pound sugarless chorizo sausage,
    thinly sliced
6 cups chicken broth
1 cup fresh or canned diced
    tomatoes
1 teaspoon dried oregano
1 teaspoon Splenda
1 bunch Italian flat-leaf parsley
Salt and pepper to taste

1. Heat the olive oil in a large soup kettle. Add the garlic and onions and cook, stirring over medium heat until the garlic has become a paste and the onions are translucent.

2. Stir in the rest of the ingredients. Taste before adding the salt and pepper; since the sausage contains sodium, you may not need any. Cover and simmer over low heat 60 minutes. Serve hot.

Creamy Fish Soup

Yields: 6 servings
Serving size: 8 ounces

stats **Per serving:**

Calories: 366.89
Protein:. . . . . .25.70 g
Carbohydrates: . . . . . .27.37 g
Sugar: . . . . .9.62 g
Fat:. . . . . .16.75 g

1 cup water
1½ cups clam broth
1 pound Idaho potatoes, peeled and
    sliced
1 pound whole pearl onions
1 pound lean cod or other white fish
    fillet, skinned and cut into bite-
    sized pieces
1 bay leaf
½ teaspoon dried thyme or 1½
    teaspoons fresh thyme
1 teaspoon Splenda
2 tablespoons whole-wheat flour
    blended with ¼ cup cold water
Freshly ground black pepper to taste
2 teaspoons soy sauce
3 cups 1% low-fat milk
½ cup heavy cream
½ cup fresh parsley, coarsely
    chopped
3 slices sugar-free cooked bacon,
    crumbled or 2 thick slices boiled
    ham, crisped

1. Bring the water and clam broth to a boil in a large soup kettle. Add the potatoes; reduce heat to a simmer. Cover and cook until the potatoes are tender.

2. Add the onions, fish, bay leaf, thyme, Splenda, flour, pepper, and soy sauce. Return to a boil; reduce heat to very low. The soup should be very thick.

3. Slowly stir in the milk and cream. Do not boil, or your soup may curdle. Remove the bay leaf. Ladle into bowls and garnish with parsley and bacon.

 tip

The clam broth adds sufficient sodium to the recipe, so no additional salt is needed.

Remove that Bay Leaf!

Bay leaves stay tough even after long cooking, and they have sharp edges. They can stick in the throat, cut the tongue, and be about as destructive as a razor in your food.

Sicilian Mussel Soup

Yields: 6 servings
Serving size: 7 ounces

 Per serving:

Calories: 236.04
Protein: . . . . 24 g
Carbohydrates: . . . . . . 14.13 g
Sugar: . . . . 3.87 g
Fat: . . . . 9.21 g

2 tablespoons olive oil
4 cloves garlic, chopped
2 shallots, chopped
1 cup water
2½ pounds mussels, scrubbed
1 (28-ounce) can crushed tomatoes
Zest and juice of ½ lemon
1 teaspoon red pepper flakes, or to
    taste
1 teaspoon Splenda
Salt and pepper to taste
1 teaspoon dried oregano
½ cup fresh Italian flat-leaf parsley,
    chopped

1. Heat the oil over medium-high heat in a four-quart soup pot. Sauté the garlic and shallots. Do not brown. Add the water and mussels. Bring to a boil and cook, stirring.

2. Using a slotted spoon, remove each mussel as it opens and place in a bowl on the side. Let the mussels cool. Add the rest of the ingredients to the pan; reduce the heat to a simmer.

3. When the mussels are cool enough to handle, twist off the top shell from each and add them back into the soup. Cook briefly, until mussels are hot again, and serve.

tip

Select mussels that are completely closed; they will open when you cook them. Discard any mussels that do not open. Remove the top half of the shell from each mussel to make them prettier to serve and easier to eat.

Lobster-and-Corn Chowder

Yields: 8 servings
Serving size: 8 ounces

 stats **Per serving:**

Calories: 174.21
Protein: . . . . .5.94 g
Carbohydrates: . . . . . .15.85 g
Sugar: . . . . .6.23 g
Fat: . . . . .8.98 g

1 tablespoon butter
½ cup sweet onion, chopped
2 tablespoons corn flour blended
    with ¼ cup cold water
1 teaspoon Splenda
1 tablespoon tomato paste
1½ cups clam broth
1 large Yukon Gold potato, peeled
    and chopped
1 tablespoon soy sauce
1 cup corn kernels
Freshly ground black pepper to taste
⅔ pound fresh or canned lobster
    meat
2 cups 1% low-fat milk
2 cups half-and-half
Salt (optional)
2 tablespoons fresh parsley for
    garnish

1. Melt the butter over medium heat in a large soup pot. Stir in the onion. Cook and stir 4 minutes, or until onion is translucent. Blend in the corn flour and Splenda. Cook another 3 minutes.

2. Add the tomato paste, clam broth, potato, and soy sauce. Reduce heat to low and cover. Cook until the potato is soft.

3. Stir in the corn and pepper. Let cook for another 3 minutes. Slowly stir in the lobster, milk, and half-and-half. Cook over low heat.

4. Add salt to taste and garnish with parsley. Serve hot with Spicy Cheese Twists (page 104).

Lobster Meat

Cooking and extracting the meat from a lobster is labor-intensive, except for the claws and the tail. You can sometimes find frozen lobster meat, frozen tail, or good fresh lobster meat at an upscale fish market. If you cook the beast yourself, save some of the broth for your chowder.

 tip

If you are going to prepare the lobster yourself, you will need two 1¼-pound lobsters, cooked and picked. Most fishmongers and fish departments in supermarkets have fresh lobster meat. The added salt may be omitted from this recipe because the soy sauce provides enough sodium.

Creamed Broccoli-and-Cheddar Soup

Yields: 4 servings
Serving size: 8 ounces

 Per serving:

Calories: 241.09
Protein: . . . . 12.97 g
Carbohydrates: . . . . . . 9.68 g
Sugar: . . . . 3.31 g
Fat: . . . . 17.12 g

1 broccoli crown
1 tablespoon whole-wheat flour
2 tablespoons cold water
3½ cups chicken broth
1 teaspoon Basic Mustard (below)
1 teaspoon Splenda
Salt and freshly ground black pepper
*   to taste*
1 teaspoon fresh lemon zest
½ cup half-and-half
4 tablespoons grated sharp Vermont
*   or Wisconsin Cheddar cheese*
⅛ teaspoon ground nutmeg
¼ cup toasted pine nuts, for garnish

1. Blanch the broccoli in boiling water 3 minutes. Drain and cool under cold running water to set the color. When cool, chop and set aside.

2. Stir flour into water; combine to make a smooth paste.

3. In a soup pot, whisk together the broth, flour paste, mustard, Splenda, salt, pepper, and lemon zest. Return the broccoli to the pot and heat, stirring. Add the half-and-half. Divide between 4 bowls.

4. Float the cheese and nutmeg on top and sprinkle with pine nuts.

You can puree the soup or leave it chunky; it's great either way.

Basic Mustard and Dijon-Style Mustard

This basic recipe is the first mustard you should learn to make—it's easy and delicious. To make, whisk ⅓ cup powdered English or Dijon mustard and ⅓ cup cold water together. Let stand to develop for 15 minutes. Serve or mix into a sauce. The analysis is: Calories: 8.18, Protein: 0.42 g, Carbohydrates: 0.32 g, Sugar: 0 g, Fat: 0.55 g. Yields: ⅓ cup; serving size: ½ teaspoon.

Creamy Pureed Mushroom Soup

Yields: 8 servings
Serving size: 8 ounces

stats **Per serving:**

Calories: 177.19
Protein:. . . . . .8.83 g
Carbohydrates: . . . . . .14.14 g
Sugar: . . . . .6.93 g
Fat:. . . . . .10 g

3 tablespoons whole-wheat flour
4 tablespoons cold water
2 tablespoons olive oil
6 shallots, chopped
1 pound of mushrooms, stemmed
 and sliced
1 teaspoon dried savory
1 teaspoon cayenne pepper, or to
 taste
1 teaspoon Splenda
Salt and pepper to taste
Juice of 1 lemon
6 cups beef broth
½ cup half-and-half
2 large pears, peeled, cored, and
 diced
½ cup whipping cream, whipped

1. Mix water with flour; combine to make a smooth paste. Set aside.

2. Heat the olive oil in a soup pot over medium heat. Add the shallots and mushrooms. Cook 5 minutes, stirring constantly.

3. Carefully mix in the next 6 ingredients one at a time, stirring constantly. Bring to a boil and reduce heat; cook 30 minutes. Working in batches, puree soup in blender.

4. Return to the soup pot. Add the half-and-half. Reduce heat to very low; sprinkle the pears around the soup. When hot, ladle into bowls.

5. Float spoonfuls of whipped cream on top of each bowl. Sprinkle with black pepper.

Cleaning Mushrooms

Do not wash or peel mushrooms; they are like sponges when it comes to water. Any bits of dirt that cling to their surface are harmless; the soil that mushrooms are grown in has been treated with thermo-phyllic bacteria, which kills all of the "bad" germs. Just use a brush or a damp towel to brush the mushrooms off, cut off the stems, and slice them lengthwise.

Irish Leek-and-Potato Soup

Yields: 6 servings
Serving size: 8 ounces

stats **Per serving:**

Calories: 263.52
Protein: . . . . .8 g
Carbohydrates: . . . . . .29.21 g
Sugar: . . . . .8.97 g
Fat: . . . . .12.15 g

*2 tablespoons butter or tub
    margarine*
4 leeks, white part only, thinly sliced
*1 large Vidalia or other sweet white
    onion*
2 tablespoons potato flour
*2 large Idaho or Yukon Gold
    potatoes, peeled and diced*
3 cups chicken broth
1 teaspoon salt, or to taste
1 teaspoon Splenda
Freshly ground black pepper to taste
1 teaspoon curry powder, or to taste
1 cup 1% low-fat milk
1½ cups half-and-half
½ bunch fresh parsley, chopped
*2 slices bacon, diced and boiled in ¼
    cup water*

1. Melt the butter in a large heavy-bottomed soup kettle over medium heat. Add the leeks and onions. Cook and stir 3–4 minutes.

2. Stir in the flour to blend well with butter. Add the potatoes, broth, salt, and Splenda. Reduce the heat and cover the pot. Cook over very low heat until the potatoes are tender.

3. Add the milk and half-and-half; stir to blend. Keep warm over low heat until ready to serve, then garnish with parsley and bacon. You can add pepper and/or curry powder for more spice if you want to.

tip

Cut leeks in half and wash them thoroughly to remove any dirt before slicing them.

White Bean-and-Tomato Soup

Yields: 12 servings
Serving size: 8 ounces

 **Per serving:**

Calories: 138.97
Protein: . . . . .8.16 g
Carbohydrates: . . . . . .20.57 g
Sugar: . . . . .3.17 g
Fat: . . . . .3.62 g

2 tablespoons olive oil
1 large Vidalia or other sweet white
    onion, chopped
2 cloves garlic, chopped
1 teaspoon Splenda
1 bunch fresh basil, torn in small
    pieces
½ bunch Italian flat-leaf parsley,
    chopped
Salt and freshly ground pepper to
    taste
1 (28-ounce) can crushed tomatoes
Juice of 1 lemon
2 (18-ounce) cans beef broth
2 (13-ounce) cans white beans,
    drained and rinsed

1. Heat the oil in a large soup kettle over medium heat. Sauté the onion and garlic. Stir in the Splenda; add the rest of the ingredients.

2. Bring to a boil. Reduce heat and cover. Simmer 15 minutes and serve.

Tomato Bisque with Sour Cream

Yields: 6 servings
Serving size: 5 ounces

 Per serving:

Calories: 58.59
Protein: . . . . 1.67 g
Carbohydrates: . . . . . . 8.74 g
Sugar: . . . . 1.93 g
Fat: . . . . 2.33 g

1 teaspoon butter or tub margarine,
    melted
1½ tablespoons potato flour
2 shallots, peeled
1 (13-ounce) can chicken broth
1 teaspoon Splenda
1 pint cherry tomatoes, stems
    removed
Salt and pepper to taste
1 teaspoon dried oregano
½ cup low-fat sour cream
Fresh chives, chopped, for garnish

1. Put everything but the sour cream and garnish into your blender; puree. Place in a pot and bring to a boil.

2. Reduce heat and simmer 10 minutes. Ladle into bowls and float sour cream on top. Sprinkle with chives and serve.

Loaded Crackers

Yummy little garnishes and snacks are often loaded with sugar and trans-fat. For instance, Campbell's cream soups are made with considerable amounts of sugar. Who knew? That's why label-reading is so important. Take your reading glasses with you to the supermarket, and find brands you can trust.

Herb Crackers

Yields: 48 crackers
Serving size: 4 crackers

 stats **Per serving:**

Calories: 130.83
Protein: . . . . 2.58 g
Carbohydrates: . . . . . . 16.25 g
Sugar: . . . . 0.62 g
Fat: . . . . 6.16 g

1½ cups all-purpose flour
½ cup whole-wheat flour
½ teaspoon salt
2 teaspoons fresh rosemary, finely
   chopped
1 teaspoon garlic powder
5 tablespoons extra-virgin olive oil,
   divided
¼ cup low-fat milk (more if needed
   to moisten dough)
1 tablespoon dried oregano leaves
1 tablespoon coarse sea salt

1. Preheat the oven to 425°F. In a large bowl, thoroughly combine the flours, salt, rosemary, and garlic powder. Stir in 4 tablespoons of olive oil.

2. Work the dough with your fingers or a food processor until it is the consistency of oatmeal. Stir milk in gradually, adding enough to make the dough hold together firmly.

3. Line a cookie sheet with parchment paper. Roll out the dough into a 12" × 16" rectangle.

4. Roll onto a rolling pin and place on the parchment paper. Cut into 1" strips. Cut across strips to make 1" squares.

5. Brush the tops of dough squares with remaining tablespoon of olive oil. Sprinkle with oregano and sea salt. Bake 15 minutes, until lightly browned. Cool. Store in an airtight container. Crackers will last a week.

Spicy Cheese Twists

Yields: 32 twists
Serving size: 2 twists

 Per serving:

Calories: 198.17
Protein: . . . . .4.88 g
Carbohydrates: . . . . . .11.93 g
Sugar: . . . . .0.41 g
Fat: . . . . .15.1 g

6 ounces unsalted butter
6 ounces cream cheese, cubed
2 ounces sharp Cheddar cheese,
    grated
2 ounces Parmesan cheese, finely
    grated
1 teaspoon sea salt
1 teaspoon Splenda
1 teaspoon dried basil leaves
1 teaspoon onion powder
1 tablespoon red hot-pepper flakes,
    or to taste
1½ cups corn flour
½ cup whole-wheat flour

1. Place all ingredients but the flour in a food processor; pulse. Slowly add the flour, a half-cup at a time; pulse until dough is just mixed and holding together. Divide dough in half. Shape into 2 oblong loaves and wrap tightly in plastic.

2. Refrigerate loaves 60 minutes. Line a cookie sheet with parchment paper. Preheat oven to 400°F. Roll one loaf of dough to 12" × 16" and ⅛" thickness.

3. Cut into 16 strips. Gently twist them and place them on the parchment paper. Bake 12 minutes.

4. Reduce heat to 350°F; bake another 6 minutes, or until crisp and golden. Let cool. Twists should be very dry and crunchy. Repeat for the second loaf.

tip

If you make extra dough and freeze it, you can always roll some twists out at the last minute.

CHAPTER

5

Salads

❧ **Some** of these recipes are for salad dressings; as lettuce is fairly negligible when it comes to carbohydrates, feel free to add any of these dressings to a plain salad. When you have to be careful is when you start adding other components to the salad (carrots, croutons, etc.)—these added carbohydrates may need to be accounted for.

continued

continued

Greens in Garlic with Pasta

Serves 4

 Per serving, without salt:

Calories:............175.47
Protein:.............7.60 g
Carbohydrates: ......25.56 g
Fat:.................5.00 g
Sat. Fat:.............0.72 g

2 teaspoons olive oil
4 cloves garlic, crushed
6 cups tightly packed, loose-leaf
    greens (baby mustard, turnip,
    chard)
2 cups cooked pasta
2 teaspoons extra-virgin olive oil
¼ cup freshly grated Parmesan
    cheese
Salt and freshly ground black pepper
    to taste (optional)

1. Place a sauté pan over medium heat. When the pan is hot, add the 2 teaspoons of olive oil and the crushed garlic. Cook, stirring frequently, until golden brown (3–5 minutes), being careful not to burn the garlic, as that makes it bitter. Add the greens; sauté until they are coated in the garlic oil. Remove from heat.

2. In a large serving bowl, add the pasta, cooked greens, 2 teaspoons extra-virgin olive oil, and Parmesan cheese; toss to mix. Season as desired and serve immediately.

Sweet or Salty?

In most cases, when you add a pinch (less than ⅛ teaspoon) of sugar to a recipe, you can reduce the amount of salt without noticing a difference. Sugar acts as a flavor enhancer and magnifies the effect of the salt.

Green Bean-and-Mushroom Salad

Serves 4

 Per serving:

Calories:............131.14
Protein:.............2.35 g
Carbohydrates: ......9.14 g
Fat:.................10.44 g
Sat. Fat:............1.43 g

2 cups fresh small green beans, ends
    trimmed
1½ cups sliced fresh mushrooms
½ cup chopped red onion
3 tablespoons extra-virgin olive,
    canola, or corn oil
1 tablespoon balsamic or red wine
    vinegar
1 clove garlic, minced
½ teaspoon sea salt (optional)
¼ teaspoon freshly ground pepper
    (optional)

1. Cook the green beans in a large pot of unsalted boiling water 5 minutes. Drain the beans in a colander that you then immediately plunge into a bowl of ice water; this stops the cooking process and retains the bright green color of the beans.

2. Once the beans are cooled, drain and place in a large bowl. If you'll be serving the salad immediately, add the mushrooms and onions to the bowl; toss to mix. (Otherwise, as recommended earlier, chill the beans separately and add them to the salad immediately before serving.)

3. To make the dressing, combine the oil and vinegar in a small bowl. Whisk together with the garlic and pour over the salad. Toss lightly and season with salt and pepper, if desired. Serve immediately.

White-and-Black Bean Salad

Serves 8

 stats **Per serving:**

Calories: 165.22
Protein: . . . . .7.43 g
Carbohydrates: . . . . . .26.77 g
Fat: . . . . .3.74 g
Sat. Fat: . . . . .0.54 g

1 cup finely chopped red onion
2 cloves garlic, minced
2 tablespoons olive oil or vegetable
    oil
⅓ cup red wine vinegar
¼ cup seeded and chopped red
    pepper
¼ cup seeded and chopped green
    pepper
2 tablespoons minced parsley
2 tablespoons granulated sugar
¼ teaspoon sea salt (optional)
¼ teaspoon pepper (optional)
1 (15-ounce) can Great Northern
    beans, rinsed and drained
1 (15-ounce) can black beans, rinsed
    and drained
Red and green pepper rings, for
    garnish

In a nonstick skillet over medium heat, sauté the onions and garlic in the oil until the onions are just beginning to soften. Remove from the heat and allow to cool until warm. Stir the vinegar, peppers, parsley, and sugar into the onions and garlic. Pour the onion mixture over combined beans in a bowl; mix well. Season with salt and pepper, if desired, and garnish with pepper rings.

Broccoli-Cauliflower Slaw

Serves 8

stats **Per serving:**

Calories:............116.80
Protein:.............5.77 g
Carbohydrates:......13.16 g
Fat:.................5.43 g
Sat Fat:.............0.94 g

4 cups raw broccoli florets
4 cups raw cauliflower
½ cup Hellmann's or Best Foods Real
*   Mayonnaise*
1 cup cottage cheese, 1% fat
3 tablespoons tarragon vinegar
1 tablespoon balsamic vinegar
⅛ cup packed brown sugar
3 tablespoons red onion

Put the broccoli and cauliflower in a food processor; pulse-process to the consistency of shredded cabbage; pour into a bowl. Place the remaining ingredients in the food processor; process until smooth. Pour the resulting dressing over the broccoli-cauliflower mixture; stir. Chill until ready to serve.

tip

Substituting cottage cheese for some of the mayonnaise cuts the fat and calories in this recipe considerably. You can cut them even more if you're able to tolerate nonfat cottage cheese and mayonnaise.

Fresh Herb Conversions

If you substitute dried herbs for the fresh ones called for in a recipe, only use ⅓ the amount.

Zesty Feta-and-Olive Salad

Serves 4

stats **Per serving:**

Calories: 108.63
Protein: . . . . 3.26 g
Carbohydrates: . . . . . . 6.36 g
Fat: . . . . 8.48 g
Sat. Fat: . . . . 2.86 g

2 ounces crumbled feta
1 small red onion, diced
½ cup chopped celery
½ cup diced cucumber
1 clove garlic, minced
1 teaspoon lemon zest
1 teaspoon orange zest
1 cup halved, very small cherry
    tomatoes
½ cup mix of green and kalamata
    olives, pitted and sliced
1 tablespoon extra-virgin olive oil
2 tablespoons minced fresh Italian
    parsley
2 teaspoons minced fresh oregano
1 teaspoon minced fresh mint
1 tablespoon minced fresh cilantro
    (optional)
Large romaine or butter lettuce
    leaves
Freshly ground black pepper

Place the feta in a large bowl; add the onion, celery, cucumber, garlic, lemon zest, orange zest, cherry tomatoes, and olives; mix. Add the olive oil and fresh herbs; toss again. Arrange the lettuce leaves on 4 salad plates and spoon the feta salad on top. Top with freshly ground pepper and serve.

Avocado-and-Peach Salad

Serves 4

stats **Per serving, without salt**

Calories:............160.28
Protein:.............2.39 g
Carbohydrates: ......15.07 g
Fat:.................11.35 g
Sat. Fat:............1.72 g

⅛ cup water
⅛ cup frozen orange juice
    concentrate
1 clove garlic, crushed
1 teaspoon rice wine vinegar
1 tablespoon extra-virgin olive oil
½ teaspoon vanilla
1½ cups tightly packed baby arugula
2 tablespoons tarragon leaves
1 avocado, peeled and diced
1 peach, peeled and diced
½ cup thinly sliced Vidalia onion
Kosher or sea salt and freshly ground
    black pepper to taste (optional)

In a measuring cup, whisk the water, orange juice concentrate, garlic, vinegar, oil, and vanilla together until well mixed. Prepare the salad by arranging layers of the arugula and tarragon, then the avocado, peach, and onions; then drizzle the salad with the orange juice vinaigrette. Season with salt and pepper, if desired, and serve.

Experiment Sensibly

When it comes to new herbs and spices, err on the side of caution. If you're not sure whether or not you like a seasoning, mix all of the other ingredients together and test a bite of the salad with a pinch of the herb or spice before you add it to the entire recipe.

Orange-Avocado Slaw

Serves 10

 Per serving, without salt

Calories: 59.87
Protein: . . . . .1.78 g
Carbohydrates: . . . . . .4.55 g
Fat: . . . . .4.60 g
Sat. Fat: . . . . .0.70 g

¼ cup orange juice
½ teaspoon curry powder
⅛ teaspoon ground cumin
¼ teaspoon sugar
1 teaspoon white wine vinegar
1 tablespoon olive oil
1 avocado, peeled and chopped
5 cups broccoli slaw mix
Sea salt and freshly ground black
    pepper to taste (optional)

In a bowl, whisk together the orange juice, curry powder, cumin, sugar, and vinegar. Add the oil in a stream, whisking until emulsified. In a large bowl, toss the avocado with the slaw mix. Drizzle with the vinaigrette. Chill until ready to serve. Season with salt and pepper, if desired.

Honey-Dijon Tuna Salad

Serves 1

 stats **Per serving:**

Calories: 194.30
Protein: . . . . .22.42 g
Carbohydrates: . . . . . .24.43 g
Fat: . . . . .1.34 g
Sat. Fat: . . . . .0.25 g

¼ cup tuna in water, drained
½ cup diced celery
¼ cup diced onion
¼ cup seeded and diced red or green
    pepper
4 ounces (half of a small container)
    nonfat plain yogurt
1 teaspoon Dijon mustard
1 teaspoon lemon juice
¼ teaspoon honey
1 tablespoon raisins
1 cup tightly packed iceberg lettuce
    (or other salad greens)

1. Use a fork to flake the tuna into a bowl. Add all the other ingredients except the lettuce; mix well. Serve on lettuce or greens.

2. Alternate serving suggestion: Mix with ½ cup of chilled, cooked pasta before dressing the salad greens; adds 1 Starch Exchange choice.

Spinach Salad with Apple-Avocado Dressing

Serves 4

stats **Per serving:**

Calories:............121.92
Protein:.............2.43 g
Carbohydrates: ......8.31 g
Fat:.................9.96 g
Sat. Fat:.............1.45 g

¼ cup unsweetened apple juice
1 teaspoon (or up to 1 tablespoon)
   cider vinegar
1 clove garlic, minced
1 teaspoon Bragg's Liquid Aminos or
   soy sauce
½ teaspoon Worcestershire sauce
2 teaspoons olive oil
1 avocado, peeled and chopped
2½ cups tightly packed spinach and
   other salad greens
½ cup thinly sliced red onion
½ cup sliced radishes
½ cup bean sprouts

In a blender or food processor, combine the juice, vinegar (the amount of which will depend on how you like your dressing), garlic, Liquid Aminos (or soy sauce), Worcestershire, oil, and avocado; process until smooth. In a large bowl, toss the salad ingredients. Pour the dressing over the salad and toss again.

Salads Don't Have to Be Fat-Free

Unless you're on a calorie-restricted diet, fat free may not be your best choice—consult your dietitian. Studies show that women who consume up to 41.7 grams of vegetable fat a day have up to a 22 percent less chance of developing type 2 diabetes. Vegetable oils—combined with a diet rich in fish, fruits, vegetables, whole grains, and nuts—are much healthier than using those chemically created fat-free foods! This type of diet is not only heart healthy, it's believed to prevent certain cancers, too. (Source: WebMD, *http://my.webmd.com*)

Greek Pasta Salad

Serves 4

 stats **Per serving:**

Calories:............419.81
Protein:.............12.12 g
Carbohydrates: ......30.94 g
Fat:.................29.34 g
Sat. Fat:.............4.88 g

1 tablespoon lemon juice
3 tablespoons olive oil
1 teaspoon dried oregano
1 teaspoon Dijon mustard
1 clove garlic, minced
2 cups cooked pasta
1 cup slivered blanched almonds
1 cup sliced cucumber
1 cup diced fresh tomato
½ cup chopped red onion
½ cup Greek olives
2 ounces crumbled feta cheese
1½ cups romaine lettuce leaves

In a large salad bowl, whisk the lemon juice together with the olive oil, oregano, mustard, and garlic. Cover and refrigerate 1 hour, or up to 12 hours. Immediately before serving, toss the pasta with the almonds, cucumbers, tomatoes, red onions, olives, and feta cheese. Serve over the lettuce.

Sweet and Savory Side Salad

For 1 serving of an easy, versatile salad or a simple dressing over salad greens, mix ¾ cup shredded carrots, ¼ cup diced celery, 1 tablespoon raisins, and 1 teaspoon frozen pineapple juice concentrate. The Nutritional Analysis is: Calories: 31.00; Protein: 0.47 g; Carbohydrate: 7.64 g; Fat: 0.07 g; Sat. Fat: 0.01 g; Cholesterol: 0.00 mg; Sodium: 15.41 mg; Fiber: 1 g.

Bleu Cheese Pasta Salad

Serves 4

stats **Per serving:**

Calories: 280.80
Carbohydrates: . . . . . .23.72 g
Fat: . . . . .11.04 g
Sat. Fat: . . . . .4.58 g
Cholesterol: . . . . .38.06 mg

1 recipe Bleu Cheese Pasta (see page 284)
4 cups tightly packed salad greens
4 slices red onion
18 large black olives, sliced
4 ounces thinly sliced or chopped chicken breast, broiled, grilled, or steamed
Nonstarchy, Free-Exchange vegetables of your choice, such as sliced cucumbers, tomato, or zucchini to taste (optional)

Prepare the Bleu Cheese Pasta (warm or chilled.) Divide the salad greens between 4 plates. Top each salad with a slice of red onion, the olives, 1 ounce of the chicken breast, and the Free-Exchange vegetables of your choice, if desired. Top with the pasta.

Taco Salad

Serves 8

 Per serving:

Calories:............426.45
Protein:.............22.64 g
Carbohydrates: ......57.61 g
Fat:.................12.62 g
Sat. Fat:.............6.64 g

1 recipe Vegetable and Bean Chili
(see page 83)
8 cups tightly packed salad greens
8 ounces Cheddar cheese, shredded
(to yield 2 cups)
8 ounces nonfat corn chips
Nonstarchy, Free-Exchange
vegetables of your choice, such
as chopped celery, onion, or
banana or jalapeño peppers
(optional)

Prepare the Vegetable and Bean Chili. Divide the salad greens between 8 large bowls. Top with the chili, Cheddar cheese, corn chips, and vegetables or peppers, if using.

Layered Salad

Serves 6

 Per serving:

Calories: 286.45
Protein: . . . . .21.09 g
Carbohydrates: . . . . . .18.14 g
Fat: . . . . .18.89 g
Sat. Fat: . . . . .14.11 g

¼ cup Hellmann's or Best Foods Real
    Mayonnaise
1¼ cups nonfat cottage cheese
½ cup nonfat plain yogurt
1 tablespoon apple cider vinegar or
    lemon juice
Pinch of sugar
6 cups shredded mixed lettuce
1½ cups diced celery
1½ cups chopped onion, any variety
1½ cups sliced carrots
1½ cups frozen green peas, thawed
6 ounces (2% fat or less) smoked
    turkey breast
6 ounces Cheddar cheese, shredded
    (to yield 1½ cups)

1. Combine the mayonnaise, cottage cheese, yogurt, vinegar (or lemon juice), and sugar in a food processor or blender; process until smooth. Set aside.

2. In a large salad bowl, layer the lettuce, celery, onion, carrots, peas, and turkey breast. Spread the mayonnaise-mixture dressing over the top of the salad. Top with the shredded cheese.

Yogurt-Mayo Sandwich Spread

Spread a little flavor! Measure ½ teaspoon drained nonfat yogurt into a paper coffee filter. Twist to secure; drain over a cup or bowl in the refrigerator for at least 1 hour. In a small bowl, combine the drained yogurt with ½ teaspoon Hellmann's or Best Foods Real Mayonnaise. Use as you would mayonnaise. A 1-teaspoon serving has: Calories: 11.52; Protein: 0.23 g; Carbohydrate: 0.86 g; Fat: 0.82 g; Sat. Fat: 0.12 g; Cholesterol: 0.70 mg; Sodium: 20.11 mg; Fiber: 0.00 g.

Golden Raisin-Smoked Turkey Salad

Yields: 4 generous-sized salads

 Per serving:

Calories:.............366.47
Protein:.............20.84 g
Carbohydrates:......61.04 g
Fat:.................7.84 g
Sat. Fat:............1.51 g

4 cups chopped broccoli
2 cups chopped cauliflower
3 shallots, chopped
1⅓ cups golden raisins
1 cup 1% cottage cheese
¼ cup Hellmann's or Best Foods Real
　　Mayonnaise
¼ cup firm silken tofu
3 tablespoons tarragon vinegar
1 tablespoon balsamic vinegar
¼ cup brown sugar
¼ pound (4 ounces) smoked turkey
　　breast, chopped
Freshly ground pepper to taste
　　(optional)
4 cups salad greens

Combine the broccoli, cauliflower, and shallots in a large bowl; stir in the raisins. In a blender or food processor, mix together the cottage cheese, mayonnaise, tofu, vinegars, and brown sugar until smooth. Toss the dressing over the broccoli, cauliflower, raisins, shallots, and turkey. Season with freshly ground pepper to taste. Chill until ready to serve, over salad greens.

Because of the smoked turkey, this salad is high in sodium. If you're on a sodium-restricted diet, consider substituting regular cooked turkey or chicken breast. Punch up the flavor by adding 1 teaspoon of Bragg's Liquid Aminos or Worcestershire sauce.

Just How Bad Is Bacon?

According to a Nutritional Analysis done by Cybersoft, Inc. (makers of the NutriBase 2001 software), when bacon is cooked until it's crisp, and drained to remove as much fat as possible, it still adds a whopping 731.52 calories! That comes out to about 39 grams of protein and 63 grams of fat, a third of which are from saturated fats (the bad guys).

Green Bean-and-Tuna Salad with Romaine Lettuce

Yields: 4 servings

Serving size: 3 ounces tuna, 4 ounces beans, ¼ head lettuce

stats **Per serving:**

Calories: 261.43
Protein: . . . . .21.03 g
Carbohydrates: . . . . . .9.77 g
Sugar: . . . . .4.23 g
Fat: . . . . .14.99 g

¼ cup extra-virgin olive oil
2 tablespoons balsamic vinegar
1 tablespoon lemon juice
Salt and pepper to taste
½ teaspoon Splenda
12 ounces fresh tuna steak
1 head romaine lettuce, rinsed,
    trimmed, spun dry, and
    shredded
1 pound fresh green beans, trimmed,
    blanched, and chilled

1. Whisk the olive oil, balsamic vinegar, lemon juice, salt, pepper, and Splenda together to make the dressing.

2. Brush the tuna with 1 teaspoon of the dressing. Grill at medium-high heat 3 minutes per side.

3. Place the lettuce on the serving plates. Add the beans; place the tuna on top. Drizzle with the dressing.

tip

Fresh tuna is best, but you can substitute canned tuna or vacuum bags of tuna.

Luncheon Salads

A nice crisp salad with plenty of veggies, some protein, and a tiny bit of oil will carry you from lunchtime until teatime. Make plenty of dressing in advance. Your dressing will always be better than commercial, and you control the sweetness by regulating the amount of Splenda you add.

Chicken, Apple, Celery, and Nut Salad

Yields: 4 servings
Serving size: ½ cup

stats **Per serving:**

Calories:............395.91
Protein:.............13.54 g
Carbohydrates: ......9.01 g
Sugar: ....4.21 g
Fat:................35.25 g

¾ cup Basic Mayonnaise (below)
Juice of ½ lime
½ teaspoon prepared Dijon mustard
Salt and pepper to taste
1 cup cooked chicken breast, diced
1 tart green apple, cored and
    chopped
2 stalks celery, chopped
½ cup walnut pieces, toasted
4 cups baby greens, rinsed and spun
    dry

Whisk the mayonnaise, lime, Dijon mustard, salt, and pepper together in a large bowl. Add the chicken, apple, celery, and walnuts, tossing to coat. Serve chilled over baby greens.

tip

This very tasty version of a Waldorf salad tastes just as good with thinly sliced deli turkey.

Basic Mayonnaise

This easy recipe is good to remember so you can whip it up in a flash. To make, set the eggs out until they reach room temperature. Blend the juice of a ½ lemon, 1½ teaspoons dry English mustard, ¼ teaspoon cayenne pepper, 1 whole egg (at room temperature), 1 teaspoon Splenda, and ½ teaspoon salt in a blender. Then add ¾ cup of olive oil, a teaspoon at a time, and let the mayonnaise thicken slowly. When thick and creamy, refrigerate. This will keep for 4–5 days. The analysis: Calories: 68.12, Protein: 0.47 g, Carbohydrates: 0.21 g, Sugar: 0.07 g, Fat: 7.28 g. Yields: 1 cup; Serving size: 2 teaspoons.

Green Bean-and-Bacon Salad with Hot Gorgonzola Dressing

Yields: 4 servings
Serving size: ⅔ cup

stats **Per serving:**

Calories: 221.23
Protein:. . . . . .9.33 g
Carbohydrates: . . . . . .11.59 g
Sugar: . . . . .5.68 g
Fat:. . . . . .15.37 g

1 small head iceberg lettuce, outer
    leaves removed, quartered
1 pound green beans, trimmed,
    rinsed, and blanched
2 slices bacon, cooked
4 ounces Gorgonzola cheese,
    crumbled
2 tablespoons red wine vinegar
½ teaspoon Splenda

1. Divide the lettuce among the 4 serving plates. Arrange the beans on top. Crumble the bacon over each serving.

2. Mix the Gorgonzola, vinegar, and Splenda in a small bowl. Microwave 30 seconds, or until the cheese is melted. Spoon the melted-cheese dressing over each salad.

Be sure to use fresh—not frozen or canned—green beans. You want them to be crunchy and crisp.

Melting Cheese

Melting seems to enrich cheese flavor, making it even more delicious than eating it cool or letting it come to room temperature, which improves the flavor even more. Try melting it for salads for even more flavor.

Grapefruit-and-Chicken Salad

Yields: 2 servings
Serving size: ¾ cup salad greens, ½ grapefruit, and 4 ounces chicken

 stats **Per serving:**

Calories: 251.46
Protein: . . . . 27.85 g
Carbohydrates: . . . . . . 16.70 g
Sugar: . . . . 13.51 g
Fat: . . . . 8.46 g

¼ cup fresh grapefruit juice, no sugar added
1 tablespoon olive oil
½ teaspoon Splenda
1 teaspoon fresh rosemary leaves, stripped from stem
Salt and pepper to taste
2 cups mixed baby field greens
1 (8-ounce) boneless, skinless chicken breast, halved lengthwise
1 ruby-red grapefruit, cut in sections

1. Whisk the grapefruit juice, olive oil, Splenda, rosemary, salt, and pepper together in a bowl to make dressing. Arrange the greens on serving plates.

2. Drizzle 2 teaspoons of dressing on the chicken. Grill the chicken over medium heat.

3. Slice the chicken and arrange it over the greens. Add the grapefruit sections; drizzle the rest of the dressing over the dish.

tip

If you find the grapefruit too tart for your taste, add more Splenda.

Grilled Vegetable Salad

Yields: 6 servings
Serving size: 1 cup

stats **Per serving:**

Calories: 163.33
Protein: . . . . 4.46 g
Carbohydrates: . . . . . . 9.36 g
Sugar: . . . . 4.77 g
Fat: . . . . 13.10 g

*Salt and freshly ground pepper to
    taste
3 Japanese eggplants, halved
4 medium zucchini, trimmed and
    quartered lengthwise
2 yellow peppers, quartered and
    cored, seeds and membranes
    removed
6 plum tomatoes, cored and halved
    lengthwise
½ cup olive oil
Juice of ½ lemon
½ cup freshly grated Parmesan
    cheese
3 cups romaine lettuce
½ cup arugula
Lemon-Herb Dressing (see below)
    to taste*

1. Heat a grill to medium-high. Salt and pepper the vegetables on both sides. Whisk the oil and lemon juice together; brush the vegetables on both sides.

2. Grill about 3 minutes per side, looking for grill marks on the eggplant and zucchini. Sprinkle with cheese.

3. Serve over the greens. Dress the greens in Lemon-Herb Dressing, if desired.

tip

You can serve the grilled veggies over pasta instead of lettuce.

Grilling Vegetables

If you make a lot of vegetables, you can always make a great salad or pasta sauce. Try grilling vegetables with sprigs of fresh mint, basil, or oregano. This is ideal for a late summer treat when everything is in season and gardens are bursting.

Lemon-Herb Dressing

Place ¼ cup lemon juice, 1 clove garlic, 2 shallots, ½ teaspoon soy sauce, 1 tablespoon dried rosemary leaves, 1 teaspoon oregano leaves, ¼ cup fresh parsley leaves, 1 teaspoon Splenda, ½ teaspoon salt, Freshly ground black pepper to taste in the blender and blend until very smooth. Pour into a bottle or jar and serve. The analysis: Calories: 2.7, Protein: 0.1 g, Carbohydrates: 0.69 g, Sugar: 0.14 g, Fat: 0.03 g. Yields: 1 cup; Serving size: 2 teaspoons.

Curried Tart Apple-and-Rice Salad

Yields: 4 servings
Serving size: ⅔ cup

stats **Per serving:**

Calories: 354.49
Protein:. . . . . .5.05 g
Carbohydrates: . . . . . .25.90 g
Sugar: . . . . .6.54 g
Fat:. . . . . .26.94 g

⅔ cup Basic Mayonnaise (page 122)
1 teaspoon Madras curry powder, or
    to taste
1 tablespoon lemon juice
2 large Granny Smith or other
    tart apples, peeled, cored, and
    chopped
½ cup red onion, finely chopped
2 cups cooked brown rice, chilled and
    fluffed with a fork
½ cup toasted pine nuts

Whisk the mayonnaise, curry powder, and lemon juice in a serving bowl. Add the apple, onion, rice, and nuts; combine well. Serve at room temperature or chill.

tip

You can make large quantities of brown rice at a time and put aside the leftovers for breakfast with fruit and yogurt, quick lunches, or dinner sides.

Wild Rice Salad with Fruit and Nuts

Yields: 4 servings
Serving size: 1 cup

 Per serving:

Calories: 377.78
Protein: . . . . .7.61 g
Carbohydrates: . . . . . .22.59 g
Sugar: . . . . .4.24 g
Fat: . . . . .30.52 g

½ cup raspberry vinegar
⅔ cup Basic Mayonnaise (page 122)
1 tablespoon fresh rosemary
Salt and pepper to taste
2 cups cooked wild rice, warmed
1 cup fresh raspberries
1 cup fresh or frozen peach slices,
    thawed if frozen
2 stalks celery, chopped
¾ cup chopped, toasted walnuts
2 cups Napa cabbage, trimmed,
    cored, and shredded

1. Whisk the vinegar, mayonnaise, rosemary, salt, and pepper together in a large serving bowl. Add the rice; fluff with a fork to coat.

2. Mix in the fruit and nuts. Mound the cabbage on serving plates; spoon the salad on top.

Wild Rice

Package directions usually underestimate the cooking time for wild rice. You may have to cook it for 60 minutes or more. You will know that it is done when it "blooms" from little spikes to tiny buds.

Lobster Salad

Yields: 4 servings
Serving size: ⅔ cup salad

Calories: 649.59
Protein: . . . . .28.12 g
Carbohydrates: . . . . . .10 g
Sugar: . . . . .3.01 g
Fat: . . . . .56.54 g

1 cup Basic Mayonnaise (page 122)
Juice of ½ lime
1 teaspoon curry powder
1 teaspoon Dijon mustard
Salt and freshly ground pepper to
 taste
1 tablespoon concentrated
 unsweetened pineapple juice
1 pound cooked lobster meat
2 cups bitter greens, such as arugula
 or watercress, rinsed and dried
 on paper towels
½ cup roasted peanuts, for garnish

1. In a large bowl, whisk the mayonnaise, lime juice, curry powder, Dijon mustard, salt, pepper, and pineapple juice together.

2. Gently fold in the cooked lobster meat. Arrange the greens on serving plates.

3. Spoon the salad over the greens and garnish with peanuts.

tip

Most fish markets sell cooked lobster meat. It's expensive, but not as much work as cooking and shelling your lobsters at home.

Greek-Style Mussel Salad

Yields: 4 servings
Serving size: 1 cup salad

stats **Per serving:**

Calories: 683.14
Protein: . . . . .43.97 g
Carbohydrates: . . . . . .22.23 g
Sugar: . . . . .9.43 g
Fat: . . . . .46.66 g

Juice of 1 lemon
zest of ½ lemon
⅔ cup extra-virgin olive oil
2 tablespoons fresh mint or 1
*   tablespoon dried mint*
1 teaspoon dried oregano
2 cloves garlic, minced
1 teaspoon cracked coriander seeds
Salt and pepper to taste
1 raw egg
2 pounds fresh mussels, steamed,
*   drained, and shelled*
2 ripe tomatoes, rinsed, cored, and
*   diced*
½ bunch green onions, chopped
2 cups fresh romaine lettuce, rinsed,
*   drained, and shredded*
2 tablespoon capers
4 large sprigs Italian flat-leaf parsley
*   for garnish*

1. Puree the lemon juice, lemon zest, olive oil, mint, oregano, garlic, coriander, salt, pepper, and eggs in a blender. Pour them into a large bowl.

2. Stir in the mussels, tomatoes, and green onions. Chill or serve at room temperature over the greens with capers sprinkled on top. Decorate each serving with a sprig of parsley.

Mediterranean Food

You can find some delicious dishes in the various coastal countries of this bountiful sea. Enjoy the sunny flavors of the Mediterranean at home by using ingredients native to the Mediterranean that can also be grown here.

Dilled-Shrimp Salad with Cucumbers

Yields: 4 servings
Serving size: 1 cup salad

stats **Per serving:**

Calories:............329.29
Protein:.............25.07 g
Carbohydrates: ......4.11 g
Sugar: ....1.60 g
Fat:.................23.51 g

1 tablespoon fresh dill or 1 teaspoon
  dried dill
½ cup sugar-free Basic Mayonnaise
  (page 122)
¼ cup all-natural, sugar-free, low-fat
  yogurt
Juice of 1 lemon
Salt and pepper to taste
Red pepper flakes to taste
1 teaspoon sweet Hungarian paprika
1 teaspoon Worcestershire sauce or
  Asian fish sauce
½ English cucumber, rinsed and diced
1 pound of cooked shrimp—frozen
  and thawed is fine, fresh is better

1. Mix the dill, mayonnaise, yogurt, lemon, spices, and Worcestershire sauce together in a bowl. Add the cucumber and shrimp; toss gently to coat with dressing.

2. Serve chilled over your favorite greens.

Bloody-Mary Tomato Aspic with Hardboiled Eggs

Yields: 8 servings
Serving size: ½ cup aspic, 2 teaspoons sauce

 Per serving:

Calories: 63.18
Protein: . . . . .5.22 g
Carbohydrates: . . . . . .5.34 g
Sugar: . . . . .3.72 g
Fat: . . . . .2.75 g

¼ cup cold water
½ ounce unflavored gelatin
1 cup boiling tomato juice with no
    added sugar
2 cups cold tomato juice with no
    added sugar
1 teaspoon soy sauce
½ teaspoon cayenne pepper, or to
    taste
Juice of ½ lime
1 teaspoon Splenda
1 teaspoon prepared horseradish
Salt and pepper to taste
4 hardboiled eggs, peeled and halved
8 teaspoons low-fat sour cream, for
    garnish

1. Place the cold water and gelatin in the bowl of a blender; let bloom 3 minutes. Start the motor and slowly add the hot tomato juice, then the cold tomato juice.

2. With the motor running, pour in the soy sauce, cayenne pepper, lime juice, Splenda, horseradish, salt, and pepper. Pour into a 4-cup mold.

3. Refrigerate 45 minutes. Add the hardboiled eggs. When firm, about 3 hours, turn out on a serving plate.

4. Spoon sour cream on each serving of this pretty salad.

Gel Is Great Fun

Aspics made with tomatoes and other veggies, plus eggs, chicken, or seafood, are wonderful! They are easy to make, can be prepared in advance, and make an elegant presentation. Rings can be stuffed with other salads to make a full-course lunch.

Pink Tomato Aspic with Shrimp

Yields: 8 servings

Serving size ½ cup

 Per serving:

Calories: 58.70
Protein: . . . . .7.09 g
Carbohydrates: . . . . . .5.72 g
Sugar: . . . . .3.66 g
Fat: . . . . .1.28 g

¼ cup cold water
½ ounce unflavored gelatin
½ cup boiling tomato juice with no
    added sugar
2 cups cold tomato juice with no
    added sugar
1 teaspoon soy sauce
Juice of ½ lemon
1 teaspoon Splenda
1 tablespoon chopped fresh dill or 1
    teaspoon dried dill
½ cup low-fat sour cream
¾ cup cooked shrimp, chopped
Whole cooked shrimp, for garnish
    (optional)

1. Place the cold water and gelatin in the bowl of a blender. Let bloom 3 minutes. Start the motor and slowly add the hot tomato juice, then the cold tomato juice.

2. With the motor running, pour in the soy sauce, lemon juice, Splenda, and dill.

3. Add the sour cream; pulse. Pour into a 4-cup ring mold and add the shrimp, stirring to even the distribution of shrimp.

Salad with Nuts and Cheese Chunks

Yields: 4 servings
Serving size: ¾ cup

 stats **Per serving:**

Calories: 479.31
Protein: . . . . .23.64 g
Carbohydrates: . . . . . .17.60 g
Sugar: . . . . .6.94 g
Fat: . . . . .36.72 g

2 cups mixed watercress and Boston
     lettuce
8 ounces Jarlsberg or other high-
     quality Swiss-style cheese, cubed
1 English cucumber, cut in spikes
2 medium carrots, peeled and cut in
     julienne strips
1 cup bean sprouts
1 yellow pepper, cored, seeds
     removed, and cut in match-stick
     size pieces
1 cup toasted walnut pieces
4 ounces of Lemon-Herb Dressing
     (page 125)

On chilled individual serving plates, stack the ingredients in the order listed. Drizzle with dressing and serve.

Color Your Salads

The more colors you have in your salad, the healthier! Intensely colored fruits and vegetables are loaded with antioxidants. These will counteract anything that's unhealthy in your body and fight infection.

Pasta Salad with Hot Peppers and Sweet Red-Pepper Dressing

Yields: 4 servings
Serving size: ⅔ cup

 **Per serving:**

Calories: 316.76
Protein: . . . . .8.07 g
Carbohydrates: . . . . . .39.72 g
Sugar: . . . . .3 g
Fat: . . . . .15.81 g

¼ cup olive oil
4 cloves garlic
1 red onion, finely chopped
4 jalapeño peppers, minced
2 chipotle peppers, minced
½ cup red wine vinegar
¼ cup Basic Mayonnaise (page 122)
Salt and freshly ground pepper to taste
⅔ pound small whole-wheat pasta
4 cups of your favorite bitter greens

1. Heat the olive oil in a large sauté pan. Add the garlic, onion, and jalapeño and chipotle peppers; cook until just slightly softened.

2. Stir in the vinegar, mayonnaise, salt, and pepper.

3. Add the whole-wheat pasta; mix well. Place the greens on a serving platter and put the pasta salad on top.

Broccoli-and-Pasta Salad

Yields: 4 servings
Serving size: ⅔ cup

stats **Per serving:**

Calories:............338.48
Protein:.............7.12 g
Carbohydrates: ......33.41 g
Sugar: ....2.17 g
Fat:.................21.06 g

Juice and zest of 1 lemon
2 tablespoons Pinot Grigio vinegar
½ cup olive oil
1 teaspoon Toasted Sesame Seed Oil
(see below)
1 teaspoon soy sauce
Salt and pepper to taste
1 teaspoon red pepper flakes, or to
taste
1 teaspoon Splenda
⅔ cup Basic Mayonnaise (page 122)
1 pound of broccoli florets, rinsed
and blanched
1 pound small whole-wheat pasta,
such as orzo

Whisk the lemon juice and zest, vinegar, oils, soy sauce, spices, Splenda, and mayonnaise in a serving bowl. Stir in the broccoli and pasta. Chill and serve.

tip

If you dress the pasta and broccoli while still hot or warm, they will take on a great deal of flavor from the dressing. Whole-grain pasta is better than regular because it's a complex carbohydrate.

Blanched Vegetables

Dropping your green veggies in boiling water for a minute or two doesn't overcook them. If you shock them in icy water afterwards, they will retain their beautiful color. "Blanch 'em and shock 'em" for vegetables that look as good as they taste.

Toasted Sesame Seed Oil

Toast ½ cup sesame seeds until golden in a large nonstick pan over medium heat. Add 1 cup oil and bring to a boil. Turn the heat to low and simmer the oil for 10 minutes or until it takes on the color of honey. Pour through cheesecloth to remove seeds. The analysis: Calories: 11, Protein: 0.06 g, Carbohydrates: 0.05 g, Sugar: 0 g, Fat: 1.25 g. Yields: 7 ounces; Serving size: ⅙ ounce.

Pasta Salad with Shrimp and Snow Pea Pods

Yields: 6 servings
Serving size: 1 cup

stats **Per serving:**

Calories:............454.35
Protein:.............17.28 g
Carbohydrates: ......40.38 g
Sugar: ....3.82 g
Fat:................24.78 g

½ cup olive oil
4 cloves garlic, chopped
1 pound raw, cleaned shrimp
1 pound snow pea pods, washed and
    trimmed
1 pound curly pasta, cooked
⅔ cup Basic Mayonnaise, plus more
    to taste (page 122)
1 teaspoon Basic Mustard (page 98)
Juice of ½ lime
Salt and pepper to taste
2 teaspoons capers
4 sprigs fresh dill to garnish

1. Heat the oil in a large pot over medium heat. Sauté the garlic about 3 minutes. Add the shrimp; toss until pink.

2. Stir in the peapods, pasta, mayonnaise, mustard, lime juice, salt, pepper, and capers. Sprinkle dill over the top and serve.

Warm Lentil Salad

Yields: 6 servings
Serving size: ¾ cup

 Per serving:

Calories: 164.63
Protein: . . . . .8.84 g
Carbohydrates: . . . . . .22.94 g
Sugar: . . . . .3.97 g
Fat: . . . . .5.02 g

1 cup dry green lentils
1 onion, peeled and stuck with 3
    whole cloves
1 clove garlic, unpeeled
3 cups water
3 cups lettuce
2 tablespoons olive oil
½ cup sweet red onion, minced
¼ cup red wine vinegar
Salt and pepper to taste
½ pound grape tomatoes, rinsed

1. Bring the lentils, onion, garlic, and water to a boil in a large saucepan. Reduce heat to low and cover. Simmer until tender, about 20–35 minutes.

2. Arrange the lettuce on salad plates. Discard the cooked onion and garlic. Drain the lentils and place in a bowl. Stir in the olive oil, red onion, vinegar, salt, pepper, and grape tomatoes. Serve on beds of lettuce.

Various Bean Salads

Just as you will see in the lentil salad, you can use chick peas, red kidney beans, and white beans to make delicious salads. If you cook the beans yourself, you can infuse them with many flavors, including onions, garlic, and spices. These beans, legumes, are excellent sources of protein and slowly digested carbs.

CHAPTER

6

Main Dishes and Casseroles

Condensed-Soup Primer

~ **Condensed** soups are the most popular ingredient shortcut in most casseroles. Your choice of which condensed soup to use can greatly affect the calorie and fat content of your dish.

For example, the average 10.75-ounce can of commercial cream-of-mushroom soup has the following nutritional breakdown: Calories: 314.15; Protein: 4.91 g; Carbohydrate: 22.57 g; Fat: 23.09 g; Sat. Fat g: 6.25; Cholesterol: 3.05 mg; Sodium: 2110.60 mg; Fiber: 0.91 g.

Now, Exchange Approximations (for homemade or canned condensed soups) will depend on the serving size and soup preparation method. You may use skim milk, soy milk, or water, or you may use nonfat dry milk and butter, which will have an obvious effect on the Nutritional Analysis. Even so, these homemade recipes are better for you than store brands.

On the surface, 314 calories for canned cream soup doesn't seem too bad when you consider that the one can of soup will probably yield at least four servings. However, when you consider the PCF Ratio (65 percent of calories are from fat!) and the sodium content, a less-healthy picture emerges.

For further comparison, commercial cream-of-celery soup has around 220 calories, cheese soup has 378, chicken mushroom has 332, cream-of-chicken has 284, and tomato soup has 207.

Many of the recipes in this chapter use simplified condensed soup that you can make at home. These condensed-soup recipes are not seasoned; instead, seasoning suggestions are made in the casserole recipes. "Salt and pepper to taste" is also assumed in all recipes, noting that salt will be determined by your own dietary restrictions.

Condensed Cream-of-Mushroom Soup

Yields: equivalent of 1 (10.75-ounce) can

 Per recipe:

Calories:.............92.46
Protein:..............3.07 g
Carbohydrates: ......20.63 g
Fat:.................0.44 g
Sat. Fat:.............0.07 g

¾ cup finely chopped fresh
    mushrooms
1 teaspoon chopped onion
1 tablespoon chopped celery
½ cup water
⅛ cup Ener-G potato flour
Optional ingredients:

1. In a microwave-safe covered container, microwave the chopped mushrooms (and the onion and celery, if using) 2 minutes, or until tender. (About ¾ cup of chopped mushrooms will yield ½ cup of steamed ones.) Reserve any resulting liquid from the steamed mushrooms, and then add enough water to equal 1 cup.

2. Place all the ingredients in a blender; process. The thickness of this soup concentrate will vary according to how much moisture remains in the mushrooms. If necessary, add 1–2 tablespoons of water to achieve a paste. Low-sodium, canned mushrooms work in this recipe, but the Nutritional Analysis assumes that fresh mushrooms are used. Adjust the sodium content accordingly.

Potato-Flour Substitute?

Instant mashed potatoes can replace potato flour; however, the amount needed will vary according to the brand of potatoes. Also, you'll need to consider other factors such as added fats and hydrogenated oils.

Condensed Cream-of-Chicken Soup, Minor's Base Method

Yields: equivalent of 1
(10.75-ounce) can

 Per recipe:

Calories:.............157.80
Protein:..............3.66 g
Carbohydrates: ......35.13 g
Fat:.................0.54 g
Sat. Fat:.............0.14 g

1 cup water
¾ teaspoon Minor's Low-Sodium
Chicken Broth Base
¼ cup Ener-G potato flour

Place all the ingredients in a blender; process until well blended. As you can tell from the Nutritional Analysis, this condensed soup made using Minor's Low-Sodium Chicken Broth Base has only ⅓ of the fat of the previous recipe, and the total calories are less, too. The biggest difference is in the amount of sodium; this version has only ⅕ (20 percent) of the sodium that is in the recipe using canned broth.

Condensed Cream-of-Chicken Soup

For the equivalent of 1 (10.75-ounce) can of condensed chicken soup, blend 1 cup canned, reduced-fat chicken broth with ¼ cup Ener-G potato flour. The recipe will last, refrigerated, for 3 days. The Nutritional Analysis for the entire recipe is: Calories: 181.20; Protein: 7.61 g; Carbohydrate: 34.14 g; Fat: 1.50 g; Sat. Fat: 0.42 g; Cholesterol: 0.00 mg; Sodium: 785.20 mg; Fiber: 2.36 g.

142

Condensed Cream-of-Celery Soup

Yields: equivalent of 1 (10.75-ounce) can

stats **Per recipe:**

Calories: 84.90
Protein: . . . . 2.00 g
Carbohydrates: . . . . . . 19.62 g
Fat: . . . . 0.19 g
Sat. Fat: . . . . 0.05 g

½ cup chopped celery
½ cup water
⅛ cup Ener-G potato flour

1. In a microwave-safe, covered container, microwave the chopped celery 2 minutes, or until tender. Do not drain off any of the resulting liquid. If necessary, add enough water to bring the steamed celery and liquid to 1 cup total.

2. Place all the ingredients in a blender; process. Use immediately, or store in a covered container in the refrigerator for use within 3 days. The thickness of this concentrate will depend upon how much moisture remains in the celery; add 1–2 tablespoons of water, if necessary, to achieve a paste.

Condensed Cream-of-Potato Soup

Yields: equivalent of 1
(10.75-ounce) can

stats **Per recipe:**

Calories: 102.78
Protein: . . . . 2.02 g
Carbohydrates: . . . . . . 23.92 g
Fat: . . . . 0.11 g
Sat. Fat: . . . . 0.03 g

½ cup peeled, diced potatoes
½ cup water
1 tablespoon Ener-G potato flour

1. Place the potatoes and water in a covered, microwave-safe bowl; microwave on high 4–5 minutes, until the potatoes are fork-tender.

2. Pour the potatoes and water into a blender, being careful of the steam. Remove the vent from the blender lid; process until smooth. Add the Ener-G potato flour 1 teaspoon at a time while the blender is running.

tip

The Nutritional Analysis for this recipe assumes you'll use the entire tablespoon of Ener-G potato flour; however, the amount needed will depend on the amount of starch in the potatoes you use. For example, new potatoes will require more Ener-G potato flour than will larger, Idaho-style potatoes.

Condensed Tomato Soup

Yields: equivalent of 1 (10.75-ounce) can

stats **Per serving:**

Calories: 136.20
Protein: . . . . 3.95 g
Carbohydrates: . . . . . . 30.61 g
Fat: . . . . 1.05 g
Sat. Fat: . . . . 0.15 g

1 cup peeled, chopped tomato, undrained
Additional tomato juices (if necessary)
¼ teaspoon baking soda
⅛ cup Ener-G potato flour

Place the tomatoes in a microwave-safe bowl; microwave on high 2–3 minutes, until tomatoes are cooked. Add additional tomato juices if necessary to bring the mixture back up to 1 cup. Add the baking soda; stir vigorously until the bubbling stops. Pour the cooked tomato mixture into a blender; add the potato flour, 1 tablespoon at a time, processing until well blended.

tip

The Nutritional Analysis for this recipe assumes you use 2 tablespoons (⅛ cup) of potato flour; however, the amount needed will depend on the ratio of tomato pulp to juice. The juicier the cooked tomatoes, the more potato flour required.

Direct Preparation

If you'll be making the soup immediately after you prepare the condensed soup recipe, you can simply add your choice of the additional 1 cup of liquid (such as skim milk, soy milk, or water) to the blender and use that method to mix the milk and soup concentrate together. Pour the combined mixture into your pan or microwave-safe dish.

Condensed Cheese Soup

Yields: equivalent of 1
(10.75-ounce) can

 Per recipe:

Calories: 314.95
Protein: . . . . 20.20 g
Carbohydrates: . . . . . . 18.19 g
Fat: . . . . 17.94 g
Sat. Fat: . . . . 11.28 g

½ cup water
⅛ cup Ener-G potato flour
¼ cup nonfat cottage cheese
2 ounces American, Cheddar, or
   Colby Cheese, shredded (to yield
   ½ cup)

Place the water, potato flour, and cottage cheese in a blender; process until well blended. Stir in the shredded cheese. The cheese will melt as the casserole is baked, prepared in the microwave, or cooked on the stovetop, according to recipe instructions.

This replacement for canned, condensed cheese soup is perfect in casserole recipes.

Be Aware of Your Exchanges

When using any of the suggested soup preparation methods, you'll need to add the appropriate Exchange Approximations for each serving amount (usually ¼ of the total) of whatever condensed soup you make. For example, broth-based soups like chicken and cream-of-mushroom or celery would be a Free Exchange. The cream-of-potato soup would add 1 Carbohydrate/Starch.

Soup Preparation Method I: Stovetop

Serves 4

 stats **Per serving, skim milk:**

Additional Calories:. .21.44
Protein:. . . . . .2.09 g
Carbohydrates: . . . . . .2.97 g
Fat:. . . . . .0.11 g
Sat. Fat:. . . . . .0.07 g

To use any of the homemade condensed-soup recipes as soup, add 1 cup of skim milk (or soy milk or water) to a pan. Stir using a spoon or whisk to blend. Cook over medium heat until mixture begins to simmer. Season according to taste.

tip

Consider the stats for both the condensed soup recipe and serving method, together.

Soup Preparation Method II: Microwave

Serves 4

stats **Per serving, skim milk:**

Additional Calories:. .21.44
Protein:. . . . . .2.09 g
Carbohydrates: . . . . . .2.97 g
Fat:. . . . . .0.11 g
Sat. Fat:. . . . . .0.07 g

Add your choice of condensed soup and 1 cup of skim milk (or soy milk or water) to a 2-quart microwave-safe dish with a cover. Stir using a spoon or whisk to blend. Microwave, covered, on high 1–3 minutes, until soup is hot. Do not boil.

Soup Preparation III:
Extra-Rich Creamed Soup

Serves 4

 Per serving:

Additional Calories:. . .70.57
Protein:. . . . . .3.62 g
Carbohydrates: . . . . . .5.19 g
Fat:. . . . . .3.98 g
Sat. Fat:. . . . . .2.48 g

1 cup skim milk
¼ cup nonfat milk powder
Condensed soup of choice
4 teaspoons unsalted butter

In a saucepan, whisk together the skim milk, milk powder, and your choice of 1 recipe of condensed soup; warm on medium-low heat. Add the butter 1 teaspoon at a time, allowing each teaspoon to melt, and stirring to fully incorporate it into the mixture before adding more. Heat to serving temperature, stirring constantly; do not allow the mixture to boil.

The butter in this extra-rich version will affect its fat content, so check with your dietitian to determine whether it's okay to make your soup this way.

Traditional Stovetop Tuna-Noodle Casserole

Serves 4

 Per serving:

Calories:............244.69
Protein:.............19.78 g
Carbohydrates: ......32.74 g
Fat:.................4.25 g
Sat. Fat:.............1.85 g

Condensed-Soup Casserole Guidelines

Note that the casseroles in this section use the condensed-soup recipes in this chapter. If you substitute canned condensed soup, be sure to adjust the Exchange Approximations when necessary.

2 cups cooked egg noodles
1 recipe Condensed Cream-of-Mushroom Soup (see page 141)
1 teaspoon steamed, chopped onion
1 tablespoon steamed, chopped celery
½ cup skim milk
1 ounce American, Cheddar, or Colby cheese, shredded (to yield ¼ cup)
1 cup frozen mixed peas and carrots
1 cup steamed, sliced fresh mushrooms
1 can water-packed tuna, drained

1. Cook the egg noodles according to package directions. Drain and return to pan. Add all the ingredients to the pan; stir to blend. Cook over medium heat, stirring occasionally, until the cheese is melted.

tip

1⅓ cups of dried egg noodles will yield 2 cups of cooked egg noodles. The Nutritional Analysis for this recipe assumes that the egg noodles were cooked without salt.

Extra-Rich Stovetop Tuna-Noodle Casserole

Add 1 medium egg (beaten) and 1 tablespoon mayonnaise to give this casserole the taste of rich, homemade egg noodles, while—at 21 percent of total calories—still maintaining a good fat ratio. It's still less than 300 calories per serving, too! The per-serving Nutritional Analysis is: Calories: 275.40; Protein: 21.18 g; Carbohydrate: 33.75 g; Fat: 6.58 g; Sat. Fat: 2.37 g; Cholesterol: 93.78 mg; Sodium: 280.75 mg; Fiber: 3.71 g.

Chicken-and-Mushroom Rice Casserole

Serves 8

stats **Per serving:**

Calories: 164.73
Protein: . . . . 9.47 g
Carbohydrates: . . . . . . 29.53 g
Fat: . . . . 1.11 g
Sat. Fat: . . . . 0.27 g

1 recipe Condensed Cream-of-
    Chicken Soup (see page 142)
1 cup diced chicken breast
1 large onion, chopped
½ cup chopped celery
1 cup uncooked rice (not instant rice)
Freshly ground black pepper to taste
    (optional)
1 teaspoon dried Herbes de Provence
    blend, optional
2 cups boiling water
2½ cups chopped broccoli florets
1 cup sliced fresh mushrooms

1. Preheat oven to 350°F. Spray a 4-quart casserole dish (large enough to prevent boil-overs in the oven) with nonstick spray. Combine the condensed soup, chicken breast, onion, celery, rice, and seasonings; mix well and place in casserole dish. Pour the boiling water over the top of the mixture; bake 30 minutes, covered.

2. Add the broccoli and mushrooms; stir. Replace the cover; return to the oven to bake an additional 20–30 minutes, or until the celery is tender and the rice has absorbed all the liquid.

Aloha Ham Microwave Casserole

Serves 4

stats **Per serving:**

Calories:.............207.53
Protein:..............13.56 g
Carbohydrates: ......32.14 g
Fat:..................2.69 g
Sat. Fat:.............0.91 g

1⅓ cups cooked rice
1 medium onion, chopped
1 recipe Condensed Cream-of-Celery
   Soup (see page 143)
1 (8-ounce) can pineapple chunks
¼ cup water
1 teaspoon brown sugar
½ pound (8 ounces) sliced lean
   baked or boiled ham
Sliced green onions, for garnish
   (optional)

1. Cook the rice according to package directions. Put the rice in a casserole dish and set aside. Place the chopped onion in a microwave-safe, covered bowl; microwave on high until tender, about 1 minute. Add the soup, pineapple with juice, water, and brown sugar to the onion. Heat, covered, on high until the mixture begins to boil, about 1 minute. Stir mixture until the brown sugar is dissolved.

2. Pour half of the soup mixture over the rice. Arrange the ham slices on top of the rice; pour the remaining soup mixture over it. Cover loosely with plastic wrap or a paper towel (to prevent splatters in the microwave); heat on high until the rice is reheated and ham is warm, about 1 minute.

tip

If you are on a sodium-restricted diet, consider substituting chicken or turkey breast for the ham.

Italian Ground-Turkey Casserole

Serves 8

stats **Per serving:**

Calories:.............297.73
Protein:.............28.98 g
Carbohydrates: ......23.36 g
Fat:.................12.17 g
Sat. Fat:.............5.62 g

*1 pound ground turkey or turkey
     sausage*
1 large onion, chopped
2 cups sliced fresh mushrooms
1 teaspoon minced garlic
1 teaspoon dried basil
¼ teaspoon dried oregano
½ teaspoon dried parsley
6 cups shredded cabbage
2 cups nonfat cottage cheese
⅛ cup Ener-G potato flour
*4 ounces Parmesan cheese, grated
     (to yield 1 cup)*
*4 ounces part-skim mozzarella
     cheese, grated (to yield 1 cup)*
*1 recipe Condensed Tomato Soup
     (see page 145)*
*1 (6-ounce) can salt-free tomato
     paste*
*1 (16-ounce) can salt-free diced
     tomatoes*

1. Place the ground turkey in a large, covered skillet over medium-low heat; allow it to steam, being careful not to brown the meat. Drain off the grease and use paper towels to blot the meat to absorb any excess fat from the turkey. Add the onion, mushrooms, minced garlic, and herbs; toss lightly. Return the cover to the skillet; steam the vegetables until they are tender, about 3 minutes. Set aside.

2. Put the shredded cabbage in a large, covered microwave-safe dish; steam until the cabbage is crisp-tender, about 5 minutes. (If your microwave doesn't have a carousel, turn the dish about halfway through the cooking time.) Drain the cabbage in a colander, being careful not to burn yourself from the steam. Press out any excess moisture.

3. Mix the cottage cheese, potato flour, and ½ of the Parmesan and mozzarella cheeses together. (Note: The potato flour acts as a bonding agent to keep the whey from separating from the cottage cheese. The tradition method of doing this is to add egg, but potato flour accomplishes the same thing without adding fat.) Add the condensed tomato soup, tomato paste, and canned tomatoes to the meat mixture; stir well.

Italian Ground-Turkey Casserole

(continued)

4. Preheat oven to 350°F. Coat a deep rectangular baking dish or roasting pan with nonstick spray. Spoon ⅓ of the meat mixture into the bottom of the pan; top with ½ of the cooked cabbage. Add another ⅓ of the meat mixture; top with the cottage cheese mixture and the rest of the cabbage. Add the remaining meat mixture; sprinkle the top of the casserole with the remaining Parmesan and mozzarella cheeses.

5. Bake 45 minutes, or until the casserole is heated through and the cheeses on top are melted and bubbling.

Base Basics

An easy way to add rich flavor to the condensed-soup or casserole recipes without adding extra calories is to use ⅛–¼ teaspoon of other Minor's bases, like Roasted Mirepoix, Onion, or Garlic.

Shrimp Microwave Casserole

Serves 4

 stats **Per serving:**

Calories:............195.53
Protein:.............17.35 g
Carbohydrates: ......27.23 g
Fat:.................1.92 g
Sat. Fat:............0.48 g

1⅓ cup uncooked egg noodles (to
    yield 4½ [½-cup] servings)
1 cup chopped green onion
1 cup chopped green pepper
1 cup sliced mushrooms
1 recipe Condensed Cream-of-Celery
    Soup (see page 143)
1 teaspoon Worcestershire sauce
4 drops Tabasco (optional)
¼ cup diced canned pimientos
½ cup pitted, chopped ripe olives
½ cup skimmed milk
½ pound (8 ounces) cooked,
    deveined, shelled shrimp

1. Cook the egg noodles according to package directions; keep warm. Place the green onion and green pepper in a covered, microwave-safe dish; microwave on high 1 minute. Add the mushroom slices; microwave another minute, or until all the vegetables are tender.

2. Add the soup, Worcestershire sauce, Tabasco (if using), pimiento, ripe olives, and milk; stir well. Microwave covered for 1–2 minutes, until the mixture is hot and bubbly.

3. Add the cooked shrimp and noodles; stir to mix. Microwave another 30 seconds–1 minute, or until the mixture is hot.

Single-Serving Beef (Almost) Stroganoff

Serves 1

stats **Per serving:**

Calories:............286.03
Protein:.............24.09 g
Carbohydrates:......36.67 g
Fat:.................5.49 g
Sat. Fat:............1.72 g

*1 tablespoon steamed or low-fat
   sautéed diced celery*
*1 teaspoon diced onion, steamed or
   low-fat sautéed*
*½ cup sliced mushrooms, steamed or
   low-fat sautéed*
*1 cup shredded, unseasoned
   cabbage, steamed*
½ cup cooked egg noodles
¼ cup nonfat cottage cheese
*1 teaspoon finely grated Parmesan
   cheese*
*1 clove roasted garlic (for roasting
   instructions, see Dry-Roasted
   Garlic on page 4)*
½ teaspoon Ener-G potato flour
*1 tablespoon nonfat yogurt or nonfat
   sour cream*
*1 ounce lean roast beef, pulled or
   cubed*
⅛ teaspoon nutmeg

1. Toss the celery, onion, mushrooms, cabbage, and noodles together in a microwave-safe, covered serving dish.

2. Put the cheeses, roasted garlic, potato flour, and yogurt (or sour cream) in a blender; process until smooth. Lightly mix the cheese sauce with the vegetables, then top the vegetables with the roast beef; sprinkle the nutmeg over the top of the dish. Microwave, covered, on high 1–2 minutes, or until heated through.

Single-Serving Smoked-Turkey Casserole

Serves 1

Per serving:

Calories: 220.64
Protein: . . . . .17.66 g
Carbohydrates: . . . . . .27.33 g
Fat: . . . . .4.80 g
Sat. Fat: . . . . .1.60 g

1 tablespoon steamed or low-fat
    sautéed diced celery
1 teaspoon diced onion, steamed
    or low-fat sautéed
1 tablespoon diced green pepper,
    steamed or low-fat sautéed
½ cup sliced mushrooms, steamed
    or low-fat sautéed
1 ounce smoked turkey, diced or
    thinly sliced
¼ cup nonfat cottage cheese
1 teaspoon finely grated Parmesan
    cheese
½ teaspoon Ener-G potato flour
½ cup cooked egg noodles

In a covered, microwave-safe bowl, combine all the ingredients; microwave on high 1–2 minutes, or until heated through.

Single-Serving Salmon Scramble

Serves 1

 Per serving:

Calories: 222.19
Protein: . . . . 21.90 g
Carbohydrates: . . . . . . 12.26 g
Fat: . . . . 10.26 g
Sat Fat: . . . . 2.55 g

1 cup chopped broccoli (fresh or
   frozen)
1 medium egg
½ teaspoon Hellmann's or Best Foods
   tartar sauce
1½ teaspoons yellow cornmeal
2 Keebler low-salt soda crackers,
   crumbled
2 ounces canned salmon, drained

1. In a microwave-safe covered bowl, steam the broccoli 5 minutes, or until tender. Drain any moisture from the broccoli; add it to a nonstick skillet treated with nonstick spray, and dry-sauté it to remove any excess moisture.

2. In another bowl, beat the egg and mix in the tartar sauce, cornmeal, cracker crumbs, and salmon. Pour the salmon mixture over the broccoli; toss to mix. Cook over medium-low heat until the egg is done, stirring the mixture occasionally with a spatula.

Single-Serving Unstuffed Cabbage and Green Peppers

Serves 1

 **Per serving:**

Calories:............206.65
Protein:.............16.44 g
Carbohydrates: ......14.43 g
Fat:.................10.03 g
Sat. Fat:............3.71 g

*3 ounces uncooked Laura's Lean Beef
    ground round*
⅛ teaspoon dried oregano
*¼ teaspoon minced dried garlic (or
    ½ clove minced fresh garlic)*
¼ teaspoon dried parsley
Dash of dried ginger
Dash of dried mustard
2 tablespoons chopped celery
2 tablespoons chopped onion
1 cup chopped green pepper
*½ cup steamed cabbage, shredded or
    rough chopped*
1 medium peeled, chopped tomato
¼ teaspoon dried basil

1. In a microwave-safe, covered dish, microwave the ground round, oregano, garlic, parsley, ginger, mustard, celery, onion, and green pepper 2 minutes. Stir the mixture, being careful not to burn yourself on the steam. Microwave on high another 2–3 minutes, or until the meat is no longer pink. Drain any fat residue or dab the beef mixture with a paper towel.

2. Heat the steamed cabbage in the microwave on high 30 seconds–1 minute, to warm it to serving temperature. Toss the chopped, raw tomato with the ground-round mixture; spoon it over the warmed cabbage. Sprinkle the dried basil over the top of the dish and serve. (If you serve this dish over ½ cup cooked rice instead of cabbage, add 1 Starch Exchange.)

Poultry

continued

continued

Oven-Fried Chicken Thighs

Serves 4

stats **Per serving, no oil:**

Calories: 73.53
Protein:. . . . . .9.46 g
Carbohydrates: . . . . . .4.65 g
Fat:. . . . . .1.69 g
Sat. Fat:. . . . . .0.42 g

Per serving, with olive oil:

Calories: 78.53
Protein:. . . . . .9.46 g
Carbohydrates: . . . . . .4.65 g
Fat:. . . . . .2.27 g
Sat. Fat:. . . . . .0.50 g

4 chicken thighs, skin removed
1 tablespoon unbleached, white all-purpose flour
1 large egg white
½ teaspoon sea salt
½ teaspoon olive oil (optional; see the "with olive oil" Nutritional Analysis)
1 tablespoon rice flour
1 tablespoon cornmeal

1. Preheat oven to 350°F. Rinse and dry the chicken thighs. Put the white flour on a plate. In a small, shallow bowl, whip the egg white together with the sea salt; add the olive oil, if using, and mix well. Put the rice flour and cornmeal on another plate; mix together. Place a rack on a baking sheet and spray both with nonstick cooking spray.

2. Roll each chicken thigh in the white flour, dip it into the egg mixture, and then roll it in the rice-flour mixture. Place the chicken thighs on the rack so they aren't touching. Bake 35–45 minutes, until the meat juices run clear.

tip

Boneless, skinless chicken-breast strips will work, although the meat tends to be drier. Allow 1 Very Lean Meat Exchange List choice for each 1-ounce serving.

Chicken Broth: Easy Slow-Cooker Method

Yield: about 4 cups
Serving size: ½ cup

 Per serving:

Calories: 67.19
Protein: . . . . .8.62 g
Carbohydrates: . . . . . .0.00 g
Fat: . . . . .3.37 g
Sat. Fat: . . . . .0.88 g

1 small onion, chopped
2 carrots, peeled and chopped
2 celery stalks and leaves, chopped
1 bay leaf
4 sprigs parsley
6 black peppercorns
¼ cup dry white wine
2 pounds chicken pieces, skin
    removed
4½ cups water

1. Add all ingredients except the water to the slow cooker. The chicken pieces and vegetables should be loosely layered and fill no more than 3/4 of the slow cooker. Add enough water to just cover the ingredients and cover the slow cooker. Use the high setting until the mixture almost reaches a boil, then reduce heat to low. Allow to simmer overnight, or up to 16 hours, checking occasionally and adding more water, if necessary.

2. Remove the chicken pieces and drain on paper towels to absorb any fat. Allow to cool, then remove the meat from the bones. Strain the vegetables from the broth and discard. (You don't want to eat vegetables cooked directly with the chicken because they will have absorbed too much of the residual fat.) Put the broth in a covered container and refrigerate for several hours or overnight, allowing the fat to congeal on top of the broth. Remove the hardened fat and discard.

Chicken Broth: Easy Slow-Cooker Method

(continued)

3. To separate the broth into small amounts for use when you steam vegetables or potatoes, fill up an ice cube tray with stock. Let freeze, then remove the cubes from the tray and store in a labeled freezer bag. (Note the size of the ice cubes. Common ice cube trays allow for ⅛ cup or 2 tablespoons of liquid per section.)

tip

The broth will be richer than what most recipes call for, so unless you need "reduced" broth, thin the broth with water as needed. Assuming you remove the fat from the broth, the Exchange Approximation for it will be a Free Exchange.

Know Your Terms

Reducing broth is the act of boiling it to decrease the amount of water, so you're left with a richer broth. Boiling nonfat, canned chicken broth won't reduce as a homemade broth would.

Another Healthy "Fried" Chicken

Serves 4

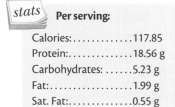 **Per serving:**

Calories:............117.85
Protein:.............18.56 g
Carbohydrates: ......5.23 g
Fat:.................1.99 g
Sat. Fat:.............0.55 g

*10 ounces raw boneless, skinless
    chicken breasts (fat trimmed off)*
½ cup nonfat plain yogurt
½ cup bread crumbs
1 teaspoon garlic powder
1 teaspoon paprika
¼ teaspoon dried thyme

1. Preheat oven to 350°F; prepare a baking pan with nonstick cooking spray. Cut the chicken breast into 4 equal pieces; marinate it in the yogurt for several minutes.

2. Mix together the bread crumbs, garlic, paprika, and thyme; dredge the chicken in the crumb mixture and arrange on prepared pan. Bake 20 minutes. To give the chicken a deep golden color, place the pan under the broiler the last 5 minutes of cooking. Watch closely to ensure the chicken "crust" doesn't burn.

Chicken Fat Facts

When faced with the decision of whether to have chicken with or without the skin, consider that ½ pound of skinless chicken breast has 9 grams of fat; a ½ pound with the skin on has 38 grams!

Buttermilk-Ranch Chicken Salad

Serves 4

 stats **Per serving:**

Calories:............146.64
Protein:.............17.97 g
Carbohydrates: ......10.63 g
Fat:.................3.68 g
Sat. Fat:.............1.24 g

1 tablespoon Hellmann's or Best
    Foods Real Mayonnaise
3 tablespoons nonfat plain yogurt
½ cup nonfat cottage cheese
½ teaspoon cider vinegar
1 teaspoon brown sugar
1 teaspoon Dijon mustard
½ cup buttermilk
2 tablespoons dried parsley
1 clove garlic, minced
2 tablespoons grated Parmesan
    cheese
¼ teaspoon sea salt (optional)
¼ teaspoon freshly ground pepper
    (optional)
1 cup chopped, cooked chicken
    breast
½ cup sliced cucumber
½ cup chopped celery
½ cup sliced carrots
4 cups salad greens
½ cup red onion slices
Fresh parsley, for garnish (optional)

1. In a blender or food processor, combine the mayonnaise, yogurt, cottage cheese, vinegar, brown sugar, mustard, buttermilk, parsley, garlic, cheese, and if using them, salt and pepper; process until smooth. Pour this dressing over the chicken, cucumber, celery, and carrots. Chill at least 2 hours.

2. To serve, arrange 1 cup of the salad greens on each of 4 serving plates. Top each salad with an equal amount of the chicken salad. Garnish with the red onion slices and fresh parsley, if desired.

Get More Mileage from Your Meals

Leftover Chicken Salad makes great sandwiches. Put it, and lots of lettuce, between two slices of bread for a quick lunch. The lettuce helps keep the bread from getting soggy if you're preparing the sandwich to go.

Molded Chicken Salad

Serves 12

stats **Per serving:**

Calories:............203.74
Protein:.............20.98 g
Carbohydrates:......5.20 g
Fat:.................10.60 g
Sat. Fat:.............3.94 g

½ cup nonfat plain yogurt
2 envelopes unflavored gelatin
¼ cup boiling water
1 teaspoon cider vinegar
1 teaspoon Dijon mustard
1 teaspoon brown sugar
1 tablespoon Hellmann's or Best
    Foods Real Mayonnaise
½ cup nonfat cottage cheese
4 ounces cream cheese
1 teaspoon celery seed
½ cup chopped dill pickle
¼ cup chopped green onion
    (scallions)
1 recipe Condensed Cream-of-
    Chicken Soup (see page 142)
1½ pounds (24 ounces) cooked,
    chopped chicken

1. Put the yogurt in a blender or food processor and sprinkle the gelatin on top; let stand 2 minutes to soften the gelatin.

2. Add the boiling water; process until the gelatin is dissolved. Add the remaining ingredients except for the chicken; process until smooth. Fold in the chopped chicken and taste for seasonings.

3. Pour into a mold or terrine treated with nonstick spray and chill until firm.

tip

Herbs like chopped chives, a little more cider vinegar, or ground black pepper won't affect Exchange Approximations.

Herbed Chicken-and-Brown Rice Dinner

Serves 4

 Per serving:

Calories: 300.49
Protein: . . . . .32.85 g
Carbohydrates: . . . . . .26.03 g
Fat: . . . . .6.19 g
Sat Fat: . . . . .0.27 g

1 tablespoon canola oil
4 (4-ounce) boneless chicken breast
    pieces, skin removed
¾ teaspoon garlic powder
¾ teaspoon dried rosemary
1 (10.5-ounce) can low-fat, reduced-
    sodium chicken broth
⅓ cup water
2 cups uncooked instant brown rice

1. Heat the oil in large nonstick skillet on medium-high. Add the chicken; sprinkle with ½ of the garlic powder and crushed rosemary. Cover, and cook 4 minutes on each side, or until cooked through. Remove the chicken from the skillet and set aside.

2. Add the broth and water to the skillet, and stir to deglaze the pan; bring to a boil. Stir in the rice and the remaining garlic powder and rosemary. Top with the chicken and cover. Cook on low heat 5 minutes. Remove from the heat and let stand, covered, 5 minutes.

Walnut Chicken with Plum Sauce

Serves 4

 Per serving:

Calories:............158.65
Protein:.............18.27 g
Carbohydrates: ......1.01 g
Fat:.................8.86 g
Sat. Fat:.............1.42 g

¾ pound (12 ounces) raw boneless,
    skinless chicken breast
1 teaspoon sherry
1 egg white
2 teaspoons peanut oil
2 drops toasted sesame oil (optional)
⅓ cup ground walnuts

1. Preheat oven to 350°F. Cut the chicken into bite-sized pieces; sprinkle with the sherry and set aside.

2. In a small bowl, beat the egg white and oils until frothy. Fold the chicken pieces into the egg mixture, then roll them in chopped walnuts. Arrange the chicken pieces on a baking sheet treated with nonstick cooking spray. Bake 10–15 minutes, or until the walnuts are lightly browned and the chicken juices run clear.

tip

The walnuts make the fat ratio of this dish high, so serve it with steamed vegetables and rice to bring the ratios into balance.

Easy Chicken Paprikash

Serves 4

 stats **Per serving, using equal amounts of light- and dark-meat chicken:**

Calories:............376.34
Protein:............21.58 g
Carbohydrates: ......58.44 g
Fat:.................6.42 g
Sat. Fat:............1.54 g

1 recipe Condensed Cream-of-Chicken Soup (see page 142)
½ cup skim milk
2 teaspoons paprika
⅛ teaspoon ground red pepper (optional)
¼ pound (4 ounces) chopped cooked, boneless, skinless chicken
1½ cups sliced steamed mushrooms
½ cup diced steamed onion
½ cup nonfat plain yogurt
4 cups cooked medium-sized egg noodles

1. In a saucepan, combine the soup, milk, paprika, and pepper (if using); whisk until well mixed. Bring to a boil over medium heat, stirring occasionally. Reduce the heat to low and stir in the chicken, mushrooms, and onion; cook until the chicken and vegetables are heated through. Stir in the yogurt.

2. To serve, put 1 cup of warm, cooked noodles on each of 4 plates. Top each portion of noodles with an equal amount of the chicken mixture. Garnish by sprinkling with additional paprika, if desired.

For Best Results . . .

Mock condensed-soup recipes are used in the dishes in this book so that you know the accurate Nutritional Analysis information. In all cases, you can substitute commercial canned, condensed soups; however, be sure to use the lower fat- and sodium-content varieties.

Chicken-and-Broccoli Casserole

Serves 4

 stats **Per serving:**

Calories:............327.80
Protein:.............25.65 g
Carbohydrates:......19.54 g
Fat:.................16.65 g
Sat. Fat:............5.99 g

2 cups broccoli
½ pound (8 ounces) cooked, chopped
    chicken
½ cup skim milk
⅛ cup (2 tablespoons) Hellmann's or
    Best Foods Real Mayonnaise
1 recipe Condensed Cream-of-
    Chicken Soup (see page 142)
¼ teaspoon curry powder
1 tablespoon lemon juice
½ cup (2 ounces) grated Cheddar
    cheese
½ cup bread crumbs
1 teaspoon melted butter
1 teaspoon olive oil

Preheat oven to 350°F. Treat an 11" × 7" casserole dish with nonstick spray. Steam the broccoli until tender; drain. Spread out the chicken on the bottom of the dish; cover it with the broccoli. Combine the milk, mayonnaise, soup, curry powder, and lemon juice; pour over broccoli. Mix together the cheese, bread crumbs, butter, and oil; sprinkle over the top of the casserole. Bake 30 minutes.

Chicken à la King

Serves 4

 Per serving:

Calories:............335.40
Protein:.............25.47 g
Carbohydrates: ......37.79 g
Fat:................9.78 g
Sat. Fat:.............2.32 g

1 recipe Condensed Cream-of-
    Chicken Soup (see page142)
¼ cup skim milk
½ teaspoon Worcestershire sauce
1 tablespoon Hellmann's or Best
    Foods Real Mayonnaise
¼ teaspoon ground black pepper
2 cups frozen mix of peas and pearl
    onions, thawed
1 cup frozen sliced carrots, thawed
1 cup sliced mushrooms, steamed
½ pound (8 ounces) cooked, chopped
    chicken
4 slices whole-wheat bread, toasted

Combine the soup, milk, Worcestershire, mayonnaise, and pepper in a saucepan; bring to a boil. Reduce heat and add the peas and pearl onions, carrots, mushrooms, and chicken. Simmer until the vegetables and chicken are heated through. Serve over toast.

Chicken-and-Green Bean Stovetop Casserole

Serves 4

 stats **Per serving:**

Calories:............305.29
Protein:..............22.85 g
Carbohydrates: ......35.59 g
Fat:.................8.31 g
Sat. Fat:.............2.06 g

1 recipe Condensed Cream-of-
    Chicken Soup (see page 142)
¼ cup skim milk
2 teaspoons Worcestershire sauce
1 teaspoon Hellmann's or Best Foods
    Real Mayonnaise
½ teaspoon onion powder
¼ teaspoon garlic powder
¼ teaspoon ground black pepper
1 (4-ounce) can sliced water
    chestnuts, drained
2½ cups frozen green beans, thawed
1 cup sliced mushrooms, steamed
½ pound (8 ounces) cooked, chopped
    chicken
1⅓ cups cooked brown, long-grain
    rice

Combine the soup, milk, Worcestershire, mayonnaise, onion and garlic powders, and pepper in a saucepan; bring to a boil. Reduce heat and add the water chestnuts, green beans, mushrooms, and chicken. Simmer until vegetables and chicken are heated through. Serve over rice.

Veggie Filler

Steamed mushrooms are a low-calorie way to add flavor to a dish and "stretch" the meat. If you don't like mushrooms, you can substitute an equal amount of other low-calorie steamed vegetables, like red and green peppers, and not significantly affect the total calories in the recipe.

Chicken Pasta with Herb Sauce

Serves 4

 Per serving:

Calories: 392.57
Protein: . . . . 26.22 g
Carbohydrates: . . . . . . 51.62 g
Fat: . . . . 8.43 g
Sat. Fat: . . . . 2.03 g

1 recipe Condensed Cream-of-
    Chicken Soup (see page 142)
¼ cup skim milk
½ teaspoon Worcestershire sauce
1 teaspoon Hellmann's or Best Foods
    Real Mayonnaise
¼ cup grated Parmesan cheese
¼ teaspoon chili powder
½ teaspoon garlic powder
¼ teaspoon dried rosemary
¼ teaspoon dried thyme
¼ teaspoon dried marjoram
1 cup sliced mushrooms, steamed
½ pound (8 ounces) cooked, chopped
    chicken
4 cups cooked pasta
Freshly ground black pepper
    (optional)

Combine the soup, milk, Worcestershire, mayonnaise, and cheese in a saucepan; bring to a boil. Reduce heat and add the chili powder, garlic powder, rosemary, thyme, and marjoram; stir well. Add the mushrooms and chicken; simmer until heated through. Serve over pasta, and top with freshly ground pepper, if desired.

Chicken-Thighs Cacciatore

Serves 4

stats **Per serving:**

Calories:............369.73
Protein:.............18.79 g
Carbohydrates:......48.19 g
Fat:................9.27 g
Sat. Fat:............2.43 g

2 teaspoons olive oil
½ cup chopped onion
2 cloves garlic, minced
4 chicken thighs, skin removed
½ cup dry red wine
1 (14½-oz.) can unsalted diced
    tomatoes, undrained
1 teaspoon dried parsley
½ teaspoon dried oregano
¼ teaspoon pepper
⅛ teaspoon sugar
¼ cup grated Parmesan cheese
4 cups cooked spaghetti
2 teaspoons extra-virgin olive oil

1. Heat a deep, nonstick skillet over medium-high heat; add 2 teaspoons of olive oil. Add the onion and sauté until transparent. Add the garlic and chicken thighs; sauté 3 minutes on each side, or until lightly browned.

2. Remove thighs from the pan; add wine, tomatoes and their juices, parsley, oregano, pepper, and sugar. Stir well; bring to a boil. Add chicken back to the pan; sprinkle Parmesan cheese over the top of the chicken and sauce. Cover, reduce heat, and simmer 10 minutes. Uncover and simmer 10 more minutes.

3. To serve, put 1 cup of cooked pasta on each of 4 plates. Top each pasta serving with a chicken thigh, then divide the sauce between the dishes. Drizzle ½ teaspoon of extra-virgin olive oil over the top of each dish, and serve. To add even more flavor to this recipe, substitute beef broth for half of the red wine.

For Cheese Lovers!

Indulge your love of extra cheese and still have a main dish that's under 400 calories. Prepare the Chicken-Thighs Cacciatore according to the recipe instructions. Top each portion with 1 tablespoon freshly grated Parmesan cheese. With the cheese, the analysis is: Calories: 398.22; Protein: 21.39 g; Carbohydrate: 48.43 g; Fat: 11.15 g; Sat. Fat: 3.62 g; Cholesterol: 43.87 mg; Sodium: 282.14 mg; Fiber: 3.81 g.

Thanksgiving Feast:
Turkey Casserole in a Pumpkin

Serves 4

stats **Per serving:**

Calories:............484.56
Protein:.............30.24 g
Carbohydrates: ......64.11 g
Fat:.................12.98 g
Sat. Fat:.............4.74 g

4 small pumpkins
1 recipe Condensed Cream-of-
*   Chicken Soup (see page 142)*
1 cup skim milk
1 cup low-fat, reduced-sodium
*   chicken broth*
1 tablespoon plus 1 teaspoon butter
½ cup steamed, diced celery
1 cup steamed, diced onion
1 cup steamed, sliced mushroom
*   slices*
1 tablespoon cognac (optional)
Parsley, thyme, and sage to taste
*   (optional)*
1⅓ cups cubed red potatoes,
*   steamed*
½ pound (8 ounces) steamed,
*   chopped oysters*
¼ pound (4 ounces) shredded cooked
*   turkey*
8 slices day-old bread, torn into
*   cubes*
2 eggs, beaten

1. Preheat oven to 375°F. Clean the pumpkins, cut off tops, and scrape out the seeds. Put on baking sheet and cover with foil or parchment paper. Bake 30 minutes, or until the inside flesh is somewhat tender but the pumpkins still retain their shapes.

2. While the pumpkins bake, prepare the dressing-style casserole by combining the soup, milk, broth, and butter in a saucepan; stir well to mix, and bring to a boil over medium heat. Lower the heat and add the celery, onion, mushrooms, and the cognac and seasonings, if using. Simmer 3 minutes. Remove from heat and allow to cool slightly.

3. In a large bowl, add the potatoes, oysters, turkey, and bread cubes; toss to mix.

4. Gradually add the eggs to the soup mixture, whisking the mixture constantly; pour the mixture over the potatoes, meat, and bread cubes. Mix well to coat the bread evenly. Divide the resulting mixture into the four pumpkins. Reduce oven temperature to 350°F and bake 30–40 minutes, or until the casserole is firm.

tip

The Analysis for this recipe assumes you'll use pumpkins that will yield ¾ cup of cooked pumpkin each.

Stovetop Grilled Turkey Breast

Serves 4

 stats **Per serving:**

Calories: 206.55
Protein: . . . . 30.80 g
Carbohydrates: . . . . . . 1.65 g
Fat: . . . . 7.64 g
Sat. Fat: . . . . 1.63 g

1 teaspoon cider vinegar
1 teaspoon garlic powder
1 teaspoon Dijon mustard
1 teaspoon brown sugar
¼ teaspoon black pepper
2 teaspoons olive oil
4 (4-ounce) turkey breast cutlets

1. In a medium bowl, combine the cider vinegar, garlic powder, mustard, brown sugar, and black pepper. Slowly whisk in the olive oil; combine thoroughly to make a thin paste.

2. Rinse the turkey cutlets and dry thoroughly on paper towels. If necessary to ensure a uniform thickness of the cutlets, put them between sheets of plastic wrap and pound to flatten them.

3. Pour the paste into a heavy-duty (freezer-style) resealable plastic bag. Add the turkey cutlets, moving them around in the mixture to coat all sides. Seal the bag, carefully squeezing out as much air as possible. Refrigerate to allow the turkey to marinate for at least 1 hour, or as long as overnight.

Stovetop Grilled Turkey Breast

(continued)

4. Place a nonstick, hard-anodized stovetop grill pan over high heat. When the pan is heated thoroughly, add the cutlets. (Depending on the amount of marinade you prefer to leave on the cutlets, you may want to use a splatter screen to prevent a mess on your stovetop.) Lower the heat to medium-high. Cook the cutlets 3 minutes on 1 side. Use tongs to turn the cutlets and cook another 3 minutes, or until the juices run clean.

tip

Cutlets prepared this way tend to cook faster than they do on an outdoor grill. If using an indoor grill that cooks both sides at once, like the George Foreman or Hamilton Beach models, allow 4–5 minutes total cooking time. You can also use a well-seasoned cast-iron skillet instead of a grill pan; however, you may need to introduce more oil to the pan to prevent the cutlets from sticking. Cooking time will be the same as with a grill pan. Be sure to adjust the Fat Exchange, if necessary.

Turkey-Mushroom Burgers

Yields: 8 large burgers

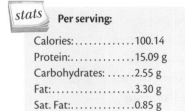

stats **Per serving:**

Calories: 100.14
Protein: . . . . 15.09 g
Carbohydrates: . . . . . . 2.55 g
Fat: . . . . 3.30 g
Sat. Fat: . . . . 0.85 g

1 pound turkey breast
1 pound fresh button mushrooms
1 tablespoon olive oil
1 teaspoon butter
1 clove garlic, minced
1 tablespoon chopped green onion
¼ teaspoon dried thyme
¼ teaspoon dried oregano
¼ teaspoon freshly ground black
   pepper
Cayenne pepper or dried red pepper
   flakes to taste (optional)

1. Cut the turkey into even pieces, about 1" square. Place the turkey cubes in the freezer 10 minutes, or long enough to allow the turkey to become somewhat firm.

2. In a covered, microwave-safe container, microwave the mushrooms on high 3–4 minutes, or until they begin to soften and sweat. Set aside to cool slightly.

3. Process the turkey in a food processor until ground, scraping down the sides of the bowl as necessary. Add the oil, butter, garlic, onion, and mushrooms (and any resulting liquid from the mushrooms); process until the mushrooms are ground, again scraping down the sides of the bowl as necessary. Add the remaining ingredients; pulse until mixed. Shape into 8 equal-sized patties. Cooking times will vary according to the method used and how thick you form the burgers.

Cranberry-Turkey Sausage

Serves 8

stats **Per serving:**

Calories: 107.40
Protein: . . . . .13.95 g
Carbohydrates: . . . . . .4.76 g
Fat: . . . . .3.31 g
Sat. Fat: . . . . .0.86 g

1 pound raw turkey breast
¼ cup cranberry-raisin chutney
¼ cup low-fat, reduced-sodium
*   chicken broth*
1 tablespoon green onion
¼ cup cornmeal
1 teaspoon dried rosemary
½ teaspoon ground black pepper
1 tablespoon olive oil
1 teaspoon butter

1. Cut the turkey into even pieces, about 1" square. Place the turkey cubes in the freezer 10 minutes, or long enough to allow the turkey to become somewhat firm. Process the turkey in a food processor until ground, scraping down the sides of the bowl as necessary.

2. Add the remaining ingredients; pulse until well blended. Form into 8 patties and "fry" in a nonstick skillet over medium heat, allowing about 4 minutes per side, or until juices run clear. (Alternatively, you can cook the patties on a lidded, indoor grill; allow about 4 minutes total, or until juices run clear.)

To substitute cooked turkey, add 1 Lean Meat Exchange per serving. Add water 1 tablespoon at a time if the mixture is too dry.

Poultry Sauces and Toppings

It's easy to prepare quick and healthy meals if you keep skinless, boneless chicken or turkey in the freezer. If you use an indoor grill, you don't even need to thaw them first. In fact, you can prepare most of the sauces and toppings in this section in the time it takes for the chicken or turkey to cook.

Pineapple-Black Bean Sauce

Serves 6

stats **Per serving:**

Calories: 166.11
Protein: . . . . .6.80 g
Carbohydrates: . . . . . .34.19 g
Fat: . . . . .0.87 g
Sat. Fat: . . . . .0.19 g

1 red pepper, sliced
¼ cup sliced green onions (white and
    green parts)
3 cloves garlic, minced
1–2 jalapeño peppers, seeded and
    minced
2 teaspoons curry powder
2 teaspoons minced gingerroot
1½ cups chicken broth (see page 162)
2 cups cubed pineapple
½ cup cranberry-raisin chutney
2 tablespoons, firmly packed light-
    brown sugar
2 tablespoons cornstarch
¼ cup cold water
2 cups cooked black beans

1. Treat a nonstick skillet with nonstick cooking spray. Heat over medium heat until hot. Sauté the red pepper, onions, garlic, jalapeño, curry powder, and ginger until the onions are tender, about 5 minutes.

2. Stir in the chicken broth, pineapple, chutney, and brown sugar; bring to a boil. Mix together the cornstarch and cold water; whisk it into the pineapple mixture. Boil, stirring constantly, until thickened, about 1 minute.

3. Stir in the black beans and continue to cook over medium heat until the beans are warmed, about 2–3 minutes. To serve, spoon the pineapple-bean sauce over chicken and serve with rice.

Proper Meat Handling

Be sure to wash any utensil that comes in contact with raw chicken in hot, soapy water, and rinse it well. This includes washing any utensil after each time it's used to baste a grilling, roasting, or baking chicken.

Christmas Colors with Yogurt Sauce

Yields: 2 cups
Serving size: ½ cup

 stats **Per serving:**

Calories: 97.05
Protein: . . . . .7.22 g
Carbohydrates: . . . . . .14.24 g
Fat: . . . . .1.43 g
Sat. Fat: . . . . .0.30 g

1 teaspoon olive oil
1 chopped, roasted or steamed red
    pepper
1 chopped, roasted or steamed green
    pepper
1 cup chopped onion, steamed
2 cups nonfat plain yogurt
Sea salt and freshly ground pepper
    to taste (optional)

Add the olive oil to a preheated nonstick skillet; sauté the peppers and onion until they're heated through. Add the yogurt; slowly bring it up to temperature, being careful not to boil it. Season with salt and pepper, if desired.

181

Honey-and-Cider Glaze for Baked Chicken

Serves 4

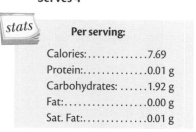

stats **Per serving, glaze only:**

Calories:............9.56
Protein:.............0.23 g
Carbohydrates: ......2.28 g
Fat:.................0.01 g
Sat. Fat:.............0.00 g

3 tablespoons cider or apple juice
½ teaspoon honey
1 teaspoon lemon juice
1 teaspoon Bragg's Liquid Aminos
½ teaspoon lemon zest

1. Preheat oven to 375°F. Combine all the ingredients in a microwave-safe bowl. Microwave on high 30 seconds. Stir until the honey is dissolved.

2. To use the glaze, arrange 4 boneless chicken pieces with the skin removed on a rack placed in a roasting pan or broiling pan. Brush or spoon 1 teaspoon of glaze over the top of each piece. Baste halfway through the cooking time, and again 5 minutes before the chicken is done. Allow the chicken to set 5 minutes before serving.

Spice-Tea Chicken Marinade

Serves 4

stats **Per serving:**

Calories:............7.69
Protein:.............0.01 g
Carbohydrates: ......1.92 g
Fat:.................0.00 g
Sat. Fat:.............0.01 g

4 Orange or Lemon Spice tea bags
2 cups boiling water
1 teaspoon honey

Steep tea bags in boiling water 4 minutes. Dissolve 1 teaspoon honey into the tea, pour it over 4 chicken pieces, and marinate 30 minutes. Occasionally turn and baste any exposed portions of chicken. Pour the tea into the roasting pan to provide moisture—discard it after cooking.

Roast Whole Chicken with Apples and Celery

Yields: 8 servings
Serving size: 4 ounces

 Per serving:

Calories:. 188.83
Protein:. . . . . .18.86 g
Carbohydrates: . . . . . .3.12 g
Sugar: . . . . .1.71 g
Fat:. . . . . .10.03 g

1 tablespoon corn flour
3 tablespoons cold water
5-pound roasting chicken
1 teaspoon salt
Freshly ground black pepper to taste
1 teaspoon Splenda
1 teaspoon dried thyme
2 teaspoons olive oil
1 lemon, thinly sliced and seeded
6 celery stalks, coarsely chopped,
    leaves reserved and separated
3 tart apples, cored, peeled, and
    quartered
1 (6") stalk fresh rosemary or 2
    tablespoons dried rosemary
1 teaspoon tamari soy sauce
1 cup chicken broth

1. Combine flour and water to form a smooth paste.

2. Rinse the chicken in cold water and pat it dry with paper towels. Rub it with salt, pepper, Splenda, and thyme, inside and out. Rub the skin with olive oil. Tease 4 lemon slices under the skin.

3. Preheat the oven to 400°F. Prepare the roasting pan with nonstick spray. Place the celery pieces in the bottom of the roasting pan.

4. Place the celery leaves, 2 apple quarters, and half of the rosemary inside the cavity of the chicken. Place the chicken in the pan; roast 20 minutes.

5. Add the rest of the apples and the tamari to the pan with the chicken. Return chicken to oven. Baste the chicken with broth every 15 minutes for 90 minutes, or until a meat thermometer inserted into a meaty part of the thigh registers 155°F.

6. Remove the chicken, apples, and celery to a serving platter. Pour juices from roasting pan into small saucepan and bring to a boil. Whisk in the flour paste and cook until thickened. Place in the freezer for a few minutes and skim off the fat. Pour into a gravy boat and serve.

Baked Chicken with Root Vegetables

Yields: 6 servings
Serving size: 4 ounces of meat and 1 cup vegetables

3½ pounds chicken, cut into 6 serving pieces
2 teaspoons olive oil
Salt and freshly ground pepper to taste
½ teaspoon freshly grated nutmeg
1 teaspoon Splenda
2 whole sweet onions, peeled and quartered
4 carrots, peeled and cut into 3" lengths
4 parsnips, peeled, halved, and cut into 3" lengths
1 celery root, peeled, quartered, thinly sliced
3 large Idaho potatoes, peeled and quartered
½ fennel bulb, cleaned and cut into chunks
1 teaspoon tamari soy sauce
1 cup chicken broth
1 tablespoon unsalted butter
½ bunch of chives, finely snipped, for garnish

1. Preheat oven to 400°F. Rub the chicken with oil and sprinkle with salt, pepper, nutmeg, and Splenda. Place chicken, bone-side up, skin down, in a large baking dish with the vegetables. Combine tamari and broth and baste chicken with the mixture.

2. Bake 15 minutes. Turn the chicken and reduce heat to 350°F. Return chicken to oven and bake, basting frequently, until the chicken is browned and the vegetables are fork-tender.

 tip

You do not have to puree the roasted vegetables in this recipe; if you prefer, leave them in big chunks, place them in a bowl, and let people serve themselves.

Baked Chicken with Root Vegetables

(continued)

3. Place the chicken on a platter. Place the vegetables on a separate platter. Drain the pan juices into a sauceboat. Put the pan juices in the freezer and skim the fat off the top if you are watching your fat intake.

4. Remove the onions from the vegetable mixture. Add the butter to the remaining vegetables; put them through a ricer or a food processor.

5. Mound the pureed veggies in a bowl. Snip the chives over the chicken and vegetables, and serve.

Root Vegetables

These are available year round, and they tend to keep for many months. Before the advent of modern-day transportation systems, root vegetables were widely used during the winter when fresh produce was scarce.

Braised Chicken Thighs with Bacon and Onions

Yields: 4 servings
Serving size: 4 ounces

stats **Per serving:**

Calories:............208.34
Protein:............25.05 g
Carbohydrates: ......4.72 g
Sugar: ....1.17 g
Fat:.................9.44 g

2 slices sugar-free bacon
4 (4-ounce) boneless, skinless chicken
    thighs
1 small yellow onion, peeled and
    chopped
4 sage leaves, torn in small pieces
Freshly ground black pepper
1 teaspoon Splenda
1½ cups low-sodium chicken broth
2 teaspoons corn or rice flour
4 tablespoons chopped parsley

1. Sauté the bacon in a large nonstick pan over medium heat. Place on a paper towel to drain. Leave ½ teaspoon of fat in the pan; sauté the chicken and onion.

2. Add the sage leaves, pepper, Splenda, and broth to the pan; cover and reduce heat to a simmer. Simmer 35–40 minutes. Crumble the bacon and add it to the pot. Cook another 5 minutes.

3. Spoon the chicken and onions onto a serving platter. Reduce broth to 1 cup. Whisk in flour and cook, whisking constantly, 3–4 minutes, or until thickened, to make gravy. Add the parsley, and pour over the chicken.

Baked Nut-Crusted Chicken Breasts

Yields: 4 servings
Serving size: 4 ounces

stats **Per serving:**

Calories:............292.57
Protein:.............29.78 g
Carbohydrates: ......3.99 g
Sugar: ....0.72 g
Fat:.................18.03 g

4 (4-ounce) boneless, skinless chicken
breasts
1 tablespoon olive oil
1 tablespoon tamari soy sauce
Juice of ½ lemon
Salt to taste
1 teaspoon cayenne pepper
1 teaspoon Splenda
½ cup ground walnuts or pecans

1. Preheat the oven to 350°F. Rinse and dry the chicken; place on paper towels.

2. Combine the oil, tamari, lemon juice, salt, cayenne pepper, and Splenda to make a paste. Spread a piece of parchment paper on a baking sheet. Rub each piece of chicken with the paste. Press the nuts into the chicken.

3. Bake 35 minutes, or until the chicken and nuts are brown. Serve hot, cold, or at room temperature.

tip

If you bake the chicken on parchment paper, you won't have to clean the pan.

Chicken Breasts with Fennel and Orange Slices

Yields: 4 servings

Serving size: 4 ounces

stats **Per serving:**

Calories: 257.92
Protein: . . . . .27.93 g
Carbohydrates: . . . . . .13.72 g
Sugar: . . . . .4.54 g
Fat: . . . . .8.64 g

¼ cup flour
Salt and freshly ground black pepper
    to taste
½ teaspoon dried tarragon
1 teaspoon Splenda
2 tablespoons olive oil
4 (4-ounce) boneless, skinless chicken
    breasts, pounded flat
½ cup red onion, peeled, sliced, and
    chopped
1 cup fennel, cleaned and thinly
    sliced
1 orange, thinly sliced
¼ cup dry white wine
¼ cup chicken broth
1 teaspoon dark soy sauce

1. On a large piece of waxed paper, mix the flour, salt, pepper, tarragon, and Splenda. Dredge the chicken breasts in the mixture; set aside.

2. Heat the oil over medium heat in a large nonstick pan. Brown the chicken on both sides. Add the vegetables to the pan.

3. Reduce heat and cook another 10 minutes, stirring every 2–3 minutes. Remove the chicken and add the orange slices, wine, broth, and soy sauce; cover and simmer another 10 minutes.

4. Return the chicken to the pan to warm it. Serve with the orange sauce and vegetables.

 tip

This elegant recipe is very delicious served with rice to sop up the sauce. Throw a few raisins and some nuts into the rice for more flavor.

To Pound or Not to Pound?

Pounding a piece of chicken breast or thigh tenderizes the meat, and the thinness allows the chicken to cook more quickly and evenly. Do you need any other reason to take a mallet, a meat pounder, or a five-pound barbell and take out your aggressions on a piece of chicken?

Chicken Breasts in Sicilian Olive Sauce

Yields: 4 servings
Serving size: 4 ounces

stats **Per serving:**

Calories: 240.25
Protein: . . . . .17 g
Carbohydrates: . . . . . .7.67 g
Sugar: . . . . .1.69 g
Fat: . . . . .15.31 g

4 chicken breast halves, bone in and
    skin on
Salt and pepper to taste
4 teaspoons Wondra quick-blending
    flour
1 tablespoon olive oil
4 cloves garlic, peeled and chopped
4 shallots
1 tablespoon fresh mint leaves, torn
    in small pieces
1 teaspoon dried oregano
1 teaspoon Splenda
16 Sicilian olives
1 cup chicken broth
1 slice hard salami, minced

1. Sprinkle the chicken with salt, pepper, and flour. Heat the oil over medium heat in a large pan. Brown the chicken, skin-side down. Turn; add the garlic and shallots. Cook 5 minutes.

2. Turn the chicken; add the mint, oregano, Splenda, olives, and broth. Cover the pan; reduce heat to a simmer. Cook 40 minutes, checking to make sure the pan doesn't dry out. Add a bit of water if the sauce gets too low.

3. Remove chicken from heat and sprinkle with salami.

tip

This dish is excellent with orzo.

Chicken Breasts with Capers

Yields: 4 servings
Serving size: 4 ounces

stats **Per serving:**

Calories:............255.97
Protein:.............28.55
Carbohydrates:......14.17 g
Sugar: ....1.4 g
Fat:.................9 g

¼ cup cornmeal
2 tablespoons flour
1 teaspoon cayenne pepper
1 teaspoon salt
1 teaspoon Splenda
¼ cup skim milk
4 boneless, skinless chicken breasts,
    thinly pounded
2 tablespoons olive oil
1 tablespoon capers
Juice of ½ lemon
½ cup chicken broth
½ cup Italian flat-leaf parsley, rinsed
    and chopped

1. Mix the cornmeal, flour, cayenne pepper, salt, and Splenda on a large piece of waxed paper. Place the milk in a bowl. Dip the chicken in the milk and then dredge it in the cornmeal mixture, pressing the dry ingredients into the chicken.

2. Heat the oil in a large nonstick pan over medium heat. Brown the chicken. Add the rest of the ingredients; cover, reduce heat, and simmer 15 minutes.

3. Serve the chicken hot, with caper sauce spooned over top.

Capers

Capers grow profusely in Sicily and other areas of the Mediterranean. The finest are the smallest, packed in brine, not salt. They add a very special flavor to soups, stews, salads, and sauces.

Chicken with Egg and Lemon over Baby Spinach

Yields: 4 servings
Serving size: 4 ounces

stats **Per serving:**

Calories: 350
Protein:. . . . . .30.89 g
Carbohydrates: . . . . . .15.3 g
Sugar: . . . . .1.47 g
Fat:. . . . . .8.75 g

4 (4-ounce) boneless, skinless chicken
     breasts, thinly pounded
Salt and pepper to taste
Pinch of flour
1 egg, beaten
2 tablespoons olive oil, divided
Juice of ½ lemon
2 (6-ounce) packages fresh, baby
     spinach
⅛ teaspoon freshly grated nutmeg

1. Sprinkle the chicken with salt, pepper, and flour. Place the beaten egg in a shallow bowl; dip the chicken in the egg. Heat 1 tablespoon of the oil in a large frying pan over medium-high heat.

2. Sauté the chicken about 4 minutes per side, or until lightly browned. Add the lemon juice to the pan.

3. Heat the rest of the oil in another sauté pan; quickly sauté the spinach. Place the spinach on warm plates, arrange the chicken on top, and pour the pan juices over the dish. Sprinkle nutmeg over the top.

tip

You can easily substitute veal scallops for the chicken.

Braised Chicken with Green Olives and Artichokes

Yields: 8 servings
Serving size: 4 ounces

stats **Per serving:**

Calories:.............186.58
Protein:..............22.17 g
Carbohydrates: ......8.34 g
Sugar: ....1.2 g
Fat:.................7.04 g

1 tablespoon corn flour
2 tablespoons cold water
2 tablespoons olive oil
8 small chicken drumsticks, thighs, or
    breast halves, skin on, bone in
Salt and pepper to taste
4 cloves garlic, chopped
4 shallots, chopped
1 tablespoon fresh rosemary or 1
    teaspoon dried rosemary
¾ cup chicken broth
¼ cup vegetable broth
½ cup green pimento-stuffed olives
1 (10-ounce) package frozen
    artichokes, thawed and sliced
    lengthwise
2 tablespoons capers, optional

1. Combine flour and water to form a smooth paste.

2. Heat the olive oil in a large frying pan over medium-high heat. Sprinkle the chicken with salt and pepper; brown it on both sides. Turn the heat to low; add the garlic, shallots, and rosemary.

3. Add the broths, olives, and artichokes; simmer 30–40 minutes. Stir the flour-water mixture into the liquid for a thicker sauce. Garnish with capers.

Grilled Turkey Thighs
with Thyme, Basil, and Butter

Yields: 6 servings
Serving size: 5 ounces

stats **Per serving:**

Calories: 312.55
Protein: . . . . .26.83 g
Carbohydrates: . . . . . .1.62 g
Sugar: . . . . .0.35 g
Fat: . . . . .21.5 g

¼ cup olive oil
¼ cup freshly squeezed lemon juice
1 tablespoon fresh thyme or 1
  teaspoon dried thyme
1 tablespoon fresh basil or 1
  teaspoon dried basil
1 teaspoon cayenne pepper
1 teaspoon onion powder
½ teaspoon garlic powder
2–2½ pounds turkey thigh, bone in,
  skin on

1. Fire up the grill. Whisk the olive oil, lemon juice, thyme, basil, cayenne pepper, onion powder, and garlic powder together in a small bowl.

2. Brush both sides of the turkey with the sauce; grill over a medium fire, brushing with sauce every few minutes. Grill until a meat thermometer inserted into the thickest part of the turkey registers 155°F.

3. Slice and serve.

tip

If you add mesquite chips to your fire, this will be even tastier. The mesquite smoke adds a lot of flavor to grilled steaks, burgers, and chicken.

Turkey Chili

Yields: 12 servings
Serving size: 6 ounces

stats **Per serving:**

Calories: 355.70
Protein: . . . . .25.4 g
Carbohydrates: . . . . . .36 g
Sugar: . . . . .6 g
Fat: . . . . .13.87 g

¼ cup cooking oil
2½ pounds lean ground turkey meat
4 sweet red onions, chopped
6 cloves garlic, chopped
4 Italian green frying peppers,
     stemmed, seeded, and chopped
2 large sweet red bell peppers,
     roasted
2 sweet yellow peppers, stemmed,
     seeded, and chopped
4 jalapeño peppers, stemmed,
     seeded, and chopped
2 tablespoons chili powder, or to
     taste
1 tablespoon dry English-style
     mustard
1 teaspoon cinnamon
1 teaspoon Dutch-process cocoa
     powder
½ cup strong cold coffee
2 tablespoons Splenda
3 (14-ounce) cans red kidney beans,
     drained and rinsed
2 (28-ounce) cans sugar-free Italian
     plum tomatoes
Salt and pepper to taste
1 teaspoon liquid smoke, or to taste

1. Heat the oil over medium heat in a large pot that has a cover. Sauté the turkey, breaking it up with a wooden spoon. Add the onions, garlic, and peppers to the pot; stir, sautéing until softened, about 12 minutes.

2. Add the chili powder to the meat mixture; stir to combine. In a separate bowl, blend the dry mustard, cinnamon, and cocoa powder with the coffee; whisk with a fork until smooth. Add to the meat mixture.

3. Stir in remaining ingredients and cover. Reduce the heat to a bare simmer. Cook for a minimum of 3 hours.

Cornish Game Hens in Red Wine-Mushroom Sauce

Yields: 4 servings
Serving size: ½ hen

 stats **Per serving:**

Calories: 397.95
Protein: . . . . .26.66 g
Carbohydrates: . . . . . .15.52 g
Sugar: . . . . .6.91 g
Fat: . . . . .22.54 g

2 (10-ounce) Cornish game hens, split
2 teaspoons olive oil
1 teaspoon salt
Pepper to taste
1 teaspoon dried thyme
12 white pearl onions, left whole
4 carrots, peeled, halved lengthwise, and cut into short sticks
⅔ cup dry red wine
1 teaspoon Splenda
1 cup sliced button mushrooms
1 tablespoon Wondra quick-blending flour

1. Preheat oven broiler to 450°F. Prepare a large roasting pan with nonstick spray. Rub each hen with olive oil on both sides.

2. Sprinkle the hens with salt, pepper, and thyme. Place them in the pan, skin-side down. Place them under the broiler 8–10 minutes, or until brown. Turn the hens. Add the onions, carrots, red wine, and Splenda to the pan; cover. Turn off broiler and reduce oven heat to 350°F.

3. Roast another 25 minutes. Add the mushrooms; stir the flour into the liquid. Stir to thicken. Drizzle the hens with the sauce, and serve with vegetables.

Red Versus White Wine

Red and white wines impart distinct flavors when they are used for cooking. You can make this exact recipe with white wine and produce a completely different result. Red wine gives a rich, deep, and subtly spicy flavor. White wine gives the dish a lighter, fruity flavor.

Sliced Turkey Breast with Mushroom Sauce

Yields: 6 servings
Serving size: 4 ounces

 **Per serving:**

Calories: 200.39
Protein: . . . . .30.32 g
Carbohydrates: . . . . . .9.71 g
Sugar: . . . . .3.85 g
Fat: . . . . .3.57 g

1 tablespoon corn flour
2 tablespoons cold water
1 tablespoon unsalted butter
1½ pounds boneless, skinless turkey
    breast
2 teaspoons corn or chestnut flour
Salt and freshly ground black pepper
    to taste
4 shallots, chopped
1 clove garlic, minced
½ pound shitake mushrooms,
    stemmed and brushed clean
½ cup white grape juice
1 teaspoon Splenda
1 teaspoon grated orange rind
⅛ teaspoon ground nutmeg
¾ cup chicken broth
½ cup milk
½ cup fresh parsley, finely chopped

1. Combine flour and water to form smooth paste.

2. Preheat the oven to 325°F.

3. Over medium heat, melt the butter in a large ovenproof casserole dish. Dust the turkey with flour, salt, and pepper.

4. Sauté the turkey on each side. Add the shallots, garlic, and mushrooms to the casserole dish; sauté, stirring constantly.

5. Add the grape juice, Splenda, orange rind, nutmeg, chicken broth, and milk. Cover the turkey with sauce; remove from the stove. Cover the casserole dish and bake in the oven 35–40 minutes.

Sliced Turkey Breast with Mushroom Sauce

(continued)

6. Arrange the turkey pieces on a serving platter and cut into serving pieces.

7. Over medium heat, whisk the flour and water mixture into the sauce to thicken it. Pour it over the turkey and sprinkle with parsley.

---

tip

If you are preparing this dish for a party, you can make it a day in advance and simply reheat it very gently just before serving.

Boneless, Skinless Turkey Breasts

Turkey breasts can masquerade as veal in a parmigiana, and they work well as a substitute for pork. Versatile and delicious, turkey breasts taste wonderful in braised, poached, and sautéed dishes.

Duck Breasts Sautéed with Fresh Cranberries

Yields: 6 servings
Serving size: 4 ounces

stats **Per serving:**

Calories:.............288.42
Protein:..............24.09 g
Carbohydrates:......13.99 g
Sugar: ....6.07 g
Fat:.................16.9 g

8 ounces fresh cranberries
½ cup Splenda
1 cup orange juice
1½ pounds boneless, skinless duck
    breasts
Salt and pepper to taste
¾ cup corn flour
2 tablespoons olive oil
⅔ cup chicken broth
1 teaspoon dried oregano leaves
1 teaspoon finely grated fresh lemon
    zest
½ cup chopped toasted pecans, for
    garnish

1. In a saucepan over medium heat, bring the cranberries, Splenda, and orange juice to a boil. As soon as the berries pop open, reduce heat to a simmer; cook 20 minutes. Taste for sweetness and add more Splenda, if necessary.

2. Slice each duck breast into 3 pieces and pound to flatten. Sprinkle with salt, pepper, and corn flour. Heat the olive oil in a large sauté pan over medium heat; brown the duck.

3. Reduce the heat to a simmer; add the cranberries and all of the other ingredients except the walnuts. Cover the pan; simmer 20 minutes.

4. Remove the duck pieces to a warm platter. Reduce the sauce to just under 1 cup, and pour it over the duck.

tip

Duck tastes absolutely wonderful with many kinds of fruit. This recipe calls for cranberries, but you can substitute cherries, berries, pears, or apples.

Fruit Sauces

If you are giving a dinner party, make your fruit sauce in advance. These sauces keep well in the refrigerator for at least a week, and they freeze beautifully. This will shorten your prep time prior to the party.

198

Duck Breasts with Cherry Glaze and Black Cherries

Yields: 6 servings
Serving size: 4 ounces

 Per serving:

Calories: 241.50
Protein: . . . . .23.35 g
Carbohydrates: . . . . . .52.11 g
Sugar: . . . . .11.18 g
Fat: . . . . .3.75 g

1 teaspoon cornstarch
¼ cup cold water
10 ounces pitted black cherries
4 ounces Splenda, or to taste
½ cup unsweetened apple juice
Juice of ½ lemon
½ teaspoon salt, plus extra for
    coating the duck
Freshly ground black pepper to taste,
    plus extra for coating the duck
1½ pounds duck breast, pounded
    thin
2 teaspoons corn or chestnut flour
2 tablespoons canola oil
¾ cup vegetable broth
2 tablespoons fresh rosemary or 2
    teaspoons dried rosemary
4 teaspoons sugar-free cherry jam

1. Combine cornstarch and water to form slurry.

2. Mix the cherries, Splenda, apple juice, lemon juice, ½ teaspoon salt, and pepper in a saucepan; bring to a boil over high heat. Add the cornstarch mixture; reduce heat, cover, and simmer 10 minutes.

3. Cut each duck breast into 3 pieces and set them on a piece of waxed paper. Sprinkle with salt, pepper, and extra cornstarch. Heat the oil in a large frying pan; quickly brown the duck. Add the broth and rosemary; cover and simmer 20 minutes.

4. Arrange the duck on a heated serving platter or warm plates. Add the cherries, and spoon the sugar-free cherry jam on top.

Grilled Quail with Olive Condiment

Yields: 2 servings
Serving size: 5 ounces

stats **Per serving:**

Calories: 389.41
Protein: . . . . 27.88 g
Carbohydrates: . . . . . . 2.57 g
Sugar: . . . . 0.01 g
Fat: . . . . 29.43 g

8 large pitted black olives, chopped
4 pitted green olives, chopped
1 teaspoon lemon zest
2 teaspoons parsley
3 teaspoons olive oil, divided
4 (4-ounce) quails, cleaned and split
*   open*
2 teaspoons olive oil
Salt and freshly ground black pepper
*   to taste*

1. Start your grill. If you are cooking over coals, make sure they have burned down to an ashy gray before cooking. If you are using gas, set your grill at medium-high.

2. Mix the olives, lemon zest, and parsley together in a small bowl with 1 teaspoon olive oil; set aside. Rub the quail with the remaining olive oil and sprinkle with salt and pepper.

3. Grill the quail about 4 minutes per side, or until nicely browned.

4. Serve with the olive mixture as a condiment.

 tip

Champagne makes a fantastic accompaniment to this romantic dish.

Quail

These tiny birds are not too easy to find in local stores, but the Internet is an excellent source of foods that aren't that easy to come by. Quail is definitely a delicacy, and makes a lovely special-occasion dish.

Pheasant with Fresh Pears

Yields: 4 servings
Serving size: 5 ounces

stats **Per serving:**

Calories:............290.29
Protein:.............34.86 g
Carbohydrates: ......7.20 g
Sugar: ....4.44 g
Fat:................11.91 g

1 (2–2 ½-pound) pheasant, cut in
    serving pieces
Salt and freshly ground pepper
1 teaspoon Splenda
2 slices sugar-free bacon, cut in strips
    crosswise
½ cup chicken broth
¼ cup dry white wine
4 sage leaves, minced
2 pears, peeled, cored, and quartered

1. Preheat the oven to 375°F. Rinse and pat
the pheasant pieces dry. Sprinkle them with
salt, pepper, and Splenda. Arrange them in
a baking pan; cover with equal amounts of
bacon strips.

2. Add the liquids to the pan; sprinkle with
sage. Grind extra pepper over the top. Roast
the pheasant pieces 35 minutes, basting
every 2–3 minutes.

3. Place on a warm serving platter or plates.
Arrange the pears around the pheasant, and
pour the juice into a sauce boat. You can
thicken the juices with Wondra flour if you
want a thick sauce.

tip

Pheasant is a very lean meat that
can be very dry; it does require some
added fat. Bacon imparts a lot of flavor, but you
can substitute low-fat spread or olive oil.

Pheasant with Asian Marinade

Yields: 4 servings
Serving size: 5 ounces

 Per serving:

Calories: 243.51
Protein: . . . . .33.74 g
Carbohydrates: . . . . . .5.97 g
Sugar: . . . . .4.3 g
Fat: . . . . .8.81 g

Juice of 1 lime
1 tablespoon olive oil
1 teaspoon tamari sauce
1 teaspoon fresh ginger, minced
1 teaspoon cayenne pepper powder,
*   mixed with 2 teaspoons water*
1 teaspoon Splenda
2 ounces unsweetened apple juice
1 pheasant, cut in 4 serving pieces
4 teaspoons sugar-free apricot jam

1. Mix the lime juice, olive oil, tamari, ginger, cayenne pepper, Splenda, and apple juice together in a small bowl to create the marinade. Place the pheasant pieces in a baking dish that you have prepared with nonstick spray. Pour the marinade over top.

2. Cover the dish with plastic wrap; refrigerate at least 60 minutes, turning after 30 minutes. Do not marinate more than 90 minutes or the meat will cook in the acid.

3. When ready to cook, preheat the oven to 350°F. Remove plastic wrap and place the dish in the oven. Roast 35–40 minutes, basting frequently with the pan juices.

4. Spoon apricot jam atop each piece of pheasant; return to oven. Continue roasting until jam melts and bubbles, about 5 minutes.

Pheasant

This delicious bird is a wonderful special-occasion dinner, but it needs to be handled delicately. Having almost no subcutaneous fat, it easily toughens and dries out completely. For this reason, it does not broil well, but you can roast a whole pheasant if you baste it or cover it with bacon or butter.

Seafood

Fish Stock

Yields: 4 cups
Serving size: 1 cup

stats **Per serving:**

Calories:............39.61
Protein:.............5.27 g
Carbohydrates:......0.00 g
Fat:.................1.89 g
Sat. Fat:.............0.47 g

*4 cups fish heads, bones, and
trimmings (approx. 1 pound)*
2 stalks celery and leaves, chopped
1 onion, chopped
1 carrot, peeled and chopped
1 bay leaf
4 sprigs fresh parsley
*Sea salt and pepper to taste
(optional)*

1. Use your own fish trimmings (saved in bag in the freezer), or ask the butcher at your local fish market or supermarket for fish trimmings. Wash the trimmings well.

2. Combine all the ingredients in a stockpot; add enough water to cover everything by 1" or so. Bring to a boil over high heat; reduce heat to low. Skim off the foam that rises to the top. Cover and simmer 20 minutes.

3. Remove from the heat and strain through a sieve; discard all solids. Refrigerate or freeze.

tip

To make stock from shellfish, simply substitute shrimp, crab, or lobster shells for the fish heads and bones.

Proper Fish Handling

Always wash your hands after handling raw fish, and wash all surfaces and utensils that the raw fish touched.

Asian-Style Fish Cakes

Serves 8

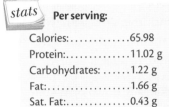

stats **Per serving:**

Calories:.............65.98
Protein:.............11.02 g
Carbohydrates: ......1.22 g
Fat:.................1.66 g
Sat. Fat:.............0.43 g

1 pound catfish fillet
2 green onions, minced
1 banana pepper, cored, seeded, and
    chopped
2 cloves garlic, minced
1 tablespoon grated or minced ginger
1 tablespoon Bragg's Liquid Aminos
1 tablespoon lemon juice
1 teaspoon lemon zest
Old Bay Seasoning to taste (optional)
Rice flour (optional)
Olive or peanut oil (optional)

1. Preheat oven to 375°F. Cut the fish into 1" pieces and combine with the green onions, banana pepper, garlic, ginger, Bragg's Liquid Aminos, lemon juice, and lemon zest in a food processor; process until chopped and mixed. (You do not want to purée this mixture; it should be a rough chop.) Add the Old Bay Seasoning, if using; stir to mix.

2. Form the fish mixture into patties of about 2 tablespoons each; you should have 16 patties total. Place the patties on a baking sheet treated with nonstick cooking spray; bake 12–15 minutes, or until crisp. (Alternatively, you can fry these in a nonstick pan about 4 minutes on each side.)

tip

For crunchy fish cakes, coat each side in the rice flour, then lightly spritz the top of the patties with the olive or peanut oil before baking as directed.

Not All Weeds Are Bad

Seaweed is an important ingredient in many processed foods, such as commercial ice cream and other foods that contain carrageenan, a thickener found in several kinds of seaweed.

Slow-Roasted Salmon

Serves 4

stats **Per serving:**

Calories:............256.96
Protein:..............25.44 g
Carbohydrates: ......0.52 g
Fat:.................16.34 g
Sat. Fat:.............3.16 g

2 teaspoons extra-virgin olive oil
4 (5-ounce) salmon fillets with skin,
    room temperature
1 cup finely minced fresh chives
Sea or kosher salt and freshly ground
    white pepper to taste (optional)
Sage sprigs, for garnish

1. Preheat oven to 250°F. Rub ½ teaspoon of the olive oil into the flesh side of each salmon fillet. Completely cover the fillets with the chives; gently press them into the flesh. Season with salt and white pepper, if desired.

2. Place the fillets skin-side down on a non-stick, oven-safe skillet or a foil-lined cookie sheet treated with nonstick spray; roast 25 minutes. Garnish with sage sprigs and serve.

Smoked-Salmon Cream Sauce

Serves 4

stats **Per serving, sauce only:**

Calories:............143.28
Protein:..............18.04 g
Carbohydrates: ......1.34 g
Fat:.................6.72 g
Sat. Fat:.............2.64 g

2 teaspoons butter
4 ounces Ducktrap River smoked
    salmon
2 cups nonfat cottage cheese
Ground nutmeg (optional)
Freshly ground white or black pepper
    (optional)

1. Melt the butter in a nonstick skillet. Cut the smoked salmon into julienne strips; sauté in the butter until heated through.

2. In a blender or food processor, blend the cottage cheese until smooth. Stir the puréed cottage cheese into the sautéed salmon; heat on low until the cottage cheese is brought to serving temperature.

3. Spoon the sauce over 4 servings of cooked pasta or toast. Top with the nutmeg and pepper, if desired.

Salmon Patties

Serves 5

 Per serving:

Calories:.............168.05
Protein:..............17.17 g
Carbohydrates: ......3.19 g
Fat:..................9.18 g
Sat. Fat:..............1.92 g

2 cups cooked salmon (no salt
    added)
6 crushed soda crackers
1 egg
½ cup skim milk
1 small onion, chopped
1 tablespoon chopped fresh parsley
1 tablespoon unbleached all-purpose
    flour
1 tablespoon olive oil
Ener-G flour (optional)

1. Place the salmon in a bowl; flake with a fork. Add the crushed crackers, egg, milk, onion, parsley, and flour; mix well. Gently form into 5 patties.

2. Heat the oil in a nonstick skillet over medium heat. (Optional: Lightly dust the patties with some Ener-G rice flour for crispier patties.) Fry on both sides until browned, about 5 minutes per side.

Crab Cakes with Sesame Crust

Serves 5

 Per serving:

Calories: 107.69
Protein: . . . . .9.04 g
Carbohydrates: . . . . . .2.93 g
Fat: . . . . .6.45 g
Sat. Fat: . . . . .1.05 g

1 pound (16 ounces) lump crabmeat
1 egg
1 tablespoon minced fresh ginger
1 small scallion, finely chopped
1 tablespoon dry sherry
1 tablespoon freshly squeezed lemon juice
6 tablespoons Hellmann's or Best Foods Real Mayonnaise
Sea salt and freshly ground white pepper to taste (optional)
Old Bay Seasoning to taste (optional)
¼ cup lightly toasted sesame seeds

1. Preheat oven to 375°F. In a large bowl, mix together the crab, egg, ginger, scallion, sherry, lemon juice, mayonnaise, and the seasonings, if using.

2. Form the mixture into 10 equal cakes. Spread the sesame seeds over a sheet pan; dip both sides of the cakes to coat them. Arrange the crab cakes on a baking sheet treated with nonstick spray. Typical baking time is 8–10 minutes (depending on how thick you make the cakes).

So, What Is Aquaculture?

"Aquaculture produces about 17 percent of the world's seafood. . . . Seaweed cultivation ranks first in volume, followed by carp, and blue mussels. In the U.S., catfish is the predominant farmed species, followed by trout, salmon, and shellfish." (Source: Ducktrap River Fish Farm's Aquaculture FAQ page at *www.ducktrap.com*)

Creamy Shrimp Pie with Rice Crust

Serves 4

 Per serving:

Calories:.............273.12
Protein:..............26.24 g
Carbohydrates: ......26.80 g
Fat:.................6.39 g
Sat. Fat:.............2.39 g

1⅓ cups cooked white rice
2 teaspoons dried parsley
2 tablespoons grated onion
1 teaspoon olive oil
1 tablespoon butter
1 clove garlic, crushed
1 pound shrimp, peeled and
    deveined
1 recipe Condensed Cream-of-
    Mushroom Soup (see page 141)
1 teaspoon lemon juice
1 cup sliced mushrooms, steamed

1. Preheat oven to 350°F. Combine the cooked rice, parsley, and onion; mix well. Use the olive oil to coat a 10" pie plate. Press the rice mixture evenly around the sides and bottom. This works best if the rice is moist; if necessary, add 1 teaspoon of water.

2. Melt the butter in a deep, nonstick skillet over medium heat; sauté the garlic. Add the shrimp; cook, stirring frequently, until pink, about 5 minutes. Add the soup and lemon juice to the skillet; stir until smooth and thoroughly heated. (If the soup seems too thick, add some water, 1 teaspoon at a time.) Stir the mushrooms into the soup mixture; pour it over the rice "crust." Bake 30 minutes, or until lightly browned on top. Serve hot.

Fat-Free Flavor

To add the flavor of sautéed mushrooms or onions without the added fat of butter or oil, roast or grill them first. Simply spread them on a baking sheet treated with nonstick spray. Roasting them for 5 minutes in a 350°F oven will be sufficient if the vegetables are sliced, and will not add additional cooking time to the recipe.

Mock Sour Cream-Baked Catfish

Serves 4

 Per serving:

Calories:............170.59
Protein:.............17.80 g
Carbohydrates: ......1.79 g
Fat:.................9.73 g
Sat. Fat:............2.17 g

1 pound (16 ounces) catfish fillets
2 teaspoons Hellmann's or Best
  Foods Real Mayonnaise
2 teaspoons all-purpose flour
½ cup plain nonfat yogurt
½ teaspoon white wine vinegar
4 teaspoons chopped pimiento-
  stuffed green olives
½ teaspoon ground celery seed
¼ teaspoon paprika
¼ teaspoon freshly ground white or
  black pepper
¼ teaspoon thyme
1 teaspoon fresh dill (or a pinch of
  dried dill per fillet)
1 lemon, cut into 4 wedges (optional)
Fresh chopped or dried parsley
  (optional)

1. Preheat oven to 350°F. Prepare a baking dish by spraying it with nonstick spray. Rinse the fillets in water, then dry between layers of paper towels. Arrange the fillets in the baking dish.

2. In a small bowl, combine the mayonnaise, flour, yogurt, vinegar, olives, celery seed, paprika, pepper, and thyme; spread the mixture over the fish and sprinkle with dill. Bake 15 minutes, or until the fish flakes when touched with a fork. Garnish with lemon wedges and parsley, if desired.

Baked Bread Crumb-Crusted Fish with Lemon

Serves 6

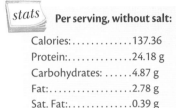 *stats* **Per serving, without salt:**

Calories:............137.36
Protein:.............24.18 g
Carbohydrates: ......4.87 g
Fat:.................2.78 g
Sat. Fat:.............0.39 g

2 large lemons
¼ cup dried breadcrumbs
1½ pounds (24 ounces) halibut fillets
Sea or kosher salt and freshly ground
    white or black pepper to taste
    (optional)

1. Preheat oven to 375°F. Wash 1 lemon and cut it into thin slices. Grate 1 tablespoon of zest from the second lemon, then juice it. Combine the grated zest and breadcrumbs in a small bowl; stir to mix; set aside.

2. Put the lemon juice in a shallow dish; arrange the lemon slices in the bottom of a baking dish treated with nonstick spray. Dip the fish pieces in the lemon juice and set them on the lemon slices in the baking dish. Sprinkle the breadcrumb mixture evenly over the fish pieces, along with the salt and pepper, if using; bake until the crumbs are lightly browned and the fish is just opaque, 10–15 minutes. (Baking time will depend on the thickness of the fish.) Serve immediately, using the lemon slices as garnish.

Lemon Infusion

Mildly flavored fish, such as catfish, cod, halibut, orange roughy, rockfish, and snapper, benefit from the distinctive flavor of lemon. Adding slices of lemon to the top of the fish allows the flavor to infuse into the fish.

Baked Red Snapper Almandine

Serves 4

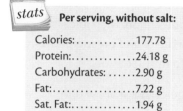

stats **Per serving, without salt:**

Calories:............177.78
Protein:.............24.18 g
Carbohydrates: ......2.90 g
Fat:.................7.22 g
Sat. Fat:.............1.94 g

1 pound (16 ounces) red snapper
   fillets
Sea or kosher salt and freshly ground
   white or black pepper to taste
   (optional)
4 teaspoons all-purpose flour
2 teaspoons olive oil
2 tablespoons ground raw almonds
2 teaspoons unsalted butter
1 tablespoon lemon juice

1. Preheat oven to 375°F. Rinse the red snapper fillets and dry between layers of paper towels. Season with salt and pepper, if using. Sprinkle the fillets with the flour, front and back.

2. In an ovenproof nonstick skillet, sauté the fillets in the olive oil until they are nicely browned on both sides. Combine the ground almonds and butter in a microwave-safe dish and microwave on high 30 seconds, or until the butter is melted; stir to combine. Pour the almond-butter mixture and the lemon juice over the fillets. Bake 3–5 minutes, or until the almonds are nicely browned.

A-Taste-of-Italy Baked Fish

Serves 4

 Per serving:

Calories: 127.91
Protein: . . . . 21.68 g
Carbohydrates: . . . . . . 7.15 g
Fat: . . . . 1.27 g
Sat. Fat: . . . . 0.41 g

1 pound (16 ounces) cod fillets
1 (14½-ounce) can stewed tomatoes
¼ teaspoon dried minced onion
½ teaspoon dried minced garlic
¼ teaspoon dried basil
¼ teaspoon dried parsley
⅛ teaspoon dried oregano
⅛ teaspoon sugar
1 tablespoon grated Parmesan
    cheese

1. Preheat oven to 375°F. Rinse the cod with cold water and pat dry with paper towels.

2. In a 2- to 3-quart baking pan or casserole treated with nonstick cooking spray, combine all the ingredients except the fish; mix. Arrange the fillets over the tomato mixture, folding thin tail ends under; spoon some of the tomato mixture over the fillets. For fillets about 1" thick, bake uncovered 20–25 minutes, or until the fish is opaque and flaky.

Baked Snapper with Orange-Rice Dressing

Serves 4

 Per serving, without salt:

Calories: 256.69
Protein: . . . . 26.03 g
Carbohydrates: . . . . . . 25.12 g
Fat: . . . . 5.19 g
Sat. Fat: . . . . 1.68 g

¼ cup chopped celery
½ cup chopped onion
½ cup orange juice
1 tablespoon lemon juice
1 teaspoon grated orange zest
1⅓ cups cooked rice
1 pound (16 ounces) red snapper
    fillets
Sea or kosher salt and freshly ground
    white or black pepper to taste
    (optional)
2 tablespoons ground raw almonds
2 teaspoons unsalted butter

1. Preheat oven to 350°F. In a microwave-safe bowl, mix the celery and onion with the juices and orange zest; microwave on high 2 minutes, or until the mixture comes to a boil. Add the rice; stir to moisten, adding some water, 1 tablespoon at a time, if necessary to thoroughly coat the rice. Cover and let stand 5 minutes.

2. Rinse the fillets and pat dry between paper towels. Prepare a baking dish with nonstick spray. Spread the rice mixture in the dish; arrange the fillets on top. Season the fillets with salt and pepper, if using. Combine the butter and almonds in a microwave-safe bowl; microwave on high 30 seconds, or until the butter is melted. Stir and spoon over the top of the fillets. Cover and bake 10 minutes. Remove the cover and bake another 5–10 minutes, or until the fish flakes easily when tested with a fork and the almonds are lightly browned.

Crunchy "Fried" Catfish Fillets

Serves 4

 Per serving, without salt:

Calories: 243.57
Protein: . . . . 20.91 g
Carbohydrates: . . . . . . 17.58 g
Fat: . . . . 9.20 g
Sat. Fat: . . . . 2.12 g

1 pound (16 ounces) farm-raised catfish fillets
1 egg white (from a large egg), room temperature
¼ cup bread crumbs
¼ cup enriched white cornmeal
1 teaspoon grated lemon zest
½ teaspoon crushed dried basil
¼ cup all-purpose flour
⅛ teaspoon kosher or sea salt (optional)
¼ teaspoon lemon pepper

1. Preheat oven to 450°F, and treat a shallow baking pan with nonstick spray. Rinse the catfish fillets and dry them between layers of paper towels.

2. In a shallow dish, beat the egg white until frothy. In another dish, combine the bread crumbs, cornmeal, lemon zest, and basil. In a third dish, combine the flour, salt (if using), and lemon pepper.

3. Dip the fish into the flour mixture to coat 1 side of each fillet. Shake off any excess flour mixture, then dip the flour-covered side of the fillet into the egg white. Next, coat the covered side of the fillet with the bread crumb mixture. Arrange the prepared fillets side by side, coated-sides up, on the prepared baking pan. Tuck in any thin edges. Bake 6–12 minutes, or until the fish flakes easily with a fork.

Zesty Crunch

Grated lemon or lime zest is a great way to give added citrus flavor to a crunchy breadcrumb topping for fish.

Baked Orange Roughy with Spicy Plum Sauce

Serves 4

 Per serving:

Calories:............221.31
Protein:.............18.60 g
Carbohydrates:......30.62 g
Fat:.................2.60 g
Sat. Fat:.............0.30 g

1 pound (16 ounces) orange roughy
  fillets
1 teaspoon paprika
1 bay leaf
1 clove garlic, crushed
1 apple, peeled, cored, and cubed
1 teaspoon grated fresh ginger
1 small red or Spanish onion,
  chopped
1 teaspoon olive oil
¼ cup Plum Sauce (see page 242)
¼ teaspoon Chinese five-spice
  powder
1 teaspoon frozen, unsweetened
  apple juice concentrate
½ teaspoon Bragg's Liquid Aminos
¼ teaspoon blackstrap molasses
1⅓ cups cooked brown rice

1. Preheat oven to 400°F. Treat a baking dish with nonstick spray. Rinse the orange roughy and pat dry between paper towels. Rub both sides of the fish with the paprika; set them in the prepared dish.

2. In a covered, microwave-safe bowl, mix the bay leaf, garlic, apple, ginger, and onion in the oil; microwave on high 3 minutes, or until the apple is tender and the onion is transparent. Stir; discard the bay leaf; top the fillets with the apple mixture. Bake uncovered 15–18 minutes, or until the fish is opaque.

3. While the fish bakes, add the plum sauce to a microwave-safe bowl. Add the 5-spice powder, apple juice concentrate, Liquid Aminos, and molasses. Microwave on high 30 seconds, stir, add a little water if needed to thin mixture, and microwave another 15 seconds. Cover until ready to serve. If necessary, bring back to temperature by microwaving the mixture another 15 seconds just prior to serving.

4. To serve, equally divide the cooked rice among 4 serving plates. Top each with an equal amount of the baked fish mixture and plum sauce mixture, drizzling the sauce atop the fish.

Sweet Onion-Baked Yellowtail Snapper

Serves 4

2 cups sliced Vidalia onions
1 tablespoon balsamic vinegar
2 teaspoons brown sugar
4 teaspoons olive oil
1 pound (16 ounces) skinless
    yellowtail snapper fillets
Sea salt and freshly ground white or
    black pepper to taste (optional)

1. In a covered microwave-safe dish, microwave the onion on high 5 minutes, or until it is transparent. Carefully remove the cover and stir in the vinegar and brown sugar. Cover and allow to set several minutes so the onion absorbs the flavors.

2. Heat a nonstick pan on medium-high and add the olive oil. Transfer the steamed onion mixture to the pan and sauté until browned but not crisp. (Be careful as the onions will burn easily because of the brown sugar; if the onion browns too quickly, lower the heat and add a few tablespoons of water.) Cook until all liquid has evaporated from the pan, stirring often. The onions should have a shiny and dark caramelized color. (This can be prepared 2–3 days in advance; store tightly covered in the refrigerator.)

3. Preheat oven to 375°F. Rinse the snapper fillets in cold water and dry between paper towels. Arrange the fillets on a baking sheet treated with nonstick spray. Spoon the caramelized onions over the tops of the fillets, pressing it to form a light "crust" over the top of the fish. Bake for 12–15 minutes, or until the fish flakes easily with a fork. Serve immediately, with Madeira sauce (optional) divided on 4 plates, with the fish placed on top.

Stir-Fried Ginger Scallops with Vegetables

Serves 4

stats **Per serving:**

Calories:............145.43
Protein:.............22.26 g
Carbohydrates:......8.35 g
Fat:.................2.68 g
Sat. Fat:............0.37 g

1 pound (16 ounces) scallops
1 teaspoon peanut or sesame oil
1 tablespoon chopped fresh ginger
2 cloves garlic, minced
1 teaspoon rice wine vinegar
2 teaspoons Bragg's Liquid Aminos
½ cup low-fat, reduced-sodium
　　chicken broth
2 cups broccoli florets
4 scallions, thinly sliced (optional)
1 teaspoon cornstarch
¼ teaspoon toasted sesame oil

1. Rinse the scallops and pat them dry between layers of paper towels. If necessary, slice the scallops so they're a uniform size. Set aside.

2. Add the peanut or sesame oil to a heated nonstick, deep skillet or wok. Sauté the ginger and garlic 1–2 minutes, being careful that the ginger doesn't burn. Add the vinegar, Liquid Aminos, and broth; bring to a boil. Remove from heat.

3. Place the broccoli and scallions in a large, covered microwave-safe dish; pour the chicken broth mixture over the top. Microwave on high 3–5 minutes, depending on how you prefer your vegetables cooked. (Keep in mind that the vegetables will continue to steam for a minute or so if the cover remains on the dish.)

Stir-Fried Ginger Scallops with Vegetables

(continued)

4. Heat the skillet or wok over medium-high heat. Add the scallops; sauté 1 minute on each side. (Do the scallops in batches, if necessary. Be careful not to overcook the scallops.) Remove the scallops from pan when done, and set aside. Drain off (but do not discard) the liquid from the broccoli; return the liquid to the bowl and transfer the broccoli to the heated skillet or wok. Stir-fry the vegetables to bring them up to serving temperature.

5. In the meantime, in a small cup or bowl, add enough water to the cornstarch to make a slurry, or roux. Whisk the slurry into the reserved broccoli liquid; microwave on high 1 minute. Add the toasted sesame oil to the broth mixture; whisk again. Pour the thickened broth mixture over the broccoli; toss to mix. Add the scallops back to the broccoli mixture; stir-fry over medium heat to return the scallops to serving temperature. Serve over rice or pasta, and adjust Exchange Approximations accordingly.

Scallops and Shrimp with White Bean Sauce

Serves 4

stats **Per serving:**

Calories:............231.32
Protein:.............26.93 g
Carbohydrates: ......18.38 g
Fat:.................4.17 g
Sat. Fat:............0.66 g

½ cup finely chopped onion, steamed
2 cloves garlic, minced
2 teaspoons olive oil, divided
¼ cup dry white wine
¼ cup tightly packed fresh parsley
    leaves
¼ cup tightly packed fresh basil
    leaves
1⅓ cups canned cannellini (white)
    beans, drained and rinsed
¼ cup low-fat, reduced-sodium
    chicken broth
½ pound (8 ounces) shrimp, shelled
    and deveined
½ pound (8 ounces) scallops

1. In a nonstick saucepan, sauté the onion and garlic in 1 teaspoon of the oil over moderately low heat until the onion is soft. Add the wine; simmer until the wine is reduced by ½. Add the parsley, basil, ⅓ cup of the beans, and the chicken broth; simmer the mixture, stirring constantly, 1 minute.

2. Transfer the bean mixture to a blender or food processor; purée. Pour the purée back into the saucepan; add the remaining beans; simmer 2 minutes.

3. In a nonstick skillet, heat the remaining 1 teaspoon of oil over moderately high heat until it is hot but not smoking. Sauté the shrimp 2 minutes on each side, or until they are cooked through. Using a slotted spoon, transfer the shrimp to a plate and cover to keep warm. Add the scallops to the skillet; sauté 1 minute on each side, or until they are cooked through. To serve, divide the bean sauce between 4 shallow bowls and arrange the shellfish over the top.

Smoked Mussels and Pasta

Serves 4

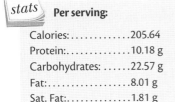

Per serving:

Calories:............205.64
Protein:.............10.18 g
Carbohydrates: ......22.57 g
Fat:.................8.01 g
Sat. Fat:............1.81 g

1⅓ cups uncooked pasta (to yield 2
    cups cooked pasta)
½ cup chopped leek
4 ounces Ducktrap River smoked
    mussels, drained of all excess oil
⅛ teaspoon cayenne pepper
½ teaspoon dried oregano
¼ cup nonfat cottage cheese
⅛ cup nonfat plain yogurt
2 teaspoons grated Parmesan cheese
2 teaspoons extra-virgin olive oil
Cracked black pepper to taste

1. Cook the pasta according to package directions; drain and set aside. In a covered, microwave-safe bowl, microwave the leek on high 2–3 minutes, or until limp and translucent. Add the mussels and cayenne pepper to the leeks; stir. Cover and microwave on high 30 seconds to heat the mussels.

2. In a blender, combine the oregano, cottage cheese, yogurt, and Parmesan cheese; process until smooth. Combine the cottage cheese and mussel mixtures; microwave on high until warm, about 30 seconds. Toss the pasta with the olive oil; stir in the mussel mixture. Divide into 4 portions and serve immediately, topped with cracked pepper.

Savory Smoke

Smoked meats impart a strong, pleasant flavor to dishes, so you can use less meat to achieve a rich taste.

Pasta and Smoked Trout with Lemon Pesto

Serves 4

 stats **Per serving:**

Calories:............209.29
Protein:.............10.29 g
Carbohydrates: ......23.49 g
Fat:.................8.33 g
Sat. Fat:............1.34 g

2 cloves garlic
2 cups fresh basil leaves, tightly
    packed
⅛ cup pine nuts, toasted (see
    page 12)
2 teaspoons fresh lemon juice
2 teaspoons water
4 teaspoons extra-virgin olive oil
4 tablespoons grated Parmesan
    cheese, divided
1⅓ cups uncooked linguini or other
    pasta (to yield 2 cups cooked
    pasta)
2 ounces Ducktrap River whole,
    boneless smoked trout
Freshly ground black pepper to taste

1. Put the garlic in the food processor; pulse until finely chopped. Add the basil, pine nuts, lemon juice, and water; process until just puréed. (Note: You can substitute fresh parsley for the basil; supplement the flavor by adding some dried basil, too, if you do.) Add the olive oil and 3 tablespoons of the Parmesan cheese; pulse until the pesto is smooth, occasionally scraping down the side of the bowl, if necessary. Set aside.

2. Cook the pasta according to package directions. While it is cooking, flake the smoked trout. When the pasta is cooked, pulse the pesto to ensure it has remained blended; toss the pesto and trout with the pasta. Sprinkle the remaining grated Parmesan cheese on top of each serving. (Although this recipe uses heart-healthy extra-virgin olive oil, it is a little higher in fat, but still low in calories. Consult your dietitian if you have any question as to whether you should include this recipe in your meal plans.) Add pepper to taste.

Smoked-Mussels Cream Sauce with Pasta

Serves 4

stats **Per serving, without flour:**

Calories:............311.88
Protein:.............22.23 g
Carbohydrates: ......27.91 g
Fat:.................10.30 g
Sat. Fat:.............3.06 g

2 teaspoons unsalted butter
2 cloves garlic, crushed
½ cup sliced leeks or green onions
½ cup dry white wine
2 cups steamed sliced mushrooms
1⅓ cups uncooked pasta (to yield 2
    cups cooked)
2 cups nonfat cottage cheese
1 teaspoon potato flour (optional)
4 ounces Ducktrap River smoked
    mussels, drained of any oil
2 teaspoons extra-virgin olive oil
Parsley to taste (optional)
Tarragon to taste (optional)
Cracked black or white pepper to
    taste (optional)

1. Melt the butter in a deep nonstick skillet. Add the garlic and leeks (or green onions); sauté just until transparent. Add the wine and bring to a boil; cook until reduced by ½. Add the mushrooms; toss in the wine mixture. Start preparing the pasta according to package directions.

2. In a blender or food processor, purée the cottage cheese. Add it to the wine-mushroom mixture; bring to serving temperature over low heat, being careful that the mixture doesn't boil. If the mixture seems too wet (if you didn't reduce the wine enough, for example), sprinkle potato flour over the mixture, stir until blended, and cook until thickened.

3. Add the mussels to the cottage cheese mixture just prior to serving, stirring well to bring the mussels to serving temperature. Serve over the pasta, tossed with the olive oil and herbs, if using. Top with cracked pepper.

Smoked-Mussels Scramble

Serves 4

stats **Per serving:**

Calories:............92.57
Protein:.............4.27 g
Carbohydrates: ......13.37 g
Fat:.................2.53 g
Sat. Fat:............0.69

4 smoked mussels (1 ounce)
1 egg
1 tablespoon unbleached all-purpose
   flour
1 tablespoon cornmeal
1 tablespoon rice flour
1 tablespoon diced, sautéed celery
1 tablespoon diced, sautéed green
   pepper
2 tablespoons diced, sautéed onion
6 ounces (2 small) diced, boiled
   potatoes
Rice flour (optional)

In a bowl, combine all the ingredients. "Fry" in a nonstick skillet sprayed with olive-oil nonstick spray. You can prepare the scramble loose or in patties.

tip

For patties, shape into balls, roll in rice flour (for extra crispness), place in skillet, and flatten with the back of a spatula. Because this is a very moist mixture, be sure to wet your hands before you shape it into balls.

Know Your Ingredients

Because smoked meats are also often high in sodium, most recipes in this book state the brand used so that the sodium counts given in the Nutritional Analysis are accurate. If you substitute another brand, consult the label and adjust the nutritional values, if necessary.

224

Smoked-Shrimp Sandwich Filling

Serves 4

 Per serving, filling only:

Calories: 103.64
Protein: . . . . 9.17 g
Carbohydrates: . . . . . . 3.14 g
Fat: . . . . 5.49 g
Sat. Fat: . . . . 2.99 g

⅛ cup (2 tablespoons) dry white
    wine
⅛ teaspoon granulated sugar
1 large roasted red pepper, chopped
1 cup thinly sliced red onion
1 clove garlic, crushed
4 ounces Ducktrap River smoked
    shrimp
2 ounces fontina cheese
Mayonnaise (optional)

1. Combine the wine and sugar in a non-stick skillet; bring to a boil. Add the roasted red pepper, red onion, and garlic. Continue to boil, stirring frequently, until the wine is absorbed by the peppers and the onion is transparent.

2. Turn off the heat; stir the shrimp and cheese into the sauce until well mixed and cheese is melted. Serve immediately on French bread.

It's good if you first spread the bread with a very thin layer of mayonnaise, and adjust the Exchange Approximations accordingly.

Smoked Shrimp-and-Cheese Quesadillas

Serves 4

 stats **Per serving:**

Calories:............271.82
Protein:.............11.47 g
Carbohydrates:......31.53 g
Fat:.................11.05 g
Sat. Fat:............3.15 g

4 (8-inch) flour tortillas
4 teaspoons olive oil
2 ounces part-skim mozzarella
    or other mild cheese (such as
    fontina or baby Swiss) or go wild
    and use goat cheese
1 jalapeño or banana pepper, finely
    chopped
2 cloves garlic, crushed
4 ounces Ducktrap River smoked
    shrimp
1 cup thinly sliced red onion
½ cup roughly chopped fresh cilantro

1. Preheat oven to 375°F. Lightly brush 1 side of each tortilla with some of the olive oil. Mix the cheese, pepper, and garlic with the remaining olive oil. Spread ¼ of the cheese mixture in the center of the oiled half of each tortilla. Top with the shrimp, red onion, and cilantro. Fold the tortilla in half to cover the ingredients.

2. Place the tortillas in a baking pan treated with nonstick spray. Bake 3–5 minutes, or until nicely browned and the cheese is melted. Serve with your choice of tomato salsa.

Cut Added Sodium

Reduce some of the sodium content (salty flavor) from smoked seafood like mussels or shrimp by rinsing them in a little water.

Fish Pie

Serves 4

stats **Per serving, without salt:**

Calories:............301.35
Protein:.............33.08 g
Carbohydrates: ......27.54 g
Fat:.................6.65 g
Sat. Fat:.............2.75 g

1 cup mock cream
¼ cup grated, low-salt Cheddar
    cheese
1 tablespoon grated Parmesan
    cheese
¼ cup red or sweet onion, steamed
¼ cup lemon juice
1 teaspoon stone-ground mustard
1 teaspoon dried parsley
½ cup sliced carrot, steamed
1 cup steamed spinach
2 ounces Ducktrap River smoked
    trout, cut into small pieces
1 pound (16 ounces) skinless cod
    fillets, cut into 1" cubes
1 hard-boiled egg, grated or finely
    chopped
¾ pound (12 ounces) potatoes,
    boiled (without salt) and diced
2 teaspoons extra-virgin olive oil
Optional seasonings to taste:
Sea or kosher salt and freshly ground
    black pepper
Ground nutmeg

1. Preheat oven to 450°F. In a nonstick sauce-pan, heat the Mock Cream; bring it to a boil. Remove from the heat and add the cheeses, onion, lemon juice, mustard, parsley, and carrots. Press the steamed spinach between layers of paper towels to remove any excess moisture.

2. Mix together the spinach, smoked trout, cod, and egg; put into a baking dish treated with nonstick spray. Pour the cheese mixture over the fish mixture.

3. In a food processor, combine the boiled potatoes, olive oil, and seasonings (if using); pulse until the potatoes are coarsely mashed. Spread the potatoes over the top of the fish mixture. Bake 25–30 minutes, or until the potatoes are golden.

Meats

Beef Broth: Easy Slow-Cooker Method

Yields: about 3 cups broth
Serving size: ½ cup

 Per serving:

Calories: 57.52
Protein: . . . . .8.95 g
Carbohydrates: . . . . . .0.00 g
Fat: . . . . .2.15 g
Sat. Fat: . . . . .0.73 g

1 pound lean round steak
1 onion, chopped
2 carrots, peeled and chopped
2 celery stalks and leaves, chopped
1 bay leaf
4 sprigs parsley
6 black peppercorns
¼ cup dry white wine
4½ cups water

1. Cut the beef into several pieces; add it to slow cooker with all of the other ingredients. Use high setting until the mixture reaches a boil, then reduce the heat to low. Allow to simmer, covered, overnight, or up to 16 hours.

2. Remove beef and drain on paper towels to absorb any fat. Strain broth; discard meat and vegetables. (You don't want to eat vegetables cooked directly with the beef because they will have absorbed too much of the residual fat.) Put broth in a covered container and refrigerate for several hours or overnight; this allows time for the fat to congeal on top of the broth. Remove hardened fat and discard. (When you remove the fat from the broth, the Exchange Approximation will be a Free Exchange.)

Broth will keep in the refrigerator for a few days. Freeze any that you won't use within that time.

Trade Secrets

Some chefs swear that a hearty beef broth requires oven-roasted bones. Place bones on a roasting tray and bake them in a 425°F oven 30–60 minutes. Blot the fat from the bones before adding them to the rest of the broth ingredients. You may need to reduce the amount of water in your slow cooker, which will produce a more concentrated broth.

Stovetop Grilled Beef Loin

Yields: 1 (5-ounce) loin
Serving size: 1 ounce

 Per serving:

Calories: 42.13
Protein: . . . . 6.00 g
Carbohydrates: . . . . . . 0.56 g
Fat: . . . . 1.69 g
Sat. Fat: . . . . 0.58 g

1 Laura's Lean Beef tenderloin fillet,
    no more than 1" thick
½ teaspoon paprika
1½ teaspoons garlic powder
⅛ teaspoon cracked black pepper
¼ teaspoon onion powder
Pinch–⅛ teaspoon cayenne pepper
    (according to taste)
⅛ teaspoon dried oregano
⅛ teaspoon dried thyme
½ teaspoon brown sugar
½ teaspoon olive oil

1. Remove the loin from the refrigerator 30 minutes before you plan to prepare it to allow it to come to room temperature. Pat the meat dry with paper towels.

2. Mix together all the dry ingredients. Rub ¼ teaspoon of the olive oil on each side of the fillet. (The olive oil is used in this recipe to help the "rub" adhere to the meat and to aid in the caramelization process.) Divide the seasoning mixture; rub it into each oiled side.

3. Heat a grill pan on high 1–2 minutes, until the pan is sizzling hot. Place beef fillet in the pan, reduce heat to medium-high, and cook 3 minutes. Use tongs to turn fillet. (Be careful not to pierce the meat.) Cook another 2 minutes for medium or 3 minutes for well done.

4. Remove from heat and let meat "rest" in the pan at least 5 minutes, allowing juices to redistribute throughout the meat and complete the cooking process—which makes for a juicier fillet.

Weights and Measures: Before and After

Exchanges are based on cooking weight of meats; however, in the case of lean pork loin trimmed of all fat, very little weight is lost during the cooking process. Therefore, the amounts given for raw pork loin in the recipes equal the cooked weights.

The Ultimate Grilled Cheeseburger Sandwich

Serves 4

stats **Per serving:**

Calories: 261.97
Protein:. . . . . .16.94 g
Carbohydrates: . . . . . .15.39 g
Fat:. . . . . .14.54 g
Sat. Fat:. . . . . .5.40 g

1 tablespoon olive oil
1 teaspoon butter
2 thick slices of 7-grain bread
    (see page 50)
1 ounce Cheddar cheese
½ pound (8 ounces) ground round
Worcestershire sauce to taste
Fresh minced garlic to taste
Balsamic vinegar to taste
Toppings of your choice, such
    as stone-ground mustard,
    mayonnaise, etc.

1. Preheat your indoor grill. Combine the olive oil and butter; use ½ of the mixture to "butter" 1 side of each slice of bread. Place the Cheddar cheese on the unbuttered side of 1 slice of bread and top with the other slice, buttered-side up.

2. Combine the ground round with the Worcestershire sauce, garlic, and balsamic vinegar, if using. Shape the ground round into a large, rectangular patty, a little larger than a slice of the bread. Grill the patty, then the cheese sandwich. (If you are using a large indoor grill, position the hamburger at the lower end, near the area where the fat drains; grill the cheese sandwich at the higher end.)

The Ultimate Grilled Cheeseburger Sandwich

(continued)

3. Once the cheese sandwich is done, separate the slices of bread, being careful not to burn yourself on the cheese. Top 1 slice with the hamburger and add your choice of condiments and fixin's.

---

tip

Allow for your choice of condiments and side dishes when you calculate additional Exchange Approximations, fats, and calories. For lean, organic (and delicious!) beef, check out Laura's Lean Beef. For information, go to *www.laurasleanbeef.com*.

The Olive Oil Factor

Once you've used an olive oil and butter mixture to "butter" the bread for a toasted or grilled sandwich, you'll never want to use just plain butter again! The olive oil helps make the bread crunchier, and imparts a subtle taste difference to the sandwich as well.

Kovbasa (Ukrainian Kielbasa)

Yields: 1½ pounds (24 ounces)
Serving size: 1 ounce

 Per serving:

Calories: 70.18
Protein: . . . . .7.99 g
Carbohydrates: . . . . . .0.00 g
Fat: . . . . .3.95 g
Sat. Fat: . . . . .1.50 g

1 pound (16 ounces) pork shoulder
½ pound (8 ounces) beef chuck
1 teaspoon freshly ground black
   pepper
½ teaspoon ground allspice
1 teaspoon garlic powder
1 teaspoon peperivka (spiced
   whiskey; see step 1 following)
Kosher or sea salt to taste (optional)

1. To prepare the peperivka, put 1 teaspoon of bourbon in a microwave-safe bowl and add a pinch of dried red pepper flakes. Microwave on high 15 seconds, or until the mixture is hot. Set aside to cool.

2. Remove all the fat from the meat. Cut the meat into cubes and put them in a food processor; grind to desired consistency.

3. Add all the remaining ingredients, including the cooled peperivka; mix until well blended.

 tip

The traditional preparation method calls for putting the sausage mixture in casings; however, it works equally well when broiled or grilled as fresh sausage patties.

Kielbasa

Yields: 1½ pounds (24 ounces)
Serving size: 1 ounce

stats **Per serving, without salt:**

Calories:............72.21
Protein:.............8.00 g
Carbohydrates: ......0.64 g
Fat:.................3.95 g
Sat. Fat:............1.50 g

1 pound (16 ounces) pork shoulder
½ pound (8 ounces) beef chuck
2 teaspoons minced garlic
1 tablespoon brown sugar
1 teaspoon freshly ground black
    pepper
½ teaspoon ground allspice
1 teaspoon fresh marjoram
Sea or kosher salt (optional)

1. Remove all fat from the meat. Cut the meat into cubes and put them in a food processor; grind to desired consistency.

2. Add the remaining ingredients; mix until well blended.

tip

You can put the sausage mixture in casings, but it works equally well broiled or grilled as patties.

Italian Sausage

Yields: about 2 pounds (32 ounces)
Serving size: 1 ounce

 Per serving, without salt:

Calories:............67.72
Protein:............7.72 g
Carbohydrates: ......0.00 g
Fat:................3.86 g
Sat. Fat:............1.45 g

2 pounds (32 ounces) pork shoulder
1 teaspoon ground black pepper
1 teaspoon dried parsley
1 teaspoon Italian-style seasoning
1 teaspoon garlic powder
¾ teaspoon crushed anise seeds
⅛ teaspoon crushed red pepper flakes
½ teaspoon paprika
½ teaspoon instant minced onion flakes
1 teaspoon kosher or sea salt (optional)

1. Remove all fat from the meat. Cut the meat into cubes and put them in a food processor; grind to desired consistency.

2. Add the remaining ingredients; mix until well blended.

tip

You can put the sausage mixture in casings, but it works equally well broiled or grilled as patties.

Simple (and Smart!) Substitutions

Game meats—buffalo, venison, elk, moose—are low in fat, as are ground chicken or turkey. Substitute one of those meats for the pork in any of the sausage recipes in this chapter.

Italian Sweet-Fennel Sausage

Yields: about 2 pounds
(32 ounces)
Serving size: 1 ounce

 Per serving, without salt:

Calories:. 69.57
Protein:. . . . . .7.73 g
Carbohydrates: . . . . . .0.47 g
Fat:. . . . . .3.86 g
Sat. Fat:. . . . . .1.45 g

1¼ teaspoons fennel seeds
¼ teaspoon cayenne pepper
2 pounds (32 ounces) pork butt
½ teaspoon black pepper
2½ teaspoons crushed garlic
1 tablespoon sugar
1 teaspoon kosher or sea salt
    (optional)

1. Toast the fennel seeds and cayenne pepper in a nonstick skillet over medium heat, stirring constantly, until the seeds just begin to darken, about 2 minutes. Set aside.

2. Remove all fat from the meat. Cut the meat into cubes and put them in a food processor; grind to desired consistency. Add the remaining ingredients and mix until well blended.

You can put the sausage mixture in casings, but it works equally well broiled or grilled as patties.

"Better the Second Day"

Ideally, sausage is made the night before and refrigerated to allow the flavors to merge. Leftover sausage can be frozen for up to 3 months.

Mock Chorizo 1

Yields: about 2 pounds
(32 ounces)
Serving size: 1 ounce

 Per serving, without salt:

Calories:............68.28
Protein:.............7.73 g
Carbohydrates: ......0.17 g
Fat:.................3.86 g
Sat. Fat:............1.45 g

2 pounds (32 ounces) lean pork
4 tablespoons chili powder
¼ teaspoon ground cloves
2 tablespoons paprika
2½ teaspoons crushed fresh garlic
1 teaspoon crushed, dried oregano
3½ tablespoons cider vinegar
1 teaspoon kosher or sea salt
     (optional)

1. Remove all fat from the meat. Cut the meat into cubes and put them in a food processor; grind to desired consistency. Add the remaining ingredients; mix until well blended.

2. Age this sausage in an airtight container in the refrigerator for 4 days before cooking. Leftover sausage can be stored in the freezer for up to 3 months.

Break from Tradition

Traditionally, chorizo is very high in fat; the chorizo recipes in this chapter are lower-fat alternatives. They make excellent replacements for adding flavor to recipes that call for bacon. In fact, 1–2 ounces of chorizo can replace an entire pound of bacon in cabbage, bean, or potato soup.

Mock Chorizo 2

Yields: about 1 pound (16 ounces)
Serving size: 1 ounce

 Per serving, without salt or soy sauce:

Calories:............70.05
Protein:.............7.75 g
Carbohydrates:......0.37 g
Fat:................3.86 g
Sat. Fat:.............1.45 g

1 pound (16 ounces) lean pork
2 tablespoons white wine vinegar
1 tablespoon dry sherry
2 teaspoons paprika
2 teaspoons chili powder
½ teaspoon dried oregano
¼ teaspoon ground cumin
½ teaspoon freshly ground black
    pepper
⅛ teaspoon ground cinnamon
⅛ teaspoon ground cloves
Pinch of ground coriander
Pinch of ground ginger
2 cloves garlic, crushed
Kosher or sea salt to taste (optional)

1. Remove all fat from the meat. Cut the meat into cubes and put them in a food processor; grind to desired consistency. Add the remaining ingredients; mix until well blended.

2. Age the sausage in an airtight container in the refrigerator for 4 days. Leftover sausage can be stored in the freezer for up to 3 months.

 tip

For a Chorizo stir-fry, consider decreasing the chili powder, adding some soy sauce or Bragg's Liquid Aminos, and increasing the garlic and ginger.

239

Mock Chorizo Moussaka

Serves 4

stats **Per serving:**
Calories:............244.31
Protein:..............17.41 g
Carbohydrates: ......25.93 g
Fat:..................8.15 g
Sat. Fat:.............2.73 g

2 ounces mock chorizo
2 cups peeled, seeded, and chopped eggplant
2 cups peeled, seeded, and chopped zucchini
4 small potatoes, peeled and thinly sliced
2 eggs
4 tablespoons grated Parmesan cheese, divided
1 cup nonfat cottage cheese
1 teaspoon Ener-G potato flour
2 teaspoons olive oil
1 teaspoon dried dill
1 teaspoon dried parsley
Pinch of nutmeg

1. Preheat oven to 350°F. Broil or grill the chorizo; set aside to drain on paper towels.

2. In a covered, microwave-safe bowl, microwave the eggplant and zucchini on high 5 minutes, or until they are steaming and just barely beginning to soften; drain and blot dry with paper towels. In a covered, microwave-safe bowl, microwave the potatoes on high 5 minutes. Set aside, covered, and allow the potatoes to steam.

3. In a bowl, beat the eggs with 2 tablespoons of the Parmesan cheese and stir in the eggplant and zucchini; set aside.

4. Put the cottage cheese, potato flour, and the remaining Parmesan cheese in a blender or food processor; process until smooth.

5. To assemble, treat a casserole dish with nonstick spray. Drain any moisture from the potatoes and pat dry with a paper towel. Toss the potatoes with the olive oil; layer across the bottom of the casserole dish. Sprinkle dill and parsley over the potatoes. Spread vegetable-egg mixture over top of the potatoes. Crumble the cooked chorizo over the top of the vegetables. Spread the cottage cheese mixture over the meat. Sprinkle nutmeg over the top of the casserole. Bake, uncovered, 20–30 minutes, or until hot and bubbly.

Rich Sausage Gravy

Serves 4

Per serving, without salt:

Calories: 120.86
Protein: . . . . 13.30 g
Carbohydrates: . . . . . . 6.31 g
Fat: . . . . 4.51 g
Sat. Fat: . . . . 1.23 g

1 cup nonfat cottage cheese
1 cup mock cream
2 ounces Kovbasa (see page 234)
2 teaspoons olive oil
1 tablespoon flour
Salt and black pepper to taste
(optional)

1. In a blender or food processor, combine the cottage cheese and Mock Cream; process until smooth. Set aside.

2. In a nonstick skillet, fry the Kovbasa until done, breaking it into small pieces as you fry it. Add the olive oil; heat until sizzling. Stir in the flour, stirring constantly to create a roux. Gradually stir in some of the cottage cheese mixture, using the back of a spatula or a whisk to blend it, stirring constantly to avoid lumps. Once you have about ½ cup of the cottage cheese mixture blended into the roux, you can add the remaining amount.

3. Continue to cook, stirring constantly, until the mixture begins to steam. Lower the heat and allow the mixture to simmer (being careful that it doesn't come to a boil) until the gravy reaches the desired consistency. Salt and pepper to taste.

Slow-Cooker Pork with Plum Sauce

Serves 4

 stats **Per serving, with Bragg's Liquid Aminos:**

Calories: 125.08
Protein: . . . . .12.97 g
Carbohydrates: . . . . . .11.35 g
Fat: . . . . .2.87 g
Sat. Fat: . . . . .0.99 g

½ pound (8 ounces) cooked,
   shredded pork
1 clove garlic, crushed
½ teaspoon grated fresh ginger
⅛ cup apple juice
¼ teaspoon dry mustard
2 teaspoons Bragg's Liquid Aminos or
   soy sauce
⅛ teaspoon dried thyme
⅛ cup plum jam
½ teaspoon cornstarch

1. In a nonstick skillet treated with nonstick spray, stir-fry the pork, garlic, and ginger.

2. In a small bowl or measuring cup, combine the remaining ingredients to make a slurry. Pour the mixture over the heated pork; mix well. Cook over low to medium heat until the mixture thickens and the juice is absorbed into the pork.

Warm Pork Salad

Serves 2

 stats **Per serving:**

Calories:............181.66
Protein:.............14.13 g
Carbohydrates: ......24.59 g
Fat:.................3.51 g
Sat. Fat:............1.08 g

2 servings of Slow-Cooker Pork with
    Plum Sauce (see recipe on page
    242)
1 teaspoon cider vinegar
¼ teaspoon Dijon mustard
2 slices red onion
1 apple, peeled, cored, and sliced
2 cups coleslaw mix
4 drops toasted sesame oil
Dash of freshly ground black pepper

1. In a nonstick skillet treated with nonstick spray, stir-fry the leftover pork until warm. Add the vinegar and mustard; mix until blended. Stir in the apple, onion, and coleslaw mix; cover and cook 2 minutes, or until the vegetables and apple just barely begin to soften.

2. Serve warm, topping salads with two drops of the sesame oil and freshly ground black pepper.

Cinnamon Grilled Pork Tenderloin

Serves 2

 stats **Per serving:**

Calories: 93.76
Protein:. . . . . .13.4 g
Carbohydrates: . . . . . .11.44 g
Fat:. . . . . .3.59 g
Sat Fat: . . . . .1.11 g

2 teaspoons Bragg's Liquid Aminos
2 teaspoons burgundy or red wine
1 teaspoon brown sugar
⅛ teaspoon honey
⅛ teaspoon garlic powder
⅛ teaspoon ground cinnamon
¼ pound (4-ounce) pork loin

1. Combine the first 6 ingredients in a large zip-top plastic bag. Add the roast and marinate in the refrigerator at least 1 hour, or up to 6 hours.

2. Grill tenderloins over hot coals until the thermometer reaches 160°F, turning while grilling. (Grilling time will depend on the thickness of the tenderloin. For example, a ¾" cut of pork grilled over medium-hot coals will take 12–14 minutes, while a cut twice as thick, or a 1½" cut, can take more than half an hour.) Allow the meat to rest up to 15 minutes, then slice thinly against the grain.

Let It Set!

Avoid the biggest cause of a dry roast! When you remove a roast from the oven, always allow it to rest for 10 minutes before you carve it. This allows the juices to redistribute through the roast (instead of draining out all over your cutting board).

MEATS

Fruited Pork-Loin Roast Casserole

Serves 4

stats **Per serving:**

Calories: 169.78
Protein: . . . . .7.36 g
Carbohydrates: . . . . . .27.49 g
Fat: . . . . .3.81 g
Sat. Fat: . . . . .1.29 g

4 small Yukon Gold potatoes, peeled
    and sliced
2 (2-ounce) pieces trimmed boneless
    pork loin, pounded flat
1 apple, peeled, cored, and sliced
4 apricot halves
1 tablespoon chopped red onion or
    shallot
⅛ cup apple cider or apple juice
Optional seasonings to taste:
Olive oil
Parmesan cheese
Salt and freshly ground pepper

1. Preheat oven to 350°F (325°F if using a glass casserole dish), and treat a casserole dish with nonstick spray.

2. Layer half of the potato slices across the bottom of the dish. Top with 1 piece of the flattened pork loin. Arrange the apple slices over the top of the loin; place the apricot halves on top of the apple. Sprinkle the red onion (or shallots) over the apricot and apples. Add the second flattened pork loin; layer the remaining potatoes atop the loin. Drizzle the apple cider (or apple juice) over the top of the casserole.

3. Cover and bake 45 minutes to 1 hour, or until the potatoes are tender. Keep the casserole covered and let it set 10 minutes after you remove it from the oven.

tip

To enhance the flavor of this dish, you can top it with the optional ingredients when it's served. Just be sure to make the appropriate Exchange Approximations adjustments if you do.

Versatile Herbs

For a change of pace, you can substitute rosemary when thyme is called for in pork recipes.

245

White Wine-and-Lemon Pork Roast

Serves 4

 stats **Per serving:**

Calories:............114.52
Protein:.............12.29 g
Carbohydrates: ......1.13 g
Fat:.................4.35 g
Sat. Fat:.............1.26 g

1 clove garlic, crushed
½ cup dry white wine
1 tablespoon lemon juice
1 teaspoon olive oil
1 tablespoon minced red onion or
    shallots
¼ teaspoon dried thyme
⅛ teaspoon ground black pepper
½ pound (8-ounce) pork loin roast

1. Make the marinade by combining the first 7 ingredients in a heavy, freezer-style plastic bag. Add the roast and marinate in the refrigerator for an hour or overnight, according to taste. (Note: Pork loin is already tender, so you're marinating the meat to impart the flavors only.)

2. Preheat oven to 350°F. Remove meat from marinade; put on a nonstick spray–treated rack in a roasting pan. Roast 20–30 minutes, or until the meat thermometer reads 150°F–170°F, depending on how well-done you prefer it.

Marmalade Marinade

Combine 1 teaspoon Dijon or stone-ground mustard, 1 tablespoon Smucker's Low-Sugar Orange Marmalade, 1 clove crushed garlic, and ¼ teaspoon dried thyme leaves. Marinate and prepare a ½ pound (8-ounce) pork loin as you would the White Wine-and-Lemon Pork Loin Roast. The Nutritional Analysis for a 2-ounce serving is: Calories: 89.52; Protein: 12.26 g; Carbohydrate: 1.90 g; Fat: 3.26 g; Sat. Fat: 1.11 g; Cholesterol: 33.45 mg; Sodium: 43.66 mg; Fiber: 0.09 g.

Pecan-Crusted Roast Pork Loin

Serves 4

 Per serving:

Calories: 147.84
Protein: . . . . .12.88 g
Carbohydrates: . . . . . .2.39 g
Fat: . . . . .9.69 g
Sat. Fat: . . . . .1.72 g

1 teaspoon olive oil
1 clove garlic, crushed
1 teaspoon brown sugar
Thyme, sage, and pepper to taste
    (optional)
½ pound (8-ounce) boneless pork
    loin roast
¼ cup chopped or ground pecans

1. Put the olive oil, crushed garlic, brown sugar, and seasonings (if using) in a heavy, freezer-style plastic bag. Work the bag until the ingredients are mixed. Add the roast to the bag; turn it to coat the meat. Marinate in the refrigerator for several hours or overnight.

2. Preheat oven to 400°F. Roll the pork loin in the chopped pecans; place it in a roasting pan. Make a tent of aluminum foil and arrange it over the pork loin, covering the nuts completely so that they won't char. Roast 10 minutes, then lower the heat to 350°F. Continue to roast another 8–15 minutes, or until the meat thermometer reads 150°F–170°F, depending on how well-done you prefer it.

Create a Celery Roasting Rack

If you prefer to bake a loin roast in a casserole alongside potatoes and carrots, elevate the roast on 2–3 stalks of celery. The celery will absorb any fat that drains from the meat so that it's not absorbed by the other vegetables. Be sure to discard the celery.

Main-Dish Pork and Beans

Serves 4

 stats **Per serving:**

Calories:............153.41
Protein:.............11.25 g
Carbohydrates: ......23.64 g
Fat:.................1.80 g
Sat. Fat:............0.57 g

1⅓ cups cooked pinto beans
2 tablespoons ketchup
¼ teaspoon Dijon mustard
¼ teaspoon dry mustard
1 teaspoon cider vinegar
4 tablespoons diced red onion
1 tablespoon 100 percent maple
    syrup
1 teaspoon brown sugar
¼ pound (4 ounces) slow-cooked,
    shredded pork
⅛ cup (2 tablespoons) apple juice
    or cider

Preheat oven to 350°F. In a casserole dish treated with nonstick spray, combine the first 8 ingredients. Layer the meat over the top of the bean mixture. Pour the apple juice (or cider) over the pork. Bake 20–30 minutes, or until the mixture is well heated and bubbling. Stir well before serving.

 tip

If you prefer thicker baked beans, after cooking, remove some of the beans and mash them. Stir them back into the dish.

Pork Broth

For about 3 cups of broth, cook 1 pound lean pork shoulder or loin (cut into pieces) with 1 onion, 2 carrots, and 2 celery stalks (all chopped); 4 sprigs parsley, 6 peppercorns, ¼ cup white wine, and 4¾ cups water in a slow-cooker. Use the high setting until mixture reaches a boil, then reduce heat to low. Allow to simmer overnight or up to 16 hours. Remove the pork, discard the vegetables, skim the fat, and freeze any broth you won't be using within a few days.

Ham-and-Artichoke Hearts Scalloped Potatoes

Serves 4

 Per serving, without salt:

Calories: 269.15
Protein: . . . . .21.49 g
Carbohydrates: . . . . . .30.65 g
Fat: . . . . .7.58 g
Sat. Fat: . . . . .4.14 g

2 cups frozen artichoke hearts
1 cup chopped onion
4 small potatoes, thinly sliced
Sea salt and freshly ground black
*   pepper to taste (optional)*
1 tablespoon lemon juice
1 tablespoon dry white wine
1 cup mock cream
½ cup nonfat cottage cheese
1 teaspoon dried parsley
1 teaspoon garlic powder
⅛ cup freshly grated Parmesan
*   cheese*
¼ pound (4 ounces) lean ham, cubed
2 ounces Cheddar cheese, grated (to
*   yield ½ cup)*

1. Preheat oven to 300°F. Thaw the artichoke hearts and pat them dry with a paper towel. In a deep casserole dish treated with nonstick spray, layer the artichokes, onion, and potatoes; lightly sprinkle salt and pepper over the top (if using).

2. In a food processor or blender, combine the lemon juice, wine, mock cream, cottage cheese, parsley, garlic powder, and Parmesan cheese; process until smooth. Pour over the layered vegetables. Top with the ham. Cover the casserole dish (with a lid or foil) and bake 35–40 minutes, or until the potatoes are cooked through.

3. Remove the cover and top with the Cheddar cheese. Return to the oven another 10 minutes, or until the cheese is melted and bubbly. Let rest 10 minutes before cutting.

tip

If you are on a sodium-restricted diet, use 4 ounces of 1 of the cooked sausage recipes in this chapter in place of the ham. Adjust the Exchange Approximations from 1 Lean Meat to 1 Medium-Fat Meat.

Simple Substitutions

Artichoke hearts are expensive. You can substitute cabbage, broccoli, or cauliflower (or a mixture of all three) for the artichokes.

Slow-Cooked Venison

Yields: about 1 pound
Serving size: 1 ounce

stats **Per serving:**

Calories:............44.77
Protein:.............8.56 g
Carbohydrates: ......0.00 g
Fat:.................0.90 g
Sat. Fat:.............0.35 g

1lb. venison roast
1–2 tablespoons cider vinegar

1. Put the venison into a ceramic-lined slow cooker, add enough water to cover, and add the vinegar; set on high. Once the mixture begins to boil, reduce temperature to low. Allow the meat to simmer 8 or more hours.

2. Drain the resulting broth from the meat and discard it. Remove any remaining fat from the meat and discard that as well. Weigh the meat and separate it into servings. The meat will keep for 1–2 days in the refrigerator, or freeze portions for use later.

Use Quality Equipment

Slow cookers with a ceramic interior maintain low temperatures better than those with a metal cooking surface.

Slow-Cooker Venison BBQ

Serves 24

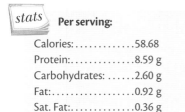 **Per serving:**

Calories: 58.68
Protein: . . . . .8.59 g
Carbohydrates: . . . . . .2.60 g
Fat: . . . . .0.92 g
Sat. Fat: . . . . .0.36 g

1½ pounds (24 ounces) Slow-Cooked
    Venison (see page 250)
1 cup water
½ cup dry white wine
½ cup Brooks Tangy Catsup
1 tablespoon red wine vinegar
1 tablespoon stone-ground mustard
1 tablespoon dried onion flakes
⅛ cup (2 tablespoons)
    Worcestershire sauce
1 teaspoon dried minced garlic
1 teaspoon cracked black pepper
1 tablespoon brown sugar

Add the cooked venison to the slow cooker. Mix all the remaining ingredients together; pour over the venison. Add additional water, if necessary, to completely cover the meat. Set the slow cooker on high until the mixture begins to boil. Reduce heat to low and simmer 2 or more hours. Adjust seasonings, if necessary.

Game Over

Instead of using the slow-cooker method to remove any gamy flavor from game meats, soak it in milk or tomato juice overnight. Drain the meat, and discard the soaking liquid.

Venison with Dried Cranberry-Vinegar Sauce

Serves 4

 stats | **Per serving, without cornstarch or flour:**

Calories:............154.14
Protein:.............17.48 g
Carbohydrates: ......4.36 g
Fat:.................6.05 g
Sat. Fat:............2.23 g

⅛ cup (2 tablespoons) dried
  cranberries
1 tablespoon sugar
3 tablespoons water
⅛ cup (2 tablespoons) champagne
  or white wine vinegar
2 teaspoons olive oil
1 tablespoon minced shallots or red
  onion
1 teaspoon minced garlic
⅛ cup (2 tablespoons) dry red wine
½ cup low-fat, reduced-sodium
  chicken broth
½ teaspoon cracked black pepper
½ pound (8 ounces) Slow-Cooked
  Venison (see page 250)
1 teaspoon cornstarch or potato
  flour
2 teaspoons butter

1. Add the cranberries, sugar, water, and champagne or vinegar to a saucepan; bring to a boil. Reduce the heat and simmer 5 minutes. Remove from heat and transfer to a food processor or blender; process until the cranberries are chopped.

2. Pour the olive oil into a heated nonstick skillet; add the shallots and garlic, and sauté 30 seconds. Deglaze the pan with the red wine; cook, stirring occasionally, until the wine is reduced by ½. Add the cranberry mixture and the chicken broth; bring to a boil. Reduce the heat to medium-low, season with the pepper, add the venison, and simmer 3 minutes, or until the meat is heated through.

3. Thicken the sauce, using a slurry of cornstarch or potato flour and 1 tablespoon of water; simmer until the sauce thickens. You'll need to cook the sauce a bit longer if you use cornstarch, in order to remove the "starchy" taste. Remove from the heat, add the butter, and whisk to incorporate the butter into the sauce.

Operate Your Appliances Safely

When puréeing hot mixtures, leave the vent uncovered on your food processor. If using a blender, either remove the vent cover from the lid or leave the lid ajar so the steam can escape.

Easy Venison Stovetop Casserole

Serves 4

stats **Per serving:**

Calories:............227.47
Protein:.............19.22 g
Carbohydrates: ......21.50 g
Fat:.................4.20 g
Sat. Fat:.............1.52 g

1 teaspoon olive oil
1 teaspoon butter
½ cup no-salt-added tomato purée
¾ cup dry red wine
2 tablespoons red currant jelly
¼ cup low-fat, reduced-sodium
    chicken broth
1 cup chopped or sliced sweet onion
1 cup thinly sliced carrots
½ pound (8 ounces) Slow-Cooked
    Venison (see page 250)
1 teaspoon arrowroot
1 tablespoon water
Freshly ground pepper to taste
⅛ cup (2 tablespoons) lemon juice
Optional garnish:
4 thin lemon slices
Fresh parsley sprigs

1. Heat the olive oil and butter in a deep, nonstick skillet. Add the tomato purée; sauté until brown. Add the red wine, red currant jelly, and chicken broth. Add the vegetables and venison; stir to coat. Bring to a boil; reduce heat, cover, and simmer 1 hour. Transfer the meat and vegetables to a heated serving dish.

2. Mix the arrowroot with the water; whisk it into the simmering pan juices to thicken. Season with pepper and stir in the lemon juice. Pour over the meat and vegetables. Garnish with lemon slices and parsley, if desired.

Venison Liverwurst

Yields: 2 pounds (32 ounces)
Serving size: 1 ounce

 Per serving, without salt:

Calories: 58.57
Protein: . . . . .10.09 g
Carbohydrates: . . . . . .0.95 g
Fat: . . . . .1.30 g
Sat. Fat: . . . . .0.46 g

1 (8" × 12") *piece of unbleached
    muslin*
1 pound (16 ounces) fresh pork liver
*1 pound (16 ounces) lean venison,
    trimmed of any fat*
*1 large sweet white onion (about 1½
    cups) finely diced*
3 tablespoons nonfat milk powder
2 teaspoons paprika
*1 teaspoon freshly fine-ground white
    pepper*
*1½ teaspoons (or to taste) kosher or
    sea salt (optional)*
1 teaspoon sugar
½ teaspoon marjoram
½ teaspoon finely ground coriander
¼ teaspoon mace
¼ teaspoon allspice
¼ teaspoon ground cardamom

1. In place of casings, prepare the muslin: Fold the muslin in half lengthwise; tightly stitch a seam across 1 of the short ends and continue along the open long side. The seam should be about ⅛ of an inch from the edge of the material. Turn the muslin casing so that the stitching is on the inside. Set it aside until you are ready to stuff it.

2. Run the liver and venison through a meat grinder using the fine disk. (Alternatively, cut the meat into cubes and freeze 20 minutes. Add the semi-frozen cubes to the bowl of your food processor and pulse until ground.) Mix well to combine the liver and venison. Transfer the ground meat to a bowl and sprinkle the remaining ingredients over the ground meat; mix thoroughly.

Venison Liverwurst

(continued)

3. Firmly pack the mixture into the muslin casing. (It's easier to get the meat packed to the bottom of the casing if you first fold the open end down over itself.) Secure the open end with a wire twist tie, butcher's twine, or cotton cord.

4. Bring enough water to a boil to cover the liverwurst in the muslin packet by 2"–3". Place a weight—such as a heavy plate—on it to keep it submerged. Bring the water to a boil; reduce the heat and simmer 3 hours. Transfer the muslin packet to a pan of ice water. When the liverwurst has cooled, refrigerate it overnight, and then remove the muslin casing. Slice into 1-ounce portions to serve. Liverwurst can be stored in the refrigerator up to 10 days.

Lamb

Baby Rack of Lamb with Zest Crust

Yields: 2 servings
Serving size: 3½ ounces

stats **Per serving:**

Calories:............325.35
Protein:.............27.76 g
Carbohydrates: ......7.91 g
Sugar: ....0.2 g
Fat:.................19.80 g

1 teaspoon lemon zest
2 tablespoons orange zest
2 tablespoons dry bread crumbs
1 teaspoon Splenda
1 tablespoon olive oil
1 teaspoon dried mint leaves
1 clove garlic, chopped
1 rack of lamb (with 6 ribs, the
    smallest you can find)
Salt and pepper to taste

1. Preheat the broiler to 450°F. Blend the first 7 ingredients together to form a nice moist paste.

2. Make sure that all fat is trimmed from the lamb. Sprinkle with salt and pepper; place in a roasting pan, bone-side up.

3. Broil 4–5 minutes. Turn and broil, meat-side up, another 4–5 minutes.

4. Remove the lamb from the oven; press the paste into the meat side. Turn off broiler and reduce oven temperature to 400°F. Bake 10–12 minutes. Remove from oven and let rest 10 minutes. Carve and serve.

Very-Hot Lamb Kabobs

Yields: 4 servings
Serving size: 4 ounces

stats **Per serving:**

Calories: 210.92
Protein: . . . . .26.14 g
Carbohydrates: . . . . . .13.02 g
Sugar: . . . . .3.66 g
Fat: . . . . .6.71 g

¼ cup lemon juice
2 tablespoons tomato paste
½ cup sugar-free tomato juice
2 tablespoons Splenda
2 teaspoons ground cayenne pepper
1 teaspoon celery salt
1 tablespoon soy sauce
½ teaspoon freshly ground black
    pepper
1 pound lean lamb, cut in 1" chunks
8 cherry tomatoes
8 large white mushrooms
8 pearl onions

1. Soak 8 wooden skewers in warm water at least 30 minutes. Preheat broiler or grill to 400°F.

2. Combine the first 8 ingredients. Place meat and marinade in a resealable plastic bag; mix well. Refrigerate and let marinate 60 minutes.

3. String the lamb, tomatoes, mushrooms, and onions on the skewers. Broil or grill until well browned on all sides, about 10 minutes, turning constantly.

Finding Great Lamb

Look for very young lamb, pink and small. Sometimes Australian and/or New Zealand lamb can be too old. American lamb can be huge but is generally okay. If you can't find any young lamb locally, you can get it on the Internet from Lobel's of New York (online at *www.lobels.com*).

Lamb Kabobs with Indian Spices

Yields: 4 servings
Serving size: 4 ounces

stats **Per serving:**

Calories: 243.18
Protein: . . . . .32.43 g
Carbohydrates: . . . . . .8.06 g
Sugar: . . . . .4.54 g
Fat: . . . . .8.9 g

1 cup plain sugar-free yogurt
Juice of ½ lime
2 cloves garlic, mashed
2 tablespoons Madras curry powder
1 teaspoon freshly grated gingerroot
1 tablespoon Splenda
Salt and freshly ground black pepper
*   to taste*
1 teaspoon dried mint leaves or 1
*   tablespoon fresh mint, minced*
1 pound lean lamb, well trimmed,
*   cut in 1" pieces*

1. Combine all ingredients to create marinade; add lamb. Marinate 4–8 hours.

2. Set grill to high heat. Dry lamb on paper towels, then string on skewers. Broil about 2 minutes per side for medium doneness.

Lamb Chops with Lavender Buds

Yields: 4 servings

Serving size: 4 ounces

 Per serving:

Calories:............234.23
Protein:.............31.5 g
Carbohydrates: ......0.91 g
Sugar: ....0.26 g
Fat:.................10.87 g

2 teaspoons lavender buds
1⅓ tablespoons unsalted butter,
    melted
1 teaspoon Splenda
Juice of ½ lemon
Salt and freshly ground black pepper
    to taste
4 (⅓ pound) thick rib lamb chops,
    bone in

1. Heat grill or broiler to 400°F. Combine all ingredients but lamb. Trim the lamb chops of all fat; paint with lavender mixture.

2. Grill 3 minutes. Brush additional lavender mixture on the chops, turn, and cook another 3 minutes. Brush again with lavender mixture, and serve.

This delicious entrée tastes very good with a vegetable risotto and side salad.

Lamb and Herbs

Lamb absolutely loves herbs. Rosemary is a natural, and so is parsley. You can also use chives and oregano. Aromatic vegetables also go well with lamb; onions, garlic, carrots, and parsnips all complement its delicate flavor. Herbs are a good, flavor-added addition to a sugar-free diet.

Rosemary-Crusted Lamb Chops

Yields: 4 servings
Serving size: 4 ounces

stats **Per serving:**

Calories: 281.33
Protein: . . . . 31.24 g
Carbohydrates: . . . . . . 1.41 g
Sugar: . . . . 0.28 g
Fat: . . . . 15.9 g

2 tablespoons olive oil
2 tablespoons fresh rosemary, finely
  minced
2 cloves garlic, chopped
Juice and zest of ½ lemon
Salt and pepper to taste
4 (⅓ pound) thick loin lamb chops,
  bone in

1. Heat your grill or broiler to 450°F. Make a paste of the first 4 ingredients. Trim the lamb chops of all fat. Sprinkle the chops with salt and pepper; brush the paste on both sides.

2. Grill the chops 5 minutes per side, or to desired doneness. Let the chops rest for a few minutes before serving.

Lamb Braised in Tomato Sauce

Yields: 6 servings
Serving size: 3½ ounces

stats **Per serving:**

Calories:............292.44
Protein:.............34.14 g
Carbohydrates: ......13.06 g
Sugar: ....6.88 g
Fat:................10.82 g

1 tablespoon olive oil
4 thick, round-bone shoulder lamb
    chops or 2 pounds lamb stew
    meat
Salt and freshly ground black pepper
    to taste
2 large white onions, chopped
4 cloves garlic, chopped
2 cups Parmelat brand sugar-free
    Italian tomatoes, crushed
1 teaspoon Splenda
¼ cup red wine vinegar
2 bay leaves
1 teaspoon dried oregano leaves
1 teaspoon dried rosemary leaves

1. Heat the olive oil in a large, heavy-bottomed soup kettle over medium-high heat. Sprinkle the lamb with salt and pepper; brown, and add the vegetables—the onions, garlic, and tomatoes.

2. Reduce heat to low; sauté the vegetables until soft. Add the rest of the ingredients. Cover and simmer 2 hours. Taste to adjust salt and pepper. Cool, and remove any fat that collects on top.

3. Fish out the bones or leave them in if you desire.

tip

You can make this dish a day ahead, refrigerate it, and skim the fat off the top just before you reheat it. Double the recipe and freeze the leftovers for an easily prepared meal later.

A House Is Not a Home Without Onions

The onion family is very diverse, ranging from sweet Vidalia onions to green onions, leeks, and garlic. Use onions liberally; they are good for you, and add a lot of flavor.

Braised Lamb Shoulder with Lemon and Onions

Yields: 4 servings
Serving size: 4 ounces

stats **Per serving:**

Calories: 257.15
Protein: . . . . .19.92 g
Carbohydrates: . . . . . .6.74 g
Sugar: . . . . .3.47 g
Fat: . . . . .16.54 g

1 teaspoon olive oil
4 (4½ ounce) round-bone shoulder
    lamb chops
Salt and pepper to taste
1 large red onion, chopped
1 teaspoon dried mint leaves or
    1 tablespoon fresh, chopped
1 teaspoon Splenda
½ cup chicken broth
⅓ cup vegetable broth
Juice of ½ lemon
½ lemon, thinly sliced, seeds removed

1. Heat the oil in a large nonstick pan over medium heat. Trim all fat from the lamb; sprinkle with salt and pepper, brown, and set aside.

2. Stir in the onions; cook until softened. Add the rest of the ingredients.

3. Reduce heat to simmer. Cover and simmer 60 minutes.

Lamb Fat

Lamb meat is sweet, but the fat is strong. When the fat is removed, the meat tastes much, much better. When you make braised lamb, you can get even more fat off it by refrigerating it until broth has cooled and fat has risen to the top. Skim the fat before reheating.

French-Style Braised Lamb Shanks

Yields: 4 servings
Serving size: 4 ounces

stats **Per serving:**

Calories:............539.63
Protein:.............39.67 g
Carbohydrates: ......42.07 g
Sugar: ....10.99 g
Fat:.................23.32 g

2 pounds lamb shanks
¼ cup whole-wheat flour
Salt and freshly ground black pepper
*   to taste*
1 tablespoon olive oil
1 large red Spanish onion, chopped
4 cloves garlic, chopped
4 carrots, chopped
4 fresh sage leaves, chopped or
*   1 teaspoon dried sage*
1 teaspoon soy sauce
1 teaspoon Splenda
1 cup fresh plum tomatoes, chopped
1 cup rich chicken stock
2 cans cannellini beans, drained and
*   rinsed*
2 slices sugar-free smoked bacon
2 cups sliced white mushrooms

1. Trim the lamb shanks of all fat. Dredge in flour, salt, and pepper. Heat olive oil in nonstick pan over medium heat. Add lamb shanks; brown on all sides.

2. Remove the shanks from the pan. Stir in onion and garlic; cook until softened.

3. Add the carrots, sage, soy sauce, Splenda, tomatoes, and chicken stock. Cover and reduce heat to a simmer. Cook 2 hours; stir in the beans.

4. Sauté the bacon in a separate nonstick pan. Drain it on paper towels. Reserve 1 teaspoon of fat and discard the rest. Sauté the mushrooms in reserved bacon fat 5 minutes. Add the mushrooms and bacon to the stewed shanks, and serve.

Shanks and Beans

Lamb shanks are mostly bone, but they still have luscious meat from the bottom of the leg. Cannellini beans are classically French, and a wonderful complement to the meat and sauce. They are a staple in the Mediterranean, and they are among the most versatile of beans.

Marinated Roast Leg of Lamb

Yields: 10 servings
Serving size: 4 ounces

 Per serving:

Calories: 364.7
Protein: . . . . 22.85 g
Carbohydrates: . . . . . . 8.24 g
Sugar: . . . . 4.33 g
Fat: . . . . 26.46 g

½ cup olive oil
¼ cup red wine vinegar
4 carrots, peeled and cut in 3"
    lengths
2 large onions, sliced
4 fresh bay leaves
10 capers
2 tablespoons rosemary leaves
2½ pound boneless leg of lamb
4 garlic cloves, slivered
Kosher salt and freshly ground black
    pepper to taste
4 anchovy filets
1 bunch Italian flat-leaf parsley,
    chopped
1 lemon, thinly sliced

1. Mix the first 7 ingredients in a large glass baking dish or enamel-coated roasting pan. Trim every bit of fat from the lamb. Make slits along the leg of lamb and insert sliced garlic cloves.

2. Sprinkle the lamb with salt and pepper. Turn it in the marinade to coat. Place the anchovy filets on top. Add the parsley and lemon.

3. Cover and refrigerate overnight, turning after 8 hours.

4. Preheat oven to 350°F. Roast the lamb 20 minutes per pound, basting with the marinade every few minutes. Let rest 15 minutes before carving.

Curried Lamb Stew

Yields: 6 servings
Serving size: 4 ounces

stats **Per serving:**

Calories:............308.15 g
Protein:.............39.25 g
Carbohydrates: ......7.91 g
Sugar: ....2.95 g
Fat:.................12.63 g

1 tablespoon peanut or canola oil
2 pounds lean boneless lamb stew
    meat
Salt and pepper to taste
2 onions, chopped
3 cloves garlic, chopped
2 teaspoons whole-wheat flour
1 tablespoon Madras curry powder,
    or to taste
1 teaspoon Splenda
1 teaspoon cayenne pepper
1 tablespoon tamarind paste mixed
    with ¼ cup water
1 cup vegetable broth
Juice of ½ lime
½ cup water (in case sauce gets too
    thick)

1. Heat the oil in a large, heavy-bottomed stew pot or soup kettle over medium-high heat. Sprinkle the lamb with salt and pepper.

2. Brown the lamb. Reduce heat to medium and add the onions and garlic; sauté until softened, about 4 minutes.

3. Move the meat and vegetables over to the side of the pan; add the flour, curry, Splenda, and cayenne, stirring constantly.

4. Stir in the rest of the ingredients. Cover, reduce heat, and simmer slowly 3 hours.

tip

This is a stew that improves with age. Make it the day before you plan to serve it.

Indian Spices

Indian cuisine can be hotter than the hottest Tex-Mex dishes. However, the cuisine can also be delicately subtle or bold and exotically delicious. The use of spices and the diversity of Indian dishes makes this culture a rich resource for a sugar-free diet.

Irish Stew

Yields: 6 servings
Serving size: 4 ounces

stats **Per serving:**

Calories:...........426.74
Protein:...........33.52 g
Carbohydrates:......28.12 g
Sugar: ....10.4 g
Fat:................15.80 g

1 tablespoon canola oil
Salt and pepper to taste
2 pounds boneless lamb stew, all fat
  removed
4 onions, chopped
2 cloves garlic, chopped
2 celery stalks with leaves, chopped
4 carrots, peeled and cut in 2"
  lengths
¼ cup white wine vinegar
1 cup beef broth
1 bay leaf
1 tablespoon dried rosemary
1 teaspoon dried sage
½ cup curly parsley, chopped
2 teaspoons chervil
1 teaspoon horseradish
2 cups mashed potatoes

1. Heat the oil in a large, heavy-bottomed soup kettle or stew pot over medium heat. Salt and pepper the lamb and brown it.

2. Reduce heat to low; stir in the onions, garlic, celery, and carrots. Add all of the other ingredients but the potatoes. Cover the pot and simmer over very low heat 2 hours.

3. When the stew is done, place in a 2-quart soufflé dish. Cover with the mashed potatoes, and run under the broiler until lightly browned.

 tip

You can increase the mashed potatoes, add more carrots to the stew, or leave them out all together.

Basque-Style Lamb Stew

Yields: 6 servings
Serving size: 4 ounces

stats **Per serving:**

Calories: 259.8
Protein: . . . . .23.97 g
Carbohydrates: . . . . . .4.12 g
Sugar: . . . . .1.65 g
Fat: . . . . .16 g

3 slices smoked bacon, cooked and
    drained
4 cloves garlic, minced
1 sprig fresh rosemary
¼ cup red wine vinegar
1½ pounds shoulder lamb, cut in
    chunks
Salt and pepper to taste
2 teaspoons olive oil
2 yellow onions, chopped
1 tablespoon sweet paprika
2 bottled sweet red roasted peppers,
    packed in oil
2 bay leaves
½ bunch Italian flat-leaf parsley,
    minced
1 cup chicken stock

1. Fry the bacon and reserve on paper towels. Mix 1 clove of garlic with the rosemary, vinegar, and lamb in a resealable plastic bag. Marinate overnight in the refrigerator, turning occasionally.

2. Discard the marinade, dry the lamb, and sprinkle it with salt and pepper. Heat the olive oil in a heavy nonstick pan over medium heat. Brown the meat; remove from the pan.

3. Sauté the rest of the garlic and the onions. Return the lamb to the pan; stir in the rest of the ingredients.

4. Reduce heat to a simmer and cover. Cook 2 hours, or until the lamb is falling off the bone. Cool, remove bones, and reheat, adding the crumbled bacon.

Basque Style

This dish draws its inspiration from Basque flavors, but it blends in traditional American flavors for a more familiar taste. The Basque region, located in Spain's northeast region, borders France, and its cuisine has long influenced European palates.

Greek Lamb-and-Eggplant Casserole

Yields: 6 servings
Serving size: 4 ounces

stats **Per serving:**

Calories: 296.11
Protein: . . . . .15.98 g
Carbohydrates: . . . . . .12.16 g
Sugar: . . . . .7.45 g
Fat: . . . . .20.84 g

2 teaspoons olive oil
2 small yellow onions, chopped
2 cloves garlic
Salt and pepper to taste
½ teaspoon cinnamon
1 teaspoon dried basil
1 teaspoon dried marjoram
1 cup sugar-free tomato sauce
1 pound ground lamb
1 medium eggplant, thinly sliced
¼ cup grated Parmesan cheese

1. Heat the olive oil in a frying pan over medium heat. Add the onion and garlic; cook until soft. Place the cooked vegetables in a large bowl.

2. Preheat the oven to 350°F. Add the salt, pepper, cinnamon, basil, marjoram, tomato sauce, and lamb to the onion and garlic; mix thoroughly.

3. Prepare a 2-quart oven-proof casserole dish with nonstick spray. Cover the bottom with eggplant slices. Add the lamb mixture; cover with more eggplant. Sprinkle with Parmesan cheese. Cover with aluminum foil.

4. Bake 60 minutes, covered. Remove aluminum foil and bake 60 minutes more. Serve with rice.

Greek Lamb-and-Pasta Casserole

Yields: 6 servings
Serving size: 4 ounces

 Per serving:

Calories:............413.21
Protein:.............25.28 g
Carbohydrates: ......25.38 g
Sugar: ....3.41 g
Fat:.................23.44 g

1 tablespoon olive oil
1 pound lean ground lamb
1 large sweet onion, chopped
4 cloves garlic, minced
½ cup currants
Salt and freshly ground pepper to taste
½ teaspoon cinnamon
1 teaspoon Splenda
1 teaspoon dried mint or 1 tablespoon fresh mint, chopped
3 cups parboiled orzo
½ cup chicken stock or broth
½ cup toasted pine nuts

1. Preheat the oven to 350°F. Prepare a casserole dish with nonstick cooking spray. Heat the olive oil in a large pan over medium heat. Sauté the meat, onion, and garlic, stirring constantly.

2. Add the currants, spices, Splenda, and mint.

3. Mix with the orzo; pour into the casserole dish. Stir in the broth. Sprinkle with pine nuts. Bake 30 minutes.

You can make this dish in advance to serve the next day or freeze and serve the next week.

Pasta, Pizza, and Potatoes

Quick Tomato Sauce

Serves 8

stats **Per serving, without salt:**

Calories: 39.85
Protein: . . . . 1.01 g
Carbohydrates: . . . . . . 5.51 g
Fat: . . . . 2.07 g
Sat. Fat: . . . . 0.28 g

2 pounds very ripe tomatoes
2 tablespoons extra-virgin olive oil
2 cloves garlic, minced
½ teaspoon ground cumin
2 large sprigs fresh thyme or ½
*   teaspoon dried thyme*
1 bay leaf
Kosher or sea salt and freshly ground
*   black pepper to taste (optional)*
3 tablespoons total of chopped
*   fresh basil, oregano, tarragon,*
*   and parsley or cilantro; or, a*
*   combination of all the listed*
*   herbs according to taste. If using*
*   dried herbs, reduce the amount*
*   to 1 tablespoon*

1. Peel and seed the tomatoes; chop them with a knife or food processor.

2. Heat a large skillet and add the olive oil. Reduce the heat to low; sauté the garlic and cumin. Add the tomatoes, thyme, bay leaf, and salt and pepper, if using. If you are using dried herbs, add them now.

3. Simmer, uncovered, over medium heat 8–10 minutes, stirring often; reduce the heat to maintain a simmer, if necessary. Simmer until the tomatoes are soft and the sauce has thickened. Discard the bay leaf and thyme sprigs. Adjust the seasoning to taste. If you are using fresh herbs, add them just before serving.

Remember . . .

The addition of ¼ teaspoon of granulated sugar in tomato sauce helps cut the acidity of the tomatoes without affecting the Exchange Approximations for the recipe.

Basic Tomato Sauce

Yields: about 5 cups
Serving size: ¼ cup

 stats **Per serving, without salt:**

Calories:. 36.54
Protein:. . . . . .0.86 g
Carbohydrates: . . . . . .5.49 g
Fat:. . . . . .1.60 g
Sat. Fat:. . . . . .0.22 g

2 tablespoons olive oil
2 cups coarsely chopped yellow
    onion
½ cup sliced carrots
2 cloves garlic, minced
4 cups canned Italian plum
    tomatoes, with juice
1 teaspoon dried oregano
1 teaspoon dried basil
¼ teaspoon sugar
Kosher or sea salt and freshly ground
    black pepper to taste (optional)
Dash of ground anise seed (optional)

1. Heat the olive oil in a large, deep skillet or saucepan over medium-high heat. Add the onions, carrots, and garlic; sauté until the onions are transparent. (For a richer-tasting sauce, allow the onions to caramelize or reach a light golden brown.)

2. Purée the tomatoes in a food processor. Add the tomatoes, herbs, and sugar to the onion mixture along with the salt, pepper, and anise, if using.

3. Simmer, partially covered, 45 minutes. Process the sauce in the food processor again if you prefer a smoother sauce.

Culinary Antacids

Stir in 2 teaspoons of Smucker's Low-Sugar Grape Jelly to tame hot chili or acidic sauce. You won't really notice the flavor of the jelly, and it will do a great job of reducing any tart, bitter, or acidic tastes in your sauce.

Uncooked Tomato Sauce

Serves 4

 Per serving, without salt:

Calories:............94
Protein:.............2.27 g
Carbohydrates: ......11.95 g
Fat:.................5.30 g
Sat. Fat:.............0.72 g

½ cup fresh basil leaves, divided
2 pounds firm ripe tomatoes, peeled,
    seeded, and chopped
2 cloves garlic, minced
4 tablespoons thinly sliced scallions
    (white and green parts)
2 tablespoons minced fresh parsley
4 teaspoons extra-virgin olive oil
1½ teaspoons red wine vinegar or
    lemon juice
¼ teaspoon sugar
Kosher or sea salt and freshly ground
    black pepper to taste (optional)

1. Chop ½ the basil leaves, and set the rest aside until later.

2. In a large bowl, combine the chopped basil, tomatoes, garlic, scallions, parsley, olive oil, vinegar or lemon juice, and sugar. Let the mixture sit at room temperature at least 4 hours, but no more than 6; season with salt and pepper, if using. Garnish with the remaining basil.

English-Muffin Pizzas

Top each ½ of an English muffin with your choice of tomato sauce. Add chopped, free-choice vegetables. Divide 1 ounce of grated mozzarella cheese between the muffin halves. Bake in a 400°F oven until the cheese bubbles, and you have a meal with 2 Carbohydrate/Starch Exchanges and 1 Medium-Fat Meat Exchange, plus the Exchange Approximation for your choice of sauce.

Fusion Lo Mein

Serves 6

 Per serving:

Calories: 126.06
Protein: . . . . .4.62 g
Carbohydrates: . . . . . .26.06 g
Fat: . . . . .1.34 g
Sat. Fat: . . . . .0.19 g

2 tablespoons rice vinegar
2 tablespoons thawed pineapple-
    orange juice from concentrate
2 teaspoons minced shallots
2 teaspoons lemon juice
1 teaspoon cornstarch
1 teaspoon Worcestershire sauce
1 teaspoon honey
2 cloves garlic, minced
1 teaspoon olive oil
¾ cup chopped green onions
1 cup diagonally sliced (¼-inch thick)
    carrots
1 cup julienned yellow bell pepper
1 cup julienned red bell pepper
3 cups small broccoli florets
1 cup fresh bean sprouts
1½ cups cooked pasta

1. In a food processor or blender, combine the vinegar, juice concentrate, shallots, lemon juice, cornstarch, Worcestershire, honey, and garlic; process until smooth.

2. Heat a wok or large nonstick skillet coated with cooking spray over medium-high heat until hot; add the olive oil. Add the onions and stir-fry 1 minute. Add the carrots, bell peppers, and broccoli; stir-fry another minute. Cover the pan and cook 2 more minutes. Add the vinegar mixture and the sprouts. Bring the mixture to a boil and cook, uncovered, 30 seconds, stirring constantly. Add the cooked pasta; toss to mix.

Roasted Butternut-Squash Pasta

Serves 4

 stats **Per serving:**

Calories:.............216.65
Protein:..............5.23 g
Carbohydrates: ......39.81 g
Fat:.................5.18 g
Sat. Fat:.............0.71 g

1 butternut squash
4 teaspoons extra-virgin olive oil
1 clove garlic, minced
1 cup chopped red onion
2 teaspoons red wine vinegar
¼ teaspoon dried oregano
2 cups cooked pasta
Freshly ground black pepper
    (optional)

1. Preheat oven to 400°F. Cut the squash in half and scoop out the seeds. Using nonstick spray, coat 1 side of each of 2 pieces of heavy-duty foil large enough to wrap the squash halves. Wrap the squash in the foil and place on a baking sheet; bake 1 hour, or until tender.

2. Scoop out the baked squash flesh and discard the rind. Rough chop the squash. Add the olive oil, garlic, and onion to a nonstick skillet; sauté until the onion is transparent. (Alternatively, put the oil, garlic, and onion in a covered, microwave-safe dish and microwave on high 2–3 minutes.)

3. Remove pan from heat; stir in the vinegar and oregano. Add the squash; stir to coat it in the onion mixture. Add the pasta; toss to mix. Season with freshly ground black pepper, if desired.

tip

For added flavor, use roasted instead of raw garlic in this recipe. Roasting the garlic causes it to caramelize, adding a natural sweetness.

Pasta with Artichokes

Serves 4

 Per serving:

Calories: 307.80
Protein: . . . . .9.75 g
Carbohydrates: . . . . . .46.66 g
Fat: . . . . .9.23 g
Sat. Fat: . . . . .1.74 g

1 (10-ounce) package frozen
    artichoke hearts
1¼ cups water
1 tablespoon lemon juice
4 teaspoons olive oil
2 cloves garlic, minced
¼ cup sun-dried tomatoes, packed in
    oil (drained and chopped)
¼ teaspoon red pepper flakes
2 teaspoons dried parsley
2 cups cooked pasta
¼ cup grated Parmesan cheese
Freshly ground black pepper to taste
    (optional)

1. Cook artichokes in water and lemon juice according to package directions; drain, reserving ¼ cup of liquid. Cool the artichokes, then cut into quarters. (Alternatively, you can decrease the amount of water to 3 tablespoons and add it with artichokes and lemon juice to a covered microwave-safe dish. Microwave according to package directions; reserve all of the liquid. This results in a stronger lemon flavor, which compensates for the lack of salt in this recipe.)

2. Heat the olive oil in a nonstick skillet over medium heat. Add garlic; sauté 1 minute. Reduce heat to low; stir in artichokes and tomatoes; simmer 1 minute. Stir in reserved artichoke liquid, red pepper flakes, and parsley; simmer 5 minutes.

3. Pour the artichoke sauce over the pasta in a large bowl; toss gently to coat. Sprinkle with cheese and top with pepper, if desired.

Garlic Toast

Large amounts of a butter- or olive oil-garlic mixture make garlic bread high in fat. For delicious results with only a touch of fat, spritz both sides of sliced bread with olive oil, and bake 6–8 minutes in a 350°F oven. Handling the toasted bread slices carefully, rub a cut garlic clove across the top of each slice.

279

Pasta with Creamed Clam Sauce

Serves 4

 Per serving:

Calories:............225.86
Protein:.............14.68 g
Carbohydrates: ......23.65 g
Fat:.................7.46 g
Sat. Fat:.............1.96 g

1 (6½-ounce) can chopped clams
4 teaspoons olive oil
1 clove garlic, minced
1 tablespoon dry white wine or dry
    vermouth
½ cup mock cream
¼ cup freshly grated Parmesan
    cheese
2 cups cooked pasta
Freshly ground black pepper to taste
    (optional)

1. Drain the canned clams and reserve the juice. Heat the olive oil in a large nonstick skillet. Add the garlic; sauté 1 minute; stir in the clams and sauté another minute. With a slotted spoon, transfer the clams to a bowl; cover to keep warm.

2. Add the wine or vermouth and reserved clam juice to the skillet; bring to a boil, and reduce by half. Lower the heat; add the Mock Cream and bring to serving temperature, being careful not to boil the cream. Stir in the Parmesan cheese; continue to heat the sauce for another minute, stirring constantly. Add the pasta; toss with the sauce.

3. Divide into 4 equal servings and serve immediately, topped with freshly ground pepper, if desired.

Pasta with Tuna Alfredo Sauce

Serves 4

stats **Per serving:**

Calories:.............278.46
Protein:..............33.25 g
Carbohydrates: ......20.80 g
Fat:..................5.42 g
Sat. Fat:.............1.85 g

1 cup nonfat cottage cheese
1 tablespoon skim milk
2 teaspoons olive oil
1 clove garlic, minced
2 (6-ounce) cans tuna packed in
   water, drained
⅛ cup (2 tablespoons) dry white
   wine
¼ cup freshly grated Parmesan
   cheese
2 cups cooked pasta
Freshly ground black pepper to taste
   (optional)

1. Process the cottage cheese and skim milk together in a food processor or blender until smooth. Set aside.

2. Heat the olive oil in a large nonstick skillet. Add the garlic and sauté 1 minute; stir in the tuna and sauté another minute. Add the wine to the skillet and bring to a boil. Lower the heat; add the cottage cheese mixture and bring to serving temperature, being careful not to let it boil. Stir in the Parmesan cheese; continue to heat the sauce 1 minute, stirring constantly. Add the pasta and toss with the sauce.

3. Divide into 4 equal servings and serve immediately, topped with freshly ground pepper, if desired.

Pasta Fagioli

Serves 8

stats **Per serving:**

Calories: 380.19
Protein: . . . . .20.37 g
Carbohydrates: . . . . . .57.48 g
Fat: . . . . .7.52 g
Sat. Fat: . . . . .1.82 g

1 (16-ounce) package ziti pasta
2 tablespoons olive oil
2 cloves garlic, minced
1½ cups sugar snap peas
1½ cups diced cooked, extra-lean (4 percent) ham
1 (16-ounce) can cannellini beans, drained
¼ cup sun-dried tomatoes packed in oil, drained and chopped
1½ cups low-fat, reduced-sodium chicken broth
½ teaspoon kosher or sea salt
¼ teaspoon cracked black pepper
¼ cup grated Parmesan cheese

1. Cook the pasta as directed on the package. Meanwhile, heat a large skillet on medium; add the olive oil. Sauté the garlic 2 minutes, being careful that it doesn't burn. Add the peas (thawed and drained, if you're using frozen); stir-fry about 3 minutes. Stir in the ham, beans, tomatoes, broth, salt, and pepper; simmer 5 minutes.

2. Toss the stir-fried bean mixture with the pasta and Parmesan cheese.

tip

The ham in this dish makes it high in sodium, so consult your dietitian before including it in your menu plan if you are on a salt-restricted diet.

Little Bits

Don't waste the unused tomato paste left in the can. Spoon out tablespoon-sized portions and place them on plastic wrap or in sandwich baggies. Seal the packages and store in the freezer. When you need tomato paste in a recipe, add the frozen paste directly to sauce; there is no need to defrost.

Macaroni Casserole

Serves 4

 Per serving, without salt:

Calories: 366.38
Protein:. . . . . .28.76 g
Carbohydrates: . . . . . .37.08 g
Fat:. . . . . .12.09 g
Sat. Fat:. . . . . .5.45 g

½ pound (8 ounces) ground turkey
1 cup chopped onion
⅛ cup (2 tablespoons) unsalted
    tomato paste
1 teaspoon dried parsley
¼ teaspoon cinnamon
Kosher or sea salt and black pepper
    to taste (optional)
1 cup skim milk
1 tablespoon Ener-G potato flour
2 cups cooked macaroni
4 ounces Cabot's 50% Light Cheddar
    Cheese, grated (to yield 1 cup)
1 recipe mock béchamel sauce

1. Preheat oven to 350°F. Fry the ground turkey in a nonstick skillet; drain off any fat and pat the meat with paper towels. Add the onion; sauté with the ground turkey until transparent. Add the tomato paste; sauté until it starts to brown. Stir in the parsley, cinnamon, and salt and pepper, if using. Remove from heat and set aside.

2. Pour the milk in a bowl and add the potato flour; whisk to mix. Stir in the macaroni and cheese.

3. Treat a 13" × 17" baking dish with nonstick spray. Pour half of the macaroni mixture into the pan. Spread the meat mixture over the macaroni. Add the rest of the macaroni, and top with the Béchamel Sauce. Bake 1 hour.

283

Bleu Cheese Pasta

Serves 4

 Per serving:

Calories: 212.46
Protein: . . . . .12.10 g
Carbohydrates: . . . . . .20.74 g
Fat: . . . . .8.75 g
Sat. Fat: . . . . .4.26 g

2 teaspoons olive oil
1 clove garlic, minced
½ cup nonfat cottage cheese
2 ounces crumbled bleu cheese
Skim milk (optional)
2 cups cooked pasta
¼ cup freshly grated Parmesan
    cheese
Freshly ground black pepper
    (optional)

1. Heat the olive oil in a large nonstick skillet. Add the garlic; sauté 1 minute. Lower the heat, stir in the cottage cheese, and bring it to serving temperature. Add the bleu cheese and stir to combine; thin the sauce with a little skim milk, if necessary.

2. Toss with the pasta; divide into 4 equal servings. Top each serving with 1 tablespoon of the Parmesan cheese and freshly ground black pepper, if desired.

Garlic Mashed Potatoes

Yields: 4 servings
Serving size: ⅔ cup

 Per serving:

Calories:............274.97
Protein:.............5.32 g
Carbohydrates: ......52.37 g
Sugar: ....4.00 g
Fat:.................5.50 g

*4 medium Idaho or Yukon Gold
    potatoes*
1 teaspoon salt
2 teaspoons olive oil
3 cloves garlic, minced
1 tablespoon unsalted butter
¼–⅓ cup milk or half-n-half
¼ teaspoon pepper
⅛ teaspoon freshly grated nutmeg

1. Peel the potatoes; slice ½" thick. Place in a large pot; cover with cold water. Add salt; bring to a boil over high heat.

2. Reduce heat to a simmer. Cook, uncovered, 15–20 minutes, or until potatoes are fork-tender.

3. While the potatoes cook, heat the olive oil in a small pan over medium heat. Sauté garlic 4–5 minutes, or until just softened; set aside.

4. Drain the potatoes; place in a bowl. Mash the potatoes with butter, milk, pepper, and nutmeg.

5. When the potatoes are smooth, stir in the garlic/oil combination. Serve hot.

285

Potato Skins Stuffed with Hot Barbecue

Yields: 4 servings
Serving size: ½ cup

 stats **Per serving:**

Calories: 389.93
Protein: . . . . .19.75 g
Carbohydrates: . . . . . .64.17 g
Sugar: . . . . .8.69 g
Fat: . . . . .5.98 g

*4 large Idaho potatoes, baked 40
    minutes at 400°F*
¼ cup milk
Salt and pepper to taste
1 onion, minced
*1 cup roasted pork tenderloin or
    roast chicken, shredded*
½ cup Barbecue Sauce (page 389)
*½ teaspoon freshly ground black
    pepper*
*4 tablespoons sharp Cheddar cheese,
    grated*

1. Remove the tops from the baked potatoes. Cut potatoes in half lengthwise. Scoop out the insides; put them in a bowl, being careful to keep the skins intact. Mash potatoes and milk, adding salt and pepper to taste. Set aside.

2. Preheat the oven to 350°F. Prepare a baking pan with nonstick spray or cover with parchment paper.

3. Spoon half of the mashed potatoes onto the skins. Add the onion, pork, and barbecue sauce; sprinkle with ground pepper. Place the stuffed potatoes on the baking pan.

4. Bake 30 minutes. Serve with grated cheese and your favorite garnishes.

tip

You can buy spit-roasted barbecued chicken from the grocery store; just make sure the sauce is sugar-free. You could also go to the deli and get preroasted sliced chicken, ready to shred.

Potatoes Are Good Food

Potatoes are very good for you, especially if you eat the skins. They are slow to digest, and are a good source of fiber. However, some potato dishes are not health friendly. Any processed and fried food is a rare treat, something you might have once every month or two, or never.

Stuffed Idaho Potatoes with Chives and Cheeses

Yields: 4 servings
Serving size: ½ cup

 Per serving:

Calories: 398.38
Protein: . . . . .14.51 g
Carbohydrates: . . . . . .52.84 g
Sugar: . . . . .5.01 g
Fat: . . . . .14.88 g

4 Idaho or Yukon Gold potatoes
⅓ cup warm 1% milk
2 tablespoons unsalted butter
⅛ teaspoon nutmeg
¼ cup fresh chives, rinsed and
    snipped
freshly ground black pepper to taste
2 ounces grated Parmesan cheese
2 ounces grated white American
    cheese

1. Scrub the potatoes, prick them with a fork, and bake them at 400°F 35–40 minutes.

2. Let cool until you can handle them. Slice off the tops; remove the insides, leaving about ¼" of pulp inside the skin. Set the skins aside.

3. Put the potato innards and the rest of the ingredients in a bowl. Using an electric mixer, beat until fairly smooth. Return to the skins; bake another 20 minutes at 300°F.

Excited Potato Starch

If you put your potatoes in a food processor or a blender to mash them, they will turn into a pasty, gluey mess. That's because the starch gets excited and separates. Instead, use a ricer or an electric mixer to mash your potatoes.

Roasted New Potatoes with Carrots and Fennel

Yields: 4 servings
Serving size: ⅔ cup

 Per serving:

Calories: 146.61
Protein: . . . . .2.66 g
Carbohydrates: . . . . . .18.18 g
Sugar: . . . . .4.89 g
Fat: . . . . .7.50 g

4 golf-ball sized new potatoes, red,
    creamery, or purple, scrubbed
    and halved
4 medium carrots, peeled, ends
    trimmed, and cut in 3" lengths
1 fennel bulb, quartered
¼ cup chicken broth
2 tablespoons olive oil
½ teaspoon caraway seeds
1 teaspoon dried thyme
salt and pepper to taste

1. Preheat the oven to 375°F. Prepare a baking sheet with nonstick cooking spray. Scrub and prepare the veggies; place them on the baking sheet.

2. Whisk the chicken broth, olive oil, caraway seeds, thyme, salt, and pepper; drizzle over the vegetables. Roast 35–40 minutes, or until the potatoes are fork-tender.

Roast Vegetables

Potatoes are just one of many great roasting vegetables! Try cauliflower, sweet peppers, onions, and celery. You can serve any of them over chilled salad greens for lunch.

Crunchy Sautéed New Potatoes

Yields: 4 servings
Serving size: 2 half-potatoes

stats **Per serving:**

Calories: 89.84
Protein: . . . . .1.00 g
Carbohydrates: . . . . . .13.00 g
Sugar: . . . . .0 g
Fat: . . . . .3.38 g

1 tablespoon olive oil
2 tablespoons water
8 medium-sized new potatoes,
    scrubbed and halved
Salt and pepper to taste

1. Add the oil and water to a nonstick pan over medium heat.

2. Place the potatoes in the pan, cut-sides down. Cover and cook 10 minutes. Remove the lid and continue to brown until the cut sides are crisp. Turn, and sprinkle with salt and pepper.

tip

Add fresh parsley just before serving for extra color and kick.

Potatoes Sautéed in Olive Oil and Herbs

Yields: 4 servings
Serving size: ⅔ cup

stats **Per serving:**

Calories:.............123.79
Protein:..............1.17 g
Carbohydrates:......13.74 g
Sugar: ....0.04 g
Fat:.................6.89 g

8 large new or fingerling potatoes,
    scrubbed and sliced ¼" thick
2 tablespoons water
2 tablespoons olive oil
¼ cup fresh Italian flat-leaf parsley,
    chopped
2 teaspoons dried rosemary or 1
    tablespoon fresh rosemary
1 teaspoon dried sage leaves or 1
    tablespoon fresh sage leaves,
    torn
Salt and pepper to taste

1. Prepare a nonstick pan with nonstick spray. Add the potatoes and water; cover, and cook 15 minutes over medium heat.

2. Remove the lid. Toss the potatoes with olive oil, herbs, salt, and pepper. Reset heat to medium-high.

3. Brown quickly, and serve.

You can use the leftover potatoes and herbs to make a great potato salad.

Cook Once, Eat Twice

Any of these recipes can be doubled, saved, and reheated for another night. Adjust the recipe if you are expecting a large number of guests. If you have leftovers, cover them tightly and refrigerate them.

Pasta with Ricotta, Garlic, and Baby Peas

Yields: 6 servings

Serving size: 1 cup

 Per serving:

Calories:............386.09
Protein:..............19.44 g
Carbohydrates: ......34.82 g
Sugar: ....3.81 g
Fat:..................19.58 g

*1 pound short pasta, such as
    macaroni*
2 tablespoons olive oil
2 cloves garlic, chopped
*1 tablespoon dried thyme or 4
    tablespoons fresh thyme*
2 whole eggs
8 ounces ricotta
5 ounces frozen baby peas
4 ounces Parmesan cheese
*6 ounces sun-dried tomatoes packed
    in oil, drained and cut in pieces*

1. Preheat the oven to 350°F. Cook pasta according to package instructions. Heat the oil in a 3-quart ovenproof casserole dish over medium-low heat.

2. Sauté the garlic 5 minutes, stirring constantly. Remove from the stove. Add the remaining ingredients; stir to mix.

3. Drain the pasta; mix with the ingredients in the casserole dish. Bake 40 minutes.

Pasta with Anchovy-Olive Sauce

Yields: 6 servings
Serving size: 1 cup

 Per serving:

Calories: 478.62
Protein: . . . . .19.47 g
Carbohydrates: . . . . . .75.12 g
Sugar: . . . . .8.73 g
Fat: . . . . .12.57 g

2 tablespoons olive oil
6 cloves garlic, chopped
4 anchovies, drained
1 teaspoon red pepper flakes
1 cup black Sicilian olives, pitted and
    chopped
1 (28-ounce) can no-sugar-added
    crushed tomatoes, in juice
1 (6-ounce) can tomato paste, no
    sugar added
½ cup fresh Italian flat-leaf parsley,
    chopped
1 pound whole-wheat spaghetti
3 quarts boiling salted water
Freshly ground black pepper to taste
½ cup freshly grated Parmesan
    cheese

1. Heat the oil in a large sauce pot over medium heat. Sauté the garlic and anchovies, stirring continuously with a wooden spoon until the anchovies melt.

2. Add the pepper flakes, olives, tomatoes, tomato paste, and parsley. Bring to a boil and reduce heat to a simmer. Cook the pasta to almost al dente; drain and add to the pot of sauce. Let it simmer a few minutes.

3. Sprinkle with cheese, and serve.

Olives

Olives add an enormous amount of flavor to just about any sauce. The taste of cooked olives is more delicate than raw olives, almost sweet. Try different brands of olives. You'll find some are vinegary, others are lemony, and still others are a combination of salty and smoky. The flavors depend on the region where they are grown and cured.

Pasta with Chicken, Green Olives, and Grape Tomatoes

Yields: 6 servings
Serving size: 1½ cups

stats **Per serving:**

Calories: 432.86
Protein: . . . . .19.36 g
Carbohydrates: . . . . . .39.50 g
Sugar: . . . . .2.56 g
Fat: . . . . .21.44 g

2 tablespoons olive oil
1 pound chicken tenders, cut in small pieces
Salt and pepper to taste
Dash of whole-wheat flour
2 cloves garlic, chopped
4 shallots, chopped
1 teaspoon Dijon-Style Mustard (page 98)
½ teaspoon Splenda
¾ cup green pitted olives, stuffed with pimentos
1 cup chicken broth
1 pound spaghetti, cooked in 3 quarts boiling, salted water
Garnish of 1 cup grape tomatoes, halved
½ cup freshly grated Parmesan cheese

1. In a large frying pan, heat the olive oil over medium heat. Sprinkle the chicken with salt, pepper, and flour. Sauté; remove from the pan.

2. Add the garlic and shallots to the pan. Cook about 3 minutes. Stir in the mustard, Splenda, olives, and broth; cook 5 minutes, stirring continuously. Return the chicken to the pot. Reduce heat to the barest simmer.

3. Cook the pasta until al dente. Add it to the pot with the chicken. Let cook another 1–2 minutes to allow flavors to combine.

4. Garnish with the tomatoes, and serve with a sprinkle of cheese.

 tip

You can buy chicken tenders fresh or frozen. Too often, they are used in fried chicken "nuggets," but they are excellent in any number of dishes and sandwiches. In fact, they are the top of the chicken breast—the filet—totally lean and excellent for a sugar-free menu.

Spaghetti with Shrimp

Yields: 6 servings
Serving size: 1 cup

stats **Per serving:**

Calories: 257.58
Protein: . . . . .21.24 g
Carbohydrates: . . . . . .34.24 g
Sugar: . . . . .1.04 g
Fat: . . . . .4.43 g

1 pound shrimp, cooked
1 tablespoon olive oil
1 quart garlicky sugar-free tomato
sauce
½ cup fresh Italian flat-leaf parsley,
chopped
1 pound linguini, cooked
1 teaspoon fresh lemon zest, for
garnish

1. Toss the cooked shrimp in the oil over medium heat 2 minutes. Add the tomato sauce and parsley; cook 5 minutes.

2. Add the cooked linguine to the shrimp sauce. Sprinkle with lemon zest, and serve immediately.

tip

Try this recipe with artichokes or sun-dried tomatoes for extra sugar-free flavor.

Storing Sauces

If you make a gallon of sauce, freeze leftovers in quart-sized containers so you always have a meal at hand. If you buy sauce, be sure it's sugar-free. Most tomato sauce has sugar added.

Ziti with Sausage and Ricotta Cheese

Yields: 6 servings
Serving size: 1¼ cup

 Per serving:

Calories:............561.91
Protein:.............41.75 g
Carbohydrates: ......26.74 g
Sugar: ....5.08 g
Fat:.................31.51 g

*½ pound Italian Sausage, cut in
   small pieces*
8 ounces ricotta cheese
½ cup Parmesan cheese
2 eggs, beaten
Salt and pepper to taste
1 tablespoon oregano
8 ounces sugar-free tomato sauce
1 pound whole-wheat ziti, cooked
4 thin slices mozzarella cheese
Grated Parmesan cheese to taste

1. Preheat the oven to 350°F. Prepare a
3-quart casserole dish with nonstick spray.

2. Steam the sausage in ¼ cup boiling water
in a frying pan over medium-high heat.

3. Combine the cheeses, egg, salt, pepper,
and oregano in a separate bowl; stir in the
sausage. Mix the cooked, drained pasta with
the cheese; pour into the casserole dish.

4. Pour the tomato sauce over the top; bake
35 minutes. Just before serving, spread the
mozzarella over the top and let it melt. Serve
the Parmesan cheese on the side.

Rotini with Smoked Salmon and Cream Cheese Sauce

Yields: 6 servings
Serving size: 1 cup

 Per serving:

Calories: 208.85
Protein: . . . . .11.71 g
Carbohydrates: . . . . . .23.96 g
Sugar: . . . . .5.03 g
Fat: . . . . .7.04 g

1 cup milk, heated
1 bunch green onions, chopped
6 ounces low-fat cream cheese, room
    temperature
4 ounces smoked salmon, cut in
    small pieces
1 teaspoon Splenda
Freshly ground black pepper to taste
1 pound rotini

1. Put a pot of water on to boil for the rotini. Meanwhile, beat the warm milk, green onions, and cream cheese together. Fold in the salmon and Splenda; sprinkle with pepper.

2. Keep the sauce warm on a burner at a very low simmer until the rotini is cooked and drained. Mix, and serve.

Smoked Salmon Versus Gravlax

Smoked salmon is pure salmon, cured by warm smoke. Gravlax is salmon that's been cured in a combination of salt and sugar, which actually cooks the fish. No matter how much you scrape off the coating, some of the sugar remains.

Warm Rotini Salad with Zucchini and Feta Cheese

Yields: 6 servings
Serving size: 1 cup

 Per serving:

Calories:............434.39
Protein:.............8.58 g
Carbohydrates: ......22.99 g
Sugar: ....2.59 g
Fat:.................35.68 g

1 cup Basic Mayonnaise (page 122)
¼ cup white wine vinegar
2 small zucchini squashes, ends
    trimmed, finely diced
½ sweet red onion, minced
½ cup fresh Italian flat-leaf parsley,
    chopped
Freshly ground black pepper to taste
1 pound whole-wheat rotini, cooked
1 cup crumbled feta cheese

1. In a large bowl, mix the mayonnaise, vinegar, zucchini squash, onion, parsley, and pepper together. Cook the pasta; drain, and add to the bowl while still hot.

2. Stir in the feta cheese. Serve hot or warm, or chill to serve later.

Tortellini with Basil and Walnuts

Yields: 2 servings
Serving size: 1½ cups

 Per serving:

Calories: 938.18
Protein: . . . . .42.61 g
Carbohydrates: . . . . . .60.02 g
Sugar: . . . . .3.22 g
Fat: . . . . .71.67 g

3 teaspoons olive oil
2 teaspoons unsalted butter
4 shallots, minced
*1 cup fresh basil leaves, finely
    chopped*
freshly ground black pepper to taste
1 cup walnut pieces, toasted
½ cup finely grated Parmesan cheese
*9-ounce box frozen cheese-filled
    tortellini*
*2 tablespoons unsalted butter,
    melted*

1. Heat the oil and butter in a large sauce pan; sauté the shallots over medium heat. Reduce to a simmer; add the basil, pepper, walnuts, and cheese.

2. Cook and drain the pasta; add to the sauce.

3. Stir to coat pasta; add melted butter, and serve.

Filled Pastas

It's important to make sure the filled pastas you buy have no sugar. Some ravioli, tortellini, and other filled pastas have sugar hidden in the fine print. An alternative is to get wonton wrappers and make your own ravioli and tortellini.

Rice, Risotto, and Wild Rice

Caribbean Coconut Rice

Yields: 6 servings
Serving size: 5 ounces

 stats **Per serving:**

Calories: 307.96
Protein: . . . . 7.88 g
Carbohydrates: . . . . . . 31.44 g
Sugar: . . . . 5.5 g
Fat: . . . . 17.92 g

1 tablespoon canola oil
1 small onion, chopped
1 cup fresh pineapple, chopped
1 cup brown or white rice
1 cup unsweetened coconut cream
2 cups water
1 teaspoon salt, or to taste
1 tablespoon chili powder, or to taste
1 teaspoon Splenda
½ cup sugar-free smoked ham

1. Heat the oil in a large saucepan over medium heat; sauté the onion. Add the rest of the ingredients.

2. Cover the pan tightly; reduce heat to low. Simmer 40 minutes, stirring occasionally. Serve hot or at room temperature.

Versatile Rice

Rice is probably the most versatile of starches. It mixes well with vegetables, herbs, fish, shellfish, poultry, and just about any meat. It can magically turn into dessert in a flash; rice pudding or a rice dessert made with lots of fruit is delicious.

Baked Rice with Vegetables

Yields: 4 servings
Serving size: 8–9 ounces

stats **Per serving:**

Calories:............308.95
Protein:.............11.44 g
Carbohydrates:......45.01
Sugar: ....5.26 g
Fat:.................8.95 g

1 tablespoon olive oil
1 medium onion, minced
1 cup long-grain rice
3 cups all-natural, sugar-free chicken
    broth
1 zucchini, grated
6 radishes, trimmed and sliced
1 cup broccoli florets, cut in small
    pieces
½ cup Parmesan cheese
1 teaspoon dried basil
½ cup Italian flat-leaf parsley,
    chopped
Salt and pepper to taste

1. Preheat oven to 350°F. Heat the olive oil in a 2-quart ovenproof casserole over medium heat; sauté the onion. After about 4 minutes, add the rice; stir to coat.

2. Add the rest of the ingredients; cover. Bake 45 minutes, stirring every 10 minutes.

tip

You can throw in some sausage, leftover chicken or whatever you have on hand to add more flavor.

Saffron Rice with Shrimp, Capers, and Pine Nuts

Yields: 4 servings
Serving size: 1 cup rice and ¼ pound shrimp

 Per serving:

Calories:............340.02
Protein:.............27.69 g
Carbohydrates: ......42.32 g
Sugar: ....1.72 g
Fat:.................5.60 g

1 tablespoon unsalted butter
2 cloves garlic, minced
1 small onion, minced
1 cup rice
1 cup clam broth
2 cups chicken broth
1 tablespoon thyme
1 teaspoon freshly ground pepper
2 teaspoons saffron threads
3 tablespoons capers
1 pound medium shrimp

1. Heat the butter in a large pot over medium heat; stir in the garlic and onion and stir, cooking until softened. Add the rice; stir to coat.

2. Add the broth, thyme, pepper and saffron. Cover and reduce heat to low. Stir the rice after 15 minutes.

3. Add the capers and shrimp after 25–30 minutes. Cover; cook another 10 minutes.

Instant Rice

It's okay to use if you're in a wild rush, but instant rice is highly processed and lacks the basic good flavor of rice. Regular rice absorbs many wonderful flavors and nutrients from the veggies and broth in the cooking liquid.

Curried Rice with Nuts

Yields: 6 servings
Serving size: 5 ounces

stats **Per serving:**

Calories:............308.61
Protein:.............9.63 g
Carbohydrates: ......36.60 g
Sugar: ....4.83 g
Fat:.................14.69 g

1 tablespoon cooking oil
1 teaspoon Toasted Sesame Seed Oil (page 135)
2 onions, chopped
2 hot chiles, stemmed, seeded, and minced
3 cloves garlic, minced
1 tablespoon Madras curry powder
1 cup rice
3 cups chicken broth
1 teaspoon salt
Freshly ground black pepper to taste
1 cup roasted unsalted peanuts

1. Heat the oils in a large pot over medium heat. Add the onions, chiles, garlic, and curry powder; cook 5 minutes.

2. Add the rice; stir to coat. Add broth, salt, and pepper. Cover; reduce heat, and simmer 40 minutes.

3. Add the peanuts; mix well. Remove from heat, and serve.

Rice with Ham, Onions, and Rosemary

Yields: 6 servings
Serving size: 6 ounces

stats **Per serving:**

Calories:............226.15
Protein:.............10.25 g
Carbohydrates: ......29.89 g
Sugar: ....3.12 g
Fat:.................6.93 g

2 tablespoons cooking oil
1 red onion, minced
1 tablespoon dried rosemary or 2
    tablespoons fresh rosemary
1 teaspoon Splenda
1 cup long-grain rice
1 cup sugar-free smoked ham
3 cups chicken broth
¼ teaspoon freshly ground black
    pepper, or to taste
1 cup sugar snap peas, ends
    trimmed, cut in halves

1. Heat the oil in a large, heavy-bottomed pot over medium flame. Add onion; cook, stirring, 4 minutes. Add rosemary; stir thoroughly.

2. Add the Splenda, rice, ham, chicken broth, and pepper. Cover; cook 40 minutes, stirring once.

3. Add the peas; stir 5 minutes, until peas are hot.

Adding Meat to a Rice Dish

Since these items generally contain a great deal of sodium, do not use any salt when including them in these dishes. Ham, bacon, and sausage add a great deal of flavor, richness, and zing to the rice dishes in this chapter. You can also use them to turn a side dish into an entrée.

Fried Rice

Yields: 4 servings
Serving size: 5 ounces

 Per serving:

Calories:............251.98
Protein:.............5.13 g
Carbohydrates: ......37.95 g
Sugar: ....2 g
Fat:.................9.16 g

2 tablespoons peanut oil
1 teaspoon Toasted Sesame Seed Oil
    (page 135)
¼ cup soy sauce
1 teaspoon Splenda
1 bunch green onions, chopped
1 tablespoon fresh gingerroot,
    minced
3 cups white or brown rice, cooked

Heat the oils in a large frying pan over medium heat. Add all of the ingredients at once. Cook 4–5 minutes, stirring often.

Brown Rice with Bacon and Apples

Yields: 4 servings
Serving size: 6 ounces

 Per serving:

Calories:............234.78
Protein:.............3.70 g
Carbohydrates: ......27.82 g
Sugar: ....6.32 g
Fat:................12.42 g

4 slices sugar-free bacon
2 tablespoons cooking oil
1 cup sweet white onion, chopped
2 tart apples, peeled, cored and
     chopped
½ cup jicama, peeled and diced
1 teaspoon freshly grated nutmeg
1 teaspoon Splenda
3 cups brown rice, cooked

1. Cook the bacon until crisp; crumble, and set aside on a fresh paper towel. In a large frying pan, heat the oil over medium heat.

2. Sauté the onion about 5 minutes. Add the apples and jicama; stir. Mix in the rest of the ingredients.

Brown Rice

Brown rice has far more nutrition and flavor than white rice. White rice loses nutrients during processing, so brown rice retains more fiber and has extra vitamin B as well. The fiber makes the rice easier to digest.

Rice with Tomatoes and Olives

Yields: 6 servings

Serving size: 4½ ounces

 Per serving:

Calories: 187.38
Protein: . . . . 3.08 g
Carbohydrates: . . . . . . 28.82 g
Sugar: . . . . 3.22 g
Fat: . . . . 7.17 g

2 tablespoons cooking oil
1 medium-sized yellow onion,
    chopped
4 Roma tomatoes, stemmed and
    diced
2 tablespoons fresh lemon juice
1 teaspoon Splenda
½ cup pitted green olives, chopped
Salt and freshly ground pepper to
    taste
1 tablespoon dried basil or ¼ cup
    fresh basil, torn in small pieces
3 cups brown rice, cooked

1. Heat oil in a large, heavy-bottomed pot over medium heat. Add the onion; sauté 4–5 minutes. Stir in the tomatoes and lemon juice.

2. Stir in the Splenda, olives, salt, pepper, basil, and rice. Cover; let sit 10–15 minutes.

Risotto with Lemons and Mascarpone Cheese

Yields: 6 servings
Serving size: 5 ounces

 Per serving:

Calories: 284.40
Protein: . . . . .6.2 g
Carbohydrates: . . . . . .48.07 g
Sugar: . . . . .1 g
Fat: . . . . .5.76 g

2 tablespoons unsalted butter
½ Meyer lemon or ¼ regular lemon,
   peeled, seeded, and chopped
1½ cups Italian short-grain arborio
   rice
1 teaspoon salt
1 tablespoon red pepper flakes
½ cup Italian flat-leaf parsley,
   chopped
5 cups chicken broth
3 tablespoons mascarpone cheese

1. Heat the butter in a large, heavy-bottomed pot over medium heat. Sauté the lemon pieces quickly;. Add the rice; stir to coat.

2. Add the salt, pepper, and parsley. Stir in the broth ½ cup at a time. Add more broth as the rice absorbs the liquid.

3. As soon as the risotto "talks" to you, add another ½ cup of hot broth. When all of the broth is absorbed, stir in the mascarpone cheese. Serve hot.

Something to Say

The key to foolproof risotto is listening to what it has to tell you. Stir until you hear a hiss at the bottom of the pot. This means it's time to add more liquid to the rice; the hiss comes from it drying out. When all of the liquid is absorbed, the risotto is done. And remember, although 5 cups of water or broth seems like a great deal, ⅓ of it evaporates or is absorbed into the rice.

Risotto with Chicken Livers

Yields: 6 servings
Serving size: 5 ounces

 Per serving:

Calories:............252.50
Protein:.............9.49 g
Carbohydrates:......38.72 g
Sugar:..............0.65 g
Fat:................5.45 g

2 cups beef broth
3 cups water
3 tablespoons olive oil, divided
1 small onion, chopped
1¼ cup arborio rice
1 teaspoon salt
Freshly ground black pepper to taste
½ pound chicken livers, cleaned and
    quartered
1 teaspoon soy sauce

1. Combine the beef broth and water; heat to a simmer. Place on a back burner over low heat.

2. Heat 1 tablespoon oil in a large, heavy-bottomed pot over medium heat. Sauté the onion. Add the rice; stir to coat. Sprinkle with salt and pepper.

3. Add the broth/water combination ½ cup at a time, stirring constantly. Wait for it to hiss before adding more broth.

4. In a separate pan, heat 2 tablespoons oil. Sauté the chicken livers about 10 minutes over medium heat. Add the soy sauce.

5. Gently mix the livers into the rice, and serve.

Risotto with Seafood

Yields: 8 main course servings, 10 side dish servings
Serving size: 5 ounces as a side; 9 ounces as a main dish

stats **Per serving:**

Calories:............337.17
Protein:.............31.98 g
Carbohydrates: ......37.55 g
Sugar: ....0.58 g
Fat:.................5.32 g

2 cups clam or shrimp-shell broth
3 cups water
2 tablespoons olive oil
4 shallots, chopped
2 cloves garlic, chopped
1½ cups arborio rice
1 teaspoon Splenda
Salt and pepper to taste
1 cup Italian flat-leaf parsley,
    chopped
Juice of 1 lemon
1 pound raw shrimp, peeled and
    cleaned
½ pound bay scallops, rinsed
1 pound Alaskan crab meat, in shells,
    cut in 1" lengths

1. Heat the broth and water together in a pot; place on a back burner over low heat.

2. Heat the oil in a large, heavy-bottomed pot over medium-high heat; sauté the garlic.

3. Stir in the rice; mix to coat. Add the broth/water combination ½ cup at a time. When half of the liquid has been used up, stir in the Splenda, salt, pepper, parsley, and lemon juice.

4. Mix in the seafood; let cook 5 minutes, or until the shrimp turns pink and the crab pieces are hot.

Risotto with Cheese and Baby Spinach

Yields: 6 servings
Serving size: 6 ounces

 Per serving:

Calories: 178.84
Protein: . . . . 7.44 g
Carbohydrates: . . . . . . 26.56 g
Sugar: . . . . 3.24 g
Fat: . . . . 5.72 g

3 cups chicken broth
2 cups skim milk
2 tablespoons olive oil
1 medium yellow onion, chopped
4 cloves garlic, chopped
1½ cups arborio rice
Salt and pepper to taste
¼ teaspoon freshly grated nutmeg
Juice and zest of ½ lemon
10 ounces fresh baby spinach, stems
    removed
1 cup freshly grated Parmesan cheese

1. Heat the broth and milk to a simmer in a saucepan; place on a back burner over low heat.

2. Heat the oil in a large, heavy-bottomed pot; sauté the onion and garlic over medium heat. Add the rice; stir to coat.

3. Stir in the salt, pepper, nutmeg, and lemon juice and zest. Start adding the milk/broth combination, ½ cup at a time. When all but ½ cup of the liquid has been incorporated into the rice, stir in the spinach.

4. Cook the spinach, adding the final ½ cup of liquid. Stir in the cheese, and serve immediately.

Vegetables and Risotto

You can add cauliflower, broccoli, tomatoes, or zucchini to risotto. Seasonal vegetables lend delicious flavor to risotto dishes, so add whatever you have on hand for more variation.

Wild Rice with Pears and Pecans

Yields: 6 servings
Serving size: 5 ounces

 Per serving:

Calories:............337.81
Protein:.............6.69 g
Carbohydrates: ......39.52 g
Sugar: ....12.97 g
Fat:.................19.07 g

1 cup wild rice
3 cups chicken broth
2 tablespoons butter
4 pears, peeled, cored, and quartered
Salt and pepper to taste
1 cup toasted pecan pieces for
*   garnish*
½ cup extra broth, if necessary

1. Preheat the oven to 350°F. Mix all of the ingredients except the pecan pieces and extra broth in a casserole dish. Cover tightly; bake 90 minutes.

2. Check the rice. Add more liquid if necessary.

Wild Rice, Snow Peas, and Water Chestnuts

Yields: 6 servings
Serving size: 5 ounces

 Per serving:

Calories: 212.10
Protein:. . . . . .6.91 g
Carbohydrates: . . . . . .30.48 g
Sugar: . . . . .4.22 g
Fat:. . . . . .7.49 g

2 tablespoons olive oil
1 small onion, chopped
1 cup wild rice
3 cups chicken broth
Salt and pepper to taste
½ pound small crisp snow peas,
    stemmed
1 cup water chestnuts, drained and
    sliced
¼ cup soy sauce
1 tablespoon Toasted Sesame Seed
    Oil (page 135)
½ cup extra broth or water, if
    necessary

1. Heat olive oil in a large heavy-bottomed pot; sauté the onion over medium heat. Add the rice, broth, salt, and pepper; cover tightly, and simmer 90 minutes.

2. Stir in the snow peas, water chestnuts, soy sauce, and sesame seed oil. Add ½ cup more broth or water if the rice is too dry. Cook and stir 5 minutes, and serve hot.

This dish's wonderful, nutty flavor is the perfect complement to broiled salmon, cod, or halibut.

Wild Rice

Wild rice is an indigenous North American grain that grows in water. It grows naturally, and can also be cultivated. It is a delicious and healthy alternative to white and brown rice and risotto.

Wild Rice with Mushrooms and Rosemary

Yields: 6 servings
Serving size: 5 ounces

 Per serving:

Calories: 165.74
Protein: . . . . 7.25 g
Carbohydrates: . . . . . . 24.39 g
Sugar: . . . . 1.2 g
Fat: . . . . 5.22 g

1 cup water
2 cups beef broth
1 cup wild rice
2 tablespoons unsalted butter, cut
    in cubes
Salt and pepper to taste
2 stalks celery, coarsely chopped
1 tablespoon dried rosemary
2 cups Italian brown or white button
    mushrooms, sliced
½ cup extra broth or water, if
    necessary

1. Preheat the oven to 350°F. Put the water, broth, rice, butter, salt, pepper, celery, and rosemary in an ovenproof casserole dish.

2. Cover tightly; bake in the oven 75 minutes.

3. Add the mushrooms. If the rice is dry, add more broth or water.

4. Cover, and cook another 30 minutes.

CHAPTER

13

Vegetables and Side Dishes

Vegetable Broth

Yields: about 2½ quarts
Serving size: ¾ cup

stats **Per serving:**

Calories:. 9.83
Protein:. . . . . .0.29 g
Carbohydrates: . . . . . .2.31 g
Fat:. . . . . .0.05 g
Sat. Fat:. . . . . .0.01 g

4 carrots, peeled and chopped
2 celery stalks and leaves, chopped
1 green bell pepper, seeded and
    chopped
2 medium zucchini, chopped
1 small onion, chopped
1 cup chopped fresh spinach
2 cups chopped leeks
½ cup chopped scallions
1 cup chopped green beans
1 cup chopped parsnips
2 bay leaves
2 cloves garlic, crushed
Sea salt and freshly ground black
    pepper (optional)
3 quarts water

1. Place all of the ingredients in a large pot; bring to a boil. Reduce the heat, cover the pan, and simmer 30 minutes, or until vegetables are tender. Discard the bay leaf. Use a slotted spoon to transfer the vegetables to a different pot; mix them with some of the broth for "Free Exchange" vegetable soup. Freeze this mixture in single-serving containers to keep on hand for a quick, heat-in-the-microwave snack.

2. Strain the remaining vegetables from the broth, purée them in a blender or food processor, and return to the broth to add dietary fiber and add some body to the broth. Cool and freeze the broth until needed.

tip

If you strain the vegetables and discard them, a ½-cup serving size of the broth will have approximately 5 calories, and will still count as 1 Free Vegetable.

Perpetual Broth

The easiest way to create vegetable broth is to keep a container in your freezer for saving the liquid from cooked vegetables. Vegetable broth makes a great addition to sauces, soups, and many other recipes. You can substitute it for meat broth in most recipes, or use it instead of water for cooking pasta, rice, or other grains.

Layered Veggie Casserole

Serves 4

stats **Per serving:**

Calories:. 84.29
Protein:. . . . . .4.50 g
Carbohydrates: . . . . . .15.51 g
Fat:. . . . . .1.35 g
Sat. Fat:. . . . . .0.75 g

1 (10-ounce) package frozen mixed
    vegetables
½ cup diced onion
½ cup diced green pepper
1 cup unsalted tomato juice
⅛ teaspoon celery seed
⅛ teaspoon dried basil
⅛ teaspoon dried oregano
⅛ teaspoon dried parsley
¼ teaspoon garlic powder
3 tablespoons grated Parmesan
    cheese, divided

1. Preheat oven to 350°F. Using a large casserole dish treated with nonstick spray, layer the frozen mixed vegetables, onion, and pepper. Mix the tomato juice with the seasonings and 2 tablespoons of the Parmesan cheese; pour it over the vegetables. Cover; bake 1 hour.

2. Uncover; sprinkle with remaining Parmesan cheese, and continue to bake 10 minutes, or until the liquid thickens and the mixture bubbles.

Season First

When you ready vegetables for steaming, add fresh or dried herbs, spices, sliced or diced onions, minced garlic, grated ginger, or just about any other seasoning you'd normally use. The seasonings will cook into the vegetables during steaming.

Creamy Polenta

Serves 4

 Per serving:

Calories:............64.37
Protein:.............5.84 g
Carbohydrates: ......9.17 g
Fat:.................0.46 g
Sat. Fat:............0.16 g

1 cup skim milk
½ cup nonfat cottage cheese
¼ cup yellow cornmeal

Add the milk and cottage cheese to a blender; process until smooth. Pour the mixture into a nonstick, heavy saucepan. Over medium heat, and stirring occasionally to prevent it from scorching, heat it until it begins to steam. Slowly stir in the cornmeal. Cook, stirring constantly, 15 minutes.

Healthy Onion Rings

Serves 4

stats **Per serving, without salt:**

Calories:............110.72
Protein:.............4.39 g
Carbohydrates: ......22.16 g
Fat:.................0.53 g
Sat. Fat:............0.11 g

1 cup yellow onion slices (¼" thick)
½ cup flour
½ cup nonfat plain yogurt
½ cup bread crumbs
Sea salt and freshly ground black
*   pepper to taste (optional)*

1. Preheat oven to 350°F. Dredge the onion slices in the flour, shaking off any excess. Dip the onions in yogurt, then dredge them through the bread crumbs.

2. Prepare a baking sheet with nonstick cooking spray. Arrange the onion rings on the pan; bake 15–20 minutes. Place the onion rings under the broiler for an additional 2 minutes to brown them. Season with salt and pepper, if desired.

Oven-Baked Red Potatoes

Serves 4

stats **Per serving:**

Calories:. 119.55
Protein:. . . . . .2.29 g
Carbohydrates: . . . . . .25.85 g
Fat:. . . . . .1.24 g
Sat. Fat:. . . . . .0.18 g

1 pound (16 ounces) small red
    potatoes, halved
¼ cup fresh lemon juice
1 teaspoon olive oil
1 teaspoon sea salt
¼ teaspoon freshly ground pepper

Preheat oven to 350°F. Arrange the potatoes in a 13" × 9" ovenproof casserole dish. Combine the remaining ingredients; pour over the potatoes. Bake 30–40 minutes, or until the potatoes are tender, turning 3–4 times to baste.

Remember the Roasting "Rack"

Use caution when roasting potatoes with meat. The potatoes will act like a sponge and soak up the fat. Your best option, of course, is to use lean cuts of meat and elevate the meat and vegetable out of the fat by putting them on a roasting rack within the pan. Or, make a "bridge" by elevating the meat on stalks of celery. Discard the celery that you've used to elevate the meat.

Baked French Fries

Serves 1

 Per serving, without salt:

Calories:............118.88
Protein:.............1.67 g
Carbohydrates: ......18.34 g
Fat:.................4.59 g
Sat. Fat:............0.63 g

1 small white potato (3 ounces)
1 teaspoon olive oil
Sea salt and freshly ground black
*   pepper to taste (optional)*

1. Preheat oven to 400°F. Wash, peel, and slice the potatoes into French-fry wedges. Wrap the slices in a paper towel to remove any excess moisture. Oil the potatoes by placing them into a plastic bag with the olive oil. Close the bag and shake the potatoes until they're evenly coated. Spread potatoes on a baking sheet treated with nonstick spray; bake 5–10 minutes.

2. Remove the pan from the oven and quickly turn the potatoes. Return the pan to the oven, and bake another 10–15 minutes, depending on how crisp you prefer your fries. Season the potatoes with salt and pepper, if your diet allows for the additional sodium.

Get a Head Start

Speed up the time it takes to bake French fries! First, cook the potatoes in the microwave for 3–4 minutes in a covered, microwave-safe dish. Allow potatoes to rest for at least 1 minute after removing the dish from the microwave. Dry potatoes with paper towels, if necessary. Arrange the potatoes on a nonstick, spray–treated baking sheet. Spray the potatoes with flavored cooking spray or a few spritzes of olive oil, and bake at 400°F for 5–8 minutes to crisp them.

Baked Potato Chips

Serves 1

 Per serving, without salt:

Calories: 118.88
Protein: . . . . .1.67 g
Carbohydrates: . . . . . .18.34 g
Fat: . . . . .4.59 g
Sat. Fat: . . . . .0.63 g

1 small white potato (3 ounces)
1 teaspoon olive oil
Sea salt and freshly ground black
*   pepper to taste (optional)*

Preheat oven to 400°F. Wash, peel, and thinly slice the potatoes. Wrap the slices in a paper towel to remove any excess moisture. Spread the potatoes on a baking sheet treated with nonstick spray; spritz them with olive oil. Bake 10–15 minutes, depending on how crisp you prefer your fries. Season the potatoes with salt and pepper, if your diet allows for the additional sodium.

tip

The Nutritional Allowance for this recipe allows for the teaspoon of olive oil. Even though you just spritz the potatoes with oil, remember that "chips" have more surface area than fries do.

Fat-Cutting Alternatives

Eliminate the oil (and thus the Fat Exchange) in the Baked French Fries and Baked Potato Chips in this chapter by using butter-flavored or olive-oil cooking spray instead.

Sweet-Potato Crisps

Serves 2

 stats **Per serving, without salt:**

Calories: 89.24
Protein: . . . . .1.31 g
Carbohydrates: . . . . . .16.10 g
Fat: . . . . .2.41 g
Sat. Fat: . . . . .0.34 g

1 small sweet potato or yam
1 teaspoon olive oil
Sea salt and freshly ground black
    pepper to taste (optional)

1. Preheat oven to 400°F. Scrub the sweet potato or yam; pierce the flesh several times with a fork. Place on a microwave-safe plate; microwave 5 minutes on high. Remove from the microwave; wrap the sweet potato in aluminum foil. Set aside 5 minutes.

2. Remove the foil, peel the potato, and cut it into "French fries." Spread the fries on a baking sheet treated with nonstick spray; spritz with the olive oil. Bake 10–15 minutes, or until crisp. Season with salt and pepper, if desired.

tip

There's a risk that sweet-potato strips (French fries) will caramelize and burn. Check them often while cooking to ensure this doesn't occur, and lower the oven temperature, if necessary.

Fluffy Buttermilk Mashed Potatoes

Serves 4

 Per serving, without salt:

Calories: 97.13
Protein: . . . . 2.12 g
Carbohydrates: . . . . . . 17.86 g
Fat: . . . . 2.14 g
Sat. Fat: . . . . 1.30 g

¾ pound (12 ounces) peeled and
    boiled potatoes
¼ cup warm buttermilk
2 teaspoons unsalted butter
Sea salt and freshly ground black
    pepper to taste (optional)

Place the potatoes in a large bowl; partially mash. Add the warm buttermilk; mix well, mashing the potatoes completely. Stir in the butter and salt and pepper (if using).

If you like your mashed potatoes creamy, add some of the potato water.

323

Roasted-Garlic Mashed Potatoes

Serves 4

 Per serving, without salt:

Calories:............126.30
Protein:.............4.44 g
Carbohydrates: ......23.00 g
Fat:.................2.48 g
Sat. Fat:.............1.36 g

4 cloves roasted garlic (for roasting
    instructions, see Dry-Roasted
    Garlic on page 4)
1 small onion, chopped
¾ pound (12 ounces) peeled, cooked
    potatoes
2 cups cauliflower, steamed and
    drained
¼ cup buttermilk
⅛ cup nonfat cottage cheese
2 teaspoons unsalted butter
Sea salt and freshly ground black
    pepper to taste (optional)

Combine all the ingredients; whip until fluffy. If the potatoes or cauliflower are overly moist, add the buttermilk gradually until the whipped mixture reaches the desired consistency.

Combining steamed cauliflower with the potatoes allows you to increase the portion size without significantly changing the flavor of the mashed potatoes.

Gravy Substitute

Instead of using gravy, sprinkle crumbled bleu cheese or grated Parmesan over mashed potatoes. Just remember that cheese is a Meat Exchange, and adjust the Exchange Approximations for each serving accordingly.

Corn Casserole

Serves 2

stats **Per serving:**

Calories:............187.89
Protein:.............11.39 g
Carbohydrates: ......32.47 g
Fat:.................2.86 g
Sat. Fat:.............1.48 g

1 tablespoon finely chopped onion
1 tablespoon finely chopped green or
    red bell pepper
1 cup frozen or fresh corn kernels
⅛ teaspoon ground mace
Dash ground white or black pepper
¾ cup skim milk
¼ cup nonfat dry milk
1 egg
1 teaspoon butter

1. Preheat oven to 325°F. In a medium-sized bowl, combine the onion, bell pepper, corn, mace, and pepper; toss to mix.

2. In a blender, combine the skim milk, dry milk, egg, and butter; process until mixed. Pour over the corn mixture; toss to mix. Pour the entire mixture into a glass casserole dish treated with nonstick spray. Bake 1 hour, or until set.

Special Spice Side Effects

Ground mace or nutmeg can elevate blood pressure or cause an irregular heartbeat in some individuals. Check with your doctor or nutritionist before you add it to your diet.

Gnocchi

Serves 8

 Per serving:

Calories:.............138.72
Protein:..............4.25 g
Carbohydrates: ......27.82 g
Fat:..................0.88 g
Sat. Fat:.............0.22 g

1 cup boiled and mashed potatoes
1 egg
2 cups all-purpose or semolina flour

1. Combine the potato, egg, and flour, in a large bowl; knead until the dough forms a ball. The finished dough should be smooth, pliable, and slightly sticky. Shape 4 equal portions of the dough into long ropes, about ¾" in diameter. On a floured surface, cut the rope into ½" pieces. Press your thumb or forefinger into each piece to create an indentation.

2. Bring a large pot of water to a boil; drop in the gnocchi, being careful that the amount you add doesn't stop the water from boiling. Cook 3–5 minutes, or until the gnocchi rise to the top. Remove the gnocchi from water with a slotted spoon. Serve immediately, or, if you make it in batches, put finished gnocchi on a platter to be set in a warm oven.

tip

As a side dish, serve gnocchi with your favorite pasta sauce or dress it with a little olive oil and herbs or Parmesan cheese. (Be sure to add the extra Exchange Approximations if you do.)

Old Country Secrets

Italian cooks sometimes toss each helping of gnocchi in a teaspoon of melted butter and sugar, then sprinkle it with cinnamon to serve it as a dessert. This adds 1 Fat Exchange and 1 Carb Exchange to the Gnocchi recipe.

Artichokes with Lemon Dipping Sauce

Yields: 4 servings
Serving size: 1 artichoke

 Per serving:

Calories: 310.98
Protein: . . . . .5.84 g
Carbohydrates: . . . . . .21.31 g
Sugar: . . . . .1.98 g
Fat: . . . . .26.93 g

4 globe artichokes, trimmed
4 quarts water
1 teaspoon ground coriander seeds
Juice of 1 lemon
1 whole egg
¼ cup unsalted butter, melted
¼ cup extra-virgin olive oil
½ cup Splenda
½ teaspoon salt
½ teaspoon paprika

1. Trim any discolored leaves off the arti-chokes. Cut off the base of the stem and the very top of each artichoke. Boil in water with coriander 18–20 minutes.

2. Whirl the lemon juice and egg in your blender. Slowly pour in the melted butter, olive oil, Splenda, salt, and paprika.

3. Serve the artichokes hot or at room tem-perature, with the sauce on the side.

Tuna-Stuffed Artichokes

Yields: 4 servings
Serving size: 1½ ounces tuna and 1 artichoke

stats **Per serving:**

Calories: 212.40
Protein: . . . . 15.46 g
Carbohydrates: . . . . . . 14.82 g
Sugar: . . . . 1.53 g
Fat: . . . . 11.58 g

4 artichokes
4 quarts water
1 (6-ounce) can tuna, well drained
½ cup fresh Italian flat-leaf parsley, chopped
1 tablespoon capers
4 tablespoons Basic Mayonnaise (page 122)
1 tablespoon lemon juice
½ teaspoon Splenda
Salt and freshly ground black pepper to taste

1. Trim any discolored leaves off the artichokes. Cut off the base of the stem and the very top of each artichoke. Boil in water 18–20 minutes.

2. Cut the stem off the artichoke. Spread leaves open and, using a grapefruit spoon or melon-ball scoop, remove the choke, leaving leaves attached to the base.

3. Mix the rest of the ingredients together. Work the tuna in between the leaves and in the hole where the choke was.

This makes an excellent lunch for a hot day. Serve with a cold soup, and you can include a pasta or rice salad to round out a satisfying and sugar-free meal.

Italian Flat-Leaf Versus Curly Parsley

Both varieties of parsley are quite good, but the Italian flat leaf has a sharper flavor; it's more peppery and makes a really great garnish or aromatic herb. Curly parsley has a different texture and a less distinct flavor. Experiment with both and decide for yourself which you prefer.

Asparagus with Chopped-Egg Sauce

Yields: 4 servings
Serving size: ¼ pound of asparagus

 Per serving:

Calories:............154.75
Protein:..............4.98 g
Carbohydrates: ......6.53 g
Sugar: ....2.94 g
Fat:.................12.16 g

4 tablespoons Basic Mayonnaise
    (page 122)
1 tablespoon Pinot Grigio vinegar
¼ cup chopped parsley
1 teaspoon Splenda
1 teaspoon lemon zest
Salt and pepper to taste
1 whole egg and 1 egg white,
    hardboiled and chopped
4 green onions, chopped
1 pound asparagus, ends trimmed

1. Mix the mayonnaise, vinegar, parsley, Splenda, lemon zest, salt and pepper, eggs, and onions in a small bowl. Steam the asparagus 5 minutes. Shock it, drain it, and place on a serving plate.

2. Arrange asparagus on a platter and drizzle sauce over it. Serve hot or at room temperature.

This is a very special side that goes extremely well with fish or shellfish. Add an extra egg and serve it on whole-wheat English muffins for lunch.

Broccoli Stir-Fry

Yields: 4 servings
Serving size: 5 ounces

 Per serving:

Calories:............293.19
Protein:.............11.81 g
Carbohydrates: ......12.57 g
Sugar: ....3.43 g
Fat:................21.12 g

1 pound broccoli florets, stems
    removed
2 tablespoons olive oil
1 tablespoon Toasted Sesame Seed
    Oil (page 135)
2 cloves garlic, chopped
2 shallots, chopped
4 ounces of chorizo, chopped
8 ounces shiitake mushrooms,
    cleaned and stemmed
2 tablespoons lemon juice
2 tablespoons soy sauce
Freshly ground black pepper to taste

1. Drop the broccoli into a pot of boiling salted water. Blanch 3 minutes, shock in cold water, and drain and dry on paper towels.

2. Place a wok over medium-high heat. Add both oils, garlic, shallots, chorizo, and mushrooms; cook, stirring, 5 minutes.

3. Return the broccoli to the pan; continue to stir-fry another 3–5 minutes. Sprinkle with lemon juice and soy sauce. Serve with plenty of freshly ground black pepper.

Broccoli is an excellent source of fiber and vitamins, which act as protective antioxidants. Every weekly menu should include two or more servings of broccoli, whether you are eating sugar-free or simply want to be healthy.

Salt Versus Soy

Soy sauce is a fine substitute for salt; you do not need to use any salt when you are using soy. You can also use herbs, such as oregano or borage, as salt substitutes. Soy sauce also has sugar, so whenever possible use tamari or sugar-free soy sauce.

Eggplant Rolls

Yields: 6 servings
Serving size: 2 rolls

 stats **Per serving:**

Calories: 175.05
Protein: . . . . 9.28 g
Carbohydrates: . . . . . . 13.77 g
Sugar: . . . . 5.48 g
Fat: . . . . 10.07 g

1 cup low-fat ricotta cheese
1 egg
¼ cup Parmesan cheese
1 teaspoon dried oregano
⅛ teaspoon or a good grinding of
    black pepper
2 medium eggplants, thinly sliced
2 tablespoons olive oil in a spray
    container
1 cup quick tomato sauce (page 274)

1. Preheat the oven to 350°F. In a bowl, whisk together the ricotta cheese, egg, Parmesan, oregano, and pepper; set aside.

2. Place the eggplant slices on a piece of parchment paper. Spray both sides with olive oil; bake 5–8 minutes.

3. Cool slightly, and spread a spoonful of the cheese mixture on each. Roll.

4. Place in a baking dish that you have prepared with nonstick spray. Cover with tomato sauce; bake 30 minutes.

 tip

Eggplants contain complex carbs, and are excellent for a sugar-free diet.

Eggplant Soufflé

Yields: 4 servings
Serving size: 3 tablespoons

 Per serving:

Calories: 133.70
Protein: . . . . .7.11 g
Carbohydrates: . . . . . .13.99 g
Sugar: . . . . .6.66 g
Fat: . . . . .6.30 g

1 medium eggplant, peeled and
    cubed
1 teaspoon salt
1 tablespoon olive oil
1 clove garlic
½ cup sweet white onion, diced
1 teaspoon dried oregano
1 teaspoon dried basil
Juice of ½ lemon
½ teaspoon salt
Freshly ground black pepper to taste
2 egg yolks
4 egg whites, beaten stiff
½ cup sugar-free tomato sauce

1. In a large bowl, sprinkle the cubed eggplant with salt. Let rest 20 minutes; squeeze out the liquid using paper towels or linen kitchen towels.

2. Preheat oven to 400°F. Prepare a 1-quart soufflé dish with nonstick cooking spray. Heat the olive oil in a nonstick sauté pan over medium flame; sauté the eggplant, garlic, and onion.

3. Remove from the heat and place in a food processor; add the herbs and pulse. Add the salt, pepper, and egg yolks; pulse until smooth.

4. Pour into the soufflé dish; fold in egg whites. Bake 35–40 minutes, or until puffed and golden. Serve with warm tomato sauce.

Eggplant

Soak or salt exceptionally large eggplants to reduce the bitterness; larger eggplants tend to be more bitter than smaller ones. The tiny white, mauve, and purple ones are always sweet. They are too young to get bitter—just like other babies.

Eggplant, Tomatoes, and Peppers

Yields: 6 servings
Serving size: one eggplant

 Per serving:

Calories: 99.87
Protein: . . . . .2.02 g
Carbohydrates: . . . . . .13.87 g
Sugar: . . . . .7.45 g
Fat: . . . . .5.09 g

2 tablespoons olive oil
6 tiny eggplants, stemmed and diced
3 cloves garlic, chopped
1 medium-sized red onion, chopped
1 sweet red bell pepper, stemmed,
    seeded, and chopped
1 sweet green bell pepper, stemmed,
    seeded, and chopped
1 tablespoon capers
4 medium-sized plum tomatoes,
    stemmed and chopped
1 teaspoon Splenda
1 teaspoon salt
20 basil leaves, rinsed and torn
1 teaspoon dried oregano
1 teaspoon red pepper flakes

1. Heat the olive oil in a large sauté or frying pan over medium-high heat. Add the eggplant, stirring constantly.

2. Every 2 minutes stir in the next ingredient. Cover, reduce heat to low, and cook 10 minutes.

 tip

You can serve this recipe as a side dish, as an hors d'oeuvre, or over salad greens. You can also spoon it into hot pasta for a nutritious lunch or supper.

Baked Yellow and Green Squash, Dressed in Herbs with Crumb Topping

Yields: 4 servings
Serving size: ⅔ cup

 Per serving:

Calories: 278.89
Protein:. . . . . .5.08 g
Carbohydrates: . . . . . .21.38 g
Sugar: . . . . .4.31 g
Fat:. . . . . .19.86 g

1 teaspoon dried oregano leaves
1 teaspoon dried rosemary leaves
½ cup unsalted butter, melted
Juice of ½ lemon
1 teaspoon salt and freshly ground
    black pepper to taste
1 large zucchini, ends removed, sliced
    ¼" thick
1 large yellow squash, ends removed,
    sliced ¼" thick
1 sweet red onion, thinly sliced
1 cup sugar-free bread crumbs

1. Preheat the oven to 350°F. Prepare a disposable bread tin with nonstick spray.

2. Whisk the herbs into the butter; add lemon juice, salt and pepper.

3. Layer the zucchini, squash, and onion in a baking dish. Sprinkle each layer with the melted butter and some bread crumbs.

4. When you get to the top, sprinkle with remaining bread crumbs, and add the rest of the melted butter. Bake 35 minutes.

You can add to the protein in this dish by putting a layer of white American or grated Fontina cheese in between the layers of squash.

Mix It Up

You can bake, steam, or sauté many different vegetables. Don't be afraid of adding some colorful peppers, a tomato or two, and some onions to just about any vegetable dish. Use whatever you have fresh and in season.

Baked Stuffed Mushrooms

Yields: 12 mushrooms
Serving size: 3 mushrooms

 stats **Per serving:**

Calories:............339.54
Protein:.............11.08 g
Carbohydrates: ......24.64 g
Sugar: ....2.85 g
Fat:.................21.98 g

12 white or brown mushrooms,
    stems trimmed
12 white or brown mushroom stems,
    chopped
¼ cup olive oil
2 cloves garlic
1 stalk celery, minced
4 shallots, minced
4 sprigs Italian flat-leaf parsley,
    stemmed and chopped
1 teaspoon oregano
1 cup sugar-free bread crumbs
½ cup freshly grated Parmesan
    cheese
¼ cup pepperoni sausage, finely
    chopped
3 tablespoons chicken broth, more if
    necessary

1. Preheat the oven to 350°F. Brush the mushrooms clean; place them on a baking sheet over parchment paper. Reserve the chopped stems.

2. Heat the olive oil in a large sauté pan over medium flame. Stir in the garlic, celery, shallots, parsley, and oregano.

3. Cook, stirring constantly. Add the chopped mushroom stems. Mix in the rest of the ingredients, moistening with the broth.

4. Pile stuffing into the mushroom caps, about 1 heaping tablespoon of filling per mushroom; bake 25 minutes. Serve hot or at room temperature.

Baked Stuffed Tomatoes with Herbs and Cashews

Yields: 4 servings
Serving size: 1 tomato, plus nuts and herbs

stats **Per serving:**

Calories:. 245.38
Protein:. . . . . .6.97 g
Carbohydrates: . . . . . .29.48 g
Sugar: . . . . .6.30 g
Fat:. . . . . .11.45 g

4 ripe, medium-sized tomatoes
4 teaspoons olive oil
1 small red onion, minced
½ cup cashews, toasted and chopped
1 cup fresh sugar-free bread crumbs
1 teaspoon dried thyme leaves or 1
    tablespoon fresh thyme
Salt and freshly ground pepper to
    taste
2 tablespoons sugar-free tomato or
    freshly squeezed lemon juice

1. Preheat oven to 350°F. Prepare a baking pan with parchment paper or nonstick spray. Cut the tops off the tomatoes; remove seeds and pulp with a melon-ball scoop or grapefruit spoon.

2. Arrange the tomatoes on the baking sheet. Heat the olive oil in a large sauté pan over medium flame.

3. Add the ingredients listed one by one. When cooked 4–5 minutes, pile into tomato shells.

4. Bake 40 minutes.

Stuffed Tomatoes

It's amazing the myriad delicious things you can stuff into tomatoes. Various vegetables, nuts, sausages, shrimp, scallops, and different herbs all make intensely flavored fillings. You can also use cooked rice, meats, and shellfish for cold stuffed tomatoes.

Spinach-Stuffed Yellow Tomatoes

Yields: 4 servings
Serving size: 1 tomato

 Per serving:

Calories:............225.01
Protein:.............11.47 g
Carbohydrates: ......20.57 g
Sugar: ....1.25 g
Fat:................12.06 g

4 ripe, medium-sized yellow
    tomatoes
1 teaspoon salt
½ teaspoon freshly ground black
    pepper, or to taste
1 teaspoon Splenda
2 tablespoons olive oil
2 cloves garlic, minced
1 (10-ounce) package frozen,
    chopped spinach, thawed, all
    moisture squeezed out
⅛ teaspoon nutmeg
Juice of ½ lemon
½ cup grated Parmesan cheese
½ cup fresh bread crumbs

1. Preheat oven to 350°F. Prepare a baking pan with parchment paper or nonstick spray. Cut the tops off the tomatoes; remove seeds and pulp with a melon-ball scoop or grapefruit spoon.

2. Place the tomatoes in the baking pan. Sprinkle the insides with salt, pepper, and Splenda.

3. Sauté the garlic 3 minutes in a sauté pan over medium heat. Add the spinach and nutmeg; sprinkle with lemon juice.

4. Remove the pan from the stove; stir in the cheese and bread crumbs. Stuff the tomatoes, and bake 30 minutes. Serve hot.

Kohlrabi with Lemon

Yields: 4 servings
Serving size: ⅔ cup

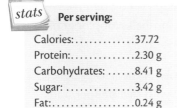 **Per serving:**

Calories: 37.72
Protein: . . . . .2.30 g
Carbohydrates: . . . . . .8.41 g
Sugar: . . . . .3.42 g
Fat: . . . . .0.24 g

1 pound kohlrabi, stems removed,
   peeled and sliced
½ cup sugar-free chicken broth
Juice of ½ lemon
Salt and pepper to taste
½ cup fresh parsley, chopped for
   garnish

Place the kohlrabi slices in a saucepan. Add the broth, lemon juice, salt, and pepper; simmer over low heat 25–30 minutes. Serve hot.

Grating Your Own Cheese

A chunk of high-grade imported Parmesan cheese will last for months in the refrigerator when stored in a plastic bag. It only takes seconds to grate cheese, and is very well worth the time. Freshly grated cheese has a stronger flavor, and you get exactly the amount you want.

Fennel with Orange Slices

Yields: 4 servings
Serving size: 1 quarter bulb

stats **Per serving:**

Calories: 107.86
Protein: . . . . 1.30 g
Carbohydrates: . . . . . . 11.56 g
Sugar: . . . . 6.48 g
Fat: . . . . 6.96 g

1 large fennel bulb, trimmed and
    quartered
2 tablespoons olive oil
½ cup freshly squeezed orange juice
1 temple or navel orange, skin on,
    seeds removed, sliced ½" thick
    for garnish

1. Preheat oven to 350°F. Place the fennel chunks in a baking pan; drizzle with oil and orange juice. Cover with aluminum foil.

2. Roast 35–40 minutes. Remove the foil covering, baste with pan juice, and broil until slightly singed. Garnish with orange slices.

tip

Fennel, also called anise, can be grilled when you've got a charcoal fire going.

Vegetable Options

You can add baby beets to fennel with delicious results, or you can make it very savory with herbs and tomatoes. During the summer, put the fronds on the grill when you are grilling fish or chicken. It's also great raw in salads.

Pumpkin Soufflé

Yields: 6 servings
Serving size: 4 tablespoons

 Per serving:

Calories:............123.23
Protein:.............4.56 g
Carbohydrates:......8.05 g
Sugar: ....2.41 g
Fat:.................9.92 g

1 (13-ounce) can pureed pumpkin,
    unsweetened
2 egg yolks
½ cup whipping cream or
    half-and-half
2 tablespoons Splenda
¼ teaspoon cloves
½ teaspoon cinnamon
¼ teaspoon nutmeg
¼ teaspoon allspice
1 teaspoon salt
1 teaspoon orange zest
5 egg whites, beaten stiff

1. Preheat the oven to 400°F. Prepare a soufflé dish with nonstick spray.

2. Put all but the egg whites in your electric mixer; beat until smooth.

3. Gently fold in the egg whites; scrape into the soufflé mold. Bake 55 minutes.

4. Check for doneness by inserting a knife. If it comes out clean, the soufflé is done. Serve immediately.

Sauerkraut with Apples and Ham

Yields: 4 servings
Serving size: ⅔ cup

 Per serving:

Calories:............127.58
Protein:.............6.87 g
Carbohydrates: ......14.77 g
Sugar: ....9.17 g
Fat:................5.32 g

1 tablespoon canola oil
½ sweet red onion, coarsely chopped
2 tart apples, cored and chopped,
    skins on
¼ pound smoked ham, diced
2 cups canned or packaged sugar-
    free sauerkraut
2 teaspoons Splenda
½ teaspoon pepper, or to taste
½ teaspoon caraway seeds

1. Heat the oil in a large frying pan over medium heat.

2. Stir in the onion and apples; sauté 4 minutes. Stir in the rest of the ingredients.

3. Cook, stirring, another 5 minutes. Serve hot.

CHAPTER 14

Sweet-Treats, Small Meals, and Snack Food

Honey-Raisin Bars

Yields: 18 bars

stats **Per serving:**

Calories:............71.23
Protein:.............1.36 g
Carbohydrates: ......12.19 g
Fat:.................2.16 g
Sat. Fat:............0.24 g

½ cup unbleached all-purpose flour
¼ teaspoon baking soda
⅛ teaspoon sea salt
¼ teaspoon cinnamon
¾ cup quick-cooking oatmeal
1 egg white, slightly beaten
2½ tablespoons sunflower oil
¼ cup honey
¼ cup skim milk
½ teaspoon vanilla
½ cup golden raisins

1. Preheat oven to 350°F. Sift the flour, soda, salt, and cinnamon together into a bowl; stir in the oatmeal.

2. In another bowl, mix the slightly beaten egg whites with the oil, honey, milk, vanilla, and raisins; add the flour mixture to liquid ingredients. Drop by teaspoon onto cookie sheets treated with nonstick spray. Bake 12–15 minutes. (Longer baking time will result in crispier cookies.) Cool on a baking rack.

3. For cookie bars, spread the mixture in an even layer on a piece of parchment paper placed on the cookie sheet; bake 15–18 minutes. Cool slightly, then use a sharp knife or pizza cutter to slice into 18 equal pieces (6 down, 3 across).

tip

If you like chewier cookies or need to cut the fat in your diet, you can substitute applesauce, plums, prunes, or mashed banana for the sunflower oil.

No-Bake Chocolate-Peanut Butter Oatmeal Cookies

Serves 12

 stats **Per serving, with granulated sugar:**

Calories: 87.02
Protein: . . . . .1.66 g
Carbohydrates: . . . . . .13.39 g
Fat: . . . . .3.14 g
Sat. Fat: . . . . .1.49 g

2 tablespoons butter
¼ cup cocoa
½ cup granulated sugar
¼ cup mock cream
Dash of sea salt
1 teaspoon vanilla
1 tablespoon peanut butter
1½ cups oatmeal

1. Add the butter to a deep, microwave-safe bowl; microwave on high 20–30 seconds, or until the butter is melted. Add the cocoa; stir to blend. Stir in the sugar, Mock Cream, and salt. Microwave on high 1 minute and 10 seconds to bring to a full boil. (Should you need to microwave the batter some more, do so in 10-second increments. You want a full boil, but because it will continue to cook for a while once it's removed from the microwave, heating it too long can cause the mixture to scorch.)

2. Add the vanilla and peanut butter; stir until mixed. Fold in the oatmeal. Drop by tablespoonful on waxed paper, and allow to cool.

Easy Graham-Cracker Goodies

A little of this rich peanut butter and cream cheese goes a long way. To make 4 treats, mix 1 teaspoon peanut butter, 1 teaspoon cream cheese, and 2 teaspoons powdered sugar until well blended. Divide between 6 whole graham crackers. Spread an equal amount of the icing on top of each graham cracker. Allow 3 open-faced squares per serving. The Analysis is: Calories: 145.65; Protein: 2.76 g; Carbohydrate: 23.22 g; Fat: 4.74 g; Sat. Fat: 1.08 g; Cholesterol: 1.83 mg; Sodium: 201.91 mg; Fiber: 1.1 g.

Powdered Sugar-Coated Cocoa Cookies

Yields: 24 cookies
Serving size: 1 cookie

 Per serving, using plums packed in heavy syrup:

Calories: 65.82
Protein: . . . . 0.88 g
Carbohydrates: . . . . . . 13.78 g
Fat: . . . . 1.36 g
Sat. Fat: . . . . 0.73 g

1 tablespoon ground flaxseed
2 tablespoons water or plum juice
2 tablespoons unsalted butter
⅜ cup cocoa powder
⅔ cup firmly packed brown sugar
½ teaspoon vanilla extract
¼ cup mashed plums
⅔ cup white rice flour
⅓ cup Ener-G potato flour
½ teaspoon baking soda
⅛ teaspoon sea salt
¼ cup powdered sugar
¹⁄₁₆ teaspoon ground black pepper
     (optional)

1. In a microwave-safe cup, combine the flax-seed with the water or plum juice; microwave on high 15–30 seconds. Stir the mixture. (It should have the consistency of a thick egg white; this mixture is an egg substitute.)

2. Add the butter to a microwave-safe mixing bowl; microwave 15–20 seconds, until the butter is melted. Add the cocoa; blend into the butter. Mix in the flaxseed mixture, along with the brown sugar and vanilla.

3. Add mashed plums to the other ingredients. (If you wish to remove the plum skins, push the fruit through a mesh sieve. The skins add some fiber to the snack, but you may not like how they look. You can use a food processor to pulverize the plum skins.) Stir to combine. Blend in the flours, baking soda, and salt until a dough forms. Refrigerate 1–2 hours, or until the mixture is firm enough to shape into balls.

Powdered Sugar-Coated Cocoa Cookies

(continued)

4. Preheat oven to 350°F. Form a heaping teaspoon of the dough into a ball, roll it in powdered sugar, and place on an ungreased cookie sheet. Use the back of a fork to flatten each cookie. Bake cookies 8–10 minutes, or until firm. Cool completely on wire racks. Season with pepper if you want to add some kick.

Comparative Analysis

Consider other substitutions, too. This analysis allows for all-purpose flour and plums canned in juice. The powdered sugar is omitted. Calories: 57.83; Protein: 0.92 g; Carbohydrate: 11.26 g; Fat: 1.37 g; Sat. Fat: 0.73 g; Cholesterol: 2.59 mg; Sodium: 41.15 mg; Fiber: 0.75 g.

Tortilla Chips

Serves 1

stats **Per serving, without sea salt:**

Calories: 60
Protein: 1
Carbohydrates: 12g
Fat: 0.5g
Sat. Fat: 0g

1 nonfat corn tortilla
Olive oil
Sea salt to taste (optional)
Seasoning blend of your choice, to
*   taste*

Preheat oven to 400°F. Spray both sides of the tortilla with olive oil. Season lightly with sea salt or any season blend. Bake the tortilla on a cookie sheet until crisp and beginning to brown, about 2–5 minutes, depending on the thickness of the tortilla. Break the tortilla into large pieces.

tip

When you buy the tortillas, look for a brand made with only cornmeal, water, and lime juice. Nutritional Analysis and Exchange Approximations will depend on the brand of tortillas and the amount of oil you use.

Black-Olive Mock Caviar

Yields: 1¼ cups
Serving size: 1 tablespoon

 Per serving:

Calories: 20.91
Protein: . . . . 0.14 g
Carbohydrates: . . . . . . 1.24 g
Fat: . . . . 1.63 g
Sat. Fat: . . . . 0.10 g

1 (5¾-ounce) can chopped black
    olives
1 (4-ounce) can chopped green chili
    peppers
1 cup diced fresh or canned no-salt-
    added tomatoes
2 tablespoons chopped green onions
1 clove garlic, minced
1 tablespoon extra-virgin olive oil
1 teaspoon red wine vinegar
Pinch of sugar
½ teaspoon freshly ground black
    pepper

In a medium-sized mixing bowl, mix together all the ingredients. Cover; chill overnight. Serve cold or at room temperature.

Snack Mix

Serves: 16
Serving Size: ½ cup

stats **Per serving, on average:**

Calories:. 125.00
Protein:. . . . . 3.00 g
Carbohydrates: . . . . . . 16.00 g
Total Fat: . . . . variable
Cholesterol:. . . . . 3.89 mg

6 cups mixed cereal (such as a
    mixture of unsweetened bran,
    oat, rice, and wheat cereals)
1 cup mini bow-knot pretzels
⅔ cup dry-roasted peanuts
⅛ cup (2 tablespoons) butter, melted
⅛ cup (2 tablespoons) olive, canola,
    or peanut oil
1 tablespoon Worcestershire sauce
¼ teaspoon garlic powder
Tabasco sauce or other liquid hot
    pepper sauce to taste (optional)

1. Preheat oven to 300°F.

2. In a large bowl, combine the cereals, pretzels, and peanuts. In another bowl, combine the butter, oil, Worcestershire, garlic powder, and Tabasco (if using). Pour over the cereal mixture; toss to coat evenly.

3. Spread the mixture on a large baking sheet; bake 30–40 minutes, stirring every 10 minutes, until crisp and dry. Cool, and store in an airtight container. Serve at room temperature.

tip

The Nutritional Analysis will depend on the type of fat and cereals used in the recipe, most notably regarding the PCF Ratio.

Zucchini with Cheese Spread

Serves 8

 stats **Per serving:**

Calories:. 38.00
Protein:. . . . . .4.00 g
Carbohydrates: . . . . . .4.00 g
Fat:. . . . . .trace
Sat. Fat:. . . . . .trace

1 large green zucchini
⅓ cup softened fat-free cream cheese
¼ cup finely chopped red bell pepper
2 teaspoons dried parsley
¼ teaspoon onion powder
¼ teaspoon dried Italian seasoning
2 drops red pepper sauce
1 green onion, thinly sliced

Peel the zucchini and cut it into ¼" slices. Mix together the remaining ingredients, except the green onion, until well blended. Spread 1–2 teaspoons of the cream cheese mixture onto each slice of zucchini; place on a serving platter. Sprinkle with green onion; cover, and refrigerate 1 hour, or until firm.

Simple Substitutions

Squash seeds are delicious when roasted, too. Serve them as snacks or as a garnish on soups or salads.

Asian Popcorn

Serves 1

 stats **Per serving:**

Calories:.............128.78
Protein:..............4.72 g
Carbohydrates: ......26.01 g
Total Fat: ....1.34 g
Sat. Fat:..............0.18 g

4 cups air-popped popcorn
1 teaspoon Bragg's Liquid Aminos or
    low-sodium soy sauce
2 teaspoons fresh lemon juice
1 teaspoon five-spice powder
¼ teaspoon ground coriander
¼ teaspoon garlic powder

1. Preheat oven to 250°F. Spread the popcorn on a nonstick cookie sheet; lightly coat with nonstick or butter-flavored cooking spray.

2. Mix together all the remaining ingredients. Drizzle the mixture over the popcorn; lightly toss to coat evenly. Bake 5 minutes; toss the popcorn and rotate the pan, then bake an additional 5 minutes. Serve warm.

Microwave Popcorn—from Scratch

To make "air-popped" popcorn in the microwave, add 1 cup of popcorn to a small brown-paper bag. Fold down the top. Spray the bag with water (or wet your hand and tap water on each side and the bottom of the bag). Microwave on high for 3 minutes, or use the popcorn setting if your microwave has it.

Keeping Snacks in Stock

Because there are no oils to go rancid, air-popped popcorn will keep for weeks if you store it in an airtight container. Pop up a large batch and keep some on hand for later. Then, depending on your mood, flavor it according to the suggestions in this section, and you'll soon have a warm, healthy snack.

Popcorn is a great snack: It's filling, it's good for you, and it's easy to prepare and keep on hand. Try the following varieties so you don't get bored.

Dilled-Ranch Popcorn—Variation

½ teaspoon ranch-style dip mix
⅛ teaspoon dried dill
⅛ teaspoon onion powder
Pinch of dried lemon peel
Italian Spiced Popcorn
1 teaspoon dried Italian herbs
⅛ teaspoon cayenne pepper
1 teaspoon grated Parmesan cheese

Mexican Popcorn—Variation

1 tablespoon dried Mexican-spiced
   salad-dressing mix
¼ teaspoon crushed dried oregano
¼ teaspoon crushed dried thyme
¼ teaspoon garlic powder

Pizza Popcorn—Variation

1 tablespoon Mrs. Dash Tomato
   Basil Garlic Blend
¼ teaspoon onion powder
1 tablespoon grated Parmesan
   cheese

Toasted Pumpkin Seeds

Serves 8

stats **Per serving, without salt:**

Calories:. 201.56
Protein:. . . . . .8.47 g
Carbohydrates: . . . . . .6.14 g
Fat:. . . . . .17.51 g
Sat. Fat:. . . . . .3.22 g

*2 cups pumpkin seeds, scooped from
a fresh pumpkin*
*1 tablespoon olive, peanut, or canola
oil*
Sea salt (optional)

1. Rinse the pumpkin seeds, removing all pulp and strings. Spread the seeds in a single layer on a large baking sheet; let them air dry at least 3 hours.

2. Preheat oven to 375°F. Drizzle the oil over the seeds; lightly sprinkle with salt, if using. (Alternative method would be to put dried pumpkin seeds in a plastic bag and add the oil. Seal the bag and toss to mix the seeds with the oil.) Toss; spread out in a single layer. Bake 15–20 minutes, until lightly browned and toasted. Stir the seeds occasionally during baking to allow for even browning. Remove the hulls to eat.

Coffee-Spice Snack Cake

Serves 16

 stats **Per serving:**

Calories: 172.00
Protein: . . . . 2.65 g
Carbohydrates: . . . . . . 36.57 g
Fat: . . . . 2.25 g
Sat. Fat: . . . . 0.40 g

1 cup honey
½ cup strong brewed coffee
1 tablespoon brandy
½ cup reduced-fat egg substitute
2 tablespoons olive oil
½ cup firmly packed brown sugar
2 cups all-purpose flour
1½ teaspoons baking powder
1½ teaspoons baking soda
½ teaspoon salt
½ teaspoon ground cinnamon
¼ teaspoon ground ginger
⅛ teaspoon ground nutmeg
⅛ teaspoon ground cloves

1. Preheat oven to 325°F. Add the honey, coffee, and brandy to a bowl; mix well. Add the egg substitute, oil, and brown sugar; beat until combined.

2. Sift together the flour, baking powder, baking soda, salt, and spices; fold into the mixture. Pour the batter into a 9" square baking dish treated with nonstick cooking spray. Bake 50–60 minutes, or until an inserted toothpick comes out clean. Slice into 16 pieces.

Hot Miniature Stromboli

Yields: 6 servings
Serving size: 3 pieces

stats **Per serving:**

Calories:.............216.71
Protein:..............15.04 g
Carbohydrates: ......2.12 g
Sugar: ....0.67 g
Fat:..................16.84 g

16 very thin slices hard salami
16 very thin slices provolone cheese
16 basil leaves
16 toothpicks
Sugar-free Dijon-style mustard (see below) or Vinaigrette (see below)

1. Preheat oven to 475°F. Prepare a cookie sheet with nonstick spray. Lay the salami slices on the cookie sheet.

2. Place a piece of cheese and a basil leaf on each piece of salami. Roll them very tightly.

3. Skewer the rolls with toothpicks; bake 6–8 minutes, or until the salami is slightly brown and the cheese melts. Carefully cut into thirds to make 18 pieces. Serve hot! Dip into mustard or salad dressing.

tip

If you're using wooden toothpicks, soak them in water for 20 minutes prior to use. You could also use metal toothpicks, but stay away from plastic toothpicks, which will melt. Most imported Italian salami is sugar-free, but ask a deli employee to check the label for you.

Sugar-free Dijon-style mustard or Vinaigrette

Blend 2 teaspoons dry Dijon mustard, ¼ cup white wine vinegar, 1 teaspoon Splenda, plus extra to taste, 1 teaspoon dried dill weed, ½ teaspoon Tamari, 1 whole egg, ½ teaspoon salt, Freshly ground white pepper to taste, ¾ cup olive oil in a blender. Pour into a jar or bottle and refrigerate. The analysis is: Calories: 67.3, Protein: 0.33 g, Carbohydrates: 0.15 g, Sugar: 0.02 g, Fat: 7.28 g. Yields: 1 cup; Serving size: 2 teaspoons.

Creamy Fruit Cup

Serves 1

 stats **Per serving, without additional applesauce or jelly:**

Calories: 128.62
Protein: . . . . 6.52 g
Carbohydrates: . . . . . . 26.42 g
Fat: . . . . 0.52 g
Sat. Fat: . . . . 0.13 g

4 ounces (½ of a small container) nonfat plain yogurt
1 tablespoon unsweetened applesauce
1 teaspoon lemon juice
½ cup cubed fresh or frozen cantaloupe
¼ cup cubed or sliced apple
6 seedless red or green grapes
Lemon zest (optional)

Mix together the yogurt, applesauce, and lemon juice; drizzle over the mixed fruit. (If you prefer a sweeter dressing, you can add another tablespoon of applesauce or blend in 2 teaspoons of Smucker's Low-Sugar Apple Jelly without increasing the number of Fruit Exchanges; adjust the calorie count accordingly.) For a more zesty (and attractive!) dish, sprinkle lemon zest over the top of the dressing.

 tip

Prepare the Creamy Fruit Cup for your lunchbox! If you do, keep the dressing and fruits in separate containers until you're ready to serve. To keep the lemon zest moist, you can mix it in with the dressing.

Just Juice?

Fruit and fruit juice provide healthy nutrients, and, in most cases, fiber, too. That's the good news. The downside is they also convert quickly to glucose. For that reason, many people can only consume them as part of a meal, rather than alone as a snack.

Tiny Italian Meatballs with Pine Nuts

Yields: 70 meatballs
Serving size: 3 meatballs

 Per serving:

Calories: 66.24
Protein: . . . . .5.40 g
Carbohydrates: . . . . . .4.96 g
Sugar: . . . . .2.19 g
Fat: . . . . .2.23 g

1 pound lean ground sirloin
3 cloves garlic, minced
½ cup dried sugar-free bread crumbs
1 whole egg, beaten
1 teaspoon Splenda
½ teaspoon ground cinnamon
1 teaspoon salt
1 teaspoon dried oregano leaves
⅔ cup pine nuts
½ cup raisins with no sugar added
    (optional)

1. Preheat oven to 375°F. Prepare 2 cookie sheets with nonstick spray. Mix all ingredients thoroughly with your fingers.

2. Roll into marble-sized meatballs, about ¾" in diameter. Bake 8–10 minutes, turning the cookie sheets once to make sure they all get equal heat.

3. Serve on toothpicks, in sauce, or in mini hero sandwiches.

Ham-Wrapped Asparagus

Yields: 36 snacks
Serving size: 3 asparagus stalks

 Per serving:

Calories: 139.01
Protein: . . . . 7.08 g
Carbohydrates: . . . . . . 11.12 g
Sugar: . . . . .0.68 g
Fat: . . . . .8.39 g

12 very thin slices sugar-free white or
    wheat bread, crusts removed
2 tablespoons unsalted butter, room
    temperature
12 slices sugar-free smoked ham
3 tablespoons mascarpone cheese,
    room temperature
12 stalks frozen asparagus, thawed
3 tablespoons unsalted butter,
    melted

1. Prepare a cookie sheet with nonstick spray.

2. Lay out the bread; spread butter on it. Place the ham on the bread. Thinly spread the mascarpone on the ham. Add a stalk of asparagus to each slice of bread.

3. Roll the asparagus, ham, and bread tightly. Put the seam face down on the cookie sheet; brush with melted butter. Freeze 2 hours, or overnight.

4. Preheat the oven to 375°F. Cut each frozen roll in 3 pieces. Bake until lightly browned, about 15 minutes. Serve hot.

Frozen Vegetables

Although most chefs prefer fresh vegetables, most of us can't get to a green market on a daily basis. Some of the best of the frozen vegetables are baby peas, asparagus, artichoke hearts, broccoli, and Brussels sprouts. Frozen, chopped spinach is very useful for omelets and other dishes; just make sure to thaw it and squeeze all of the liquid out prior to using.

Crispy Sesame Chicken Tenders

Yields: 6 servings
Serving size: 3 pieces

 Per serving:

Calories: 156.42
Protein: . . . . .7.06 g
Carbohydrates: . . . . . .9.14 g
Sugar: . . . . .0.53 g
Fat: . . . . .10.64 g

6 chicken tenders, cut into 18 bite-
    sized pieces
¼ cup soy sauce
Juice of ½ lime
1 teaspoon Splenda
¼ teaspoon cayenne pepper
½ cup white sesame seeds

1. Cut the tenders in bite-sized pieces. Mix the soy sauce, lime, Splenda, and cayenne pepper in a resealable plastic bag. Add the tenders; shake to coat the chicken. Let marinate 20–30 minutes.

2. Preheat the broiler to 350°F. Prepare a cookie sheet with nonstick spray or coat it with aluminum foil.

3. Sprinkle the sesame seeds on a piece of waxed paper. Drain the tenders; press the seeds into the chicken pieces. Discard the marinade.

4. Broil, turning occasionally, 10 minutes. Reduce heat to 225°F; bake another 5 minutes. Serve hot.

Barbecue Wings

Yield 10: servings
Serving size: 3 whole wings

stats **Per serving:**

Calories: 179.09
Protein: . . . . 12.63 g
Carbohydrates: . . . . . . 7.20 g
Sugar: . . . . 1.83 g
Fat: . . . . 10.53 g

30 whole wings
1 quart water
1 cup Barbecue Sauce (page 389)
Tabasco sauce to taste

1. Remove the wing tips and halve the wings. Meanwhile, bring water to a boil.

2. Drop the wings into boiling water. Cover; reduce heat and boil gently 10 minutes. Pre-heat the broiler or indoor grill to 400°F.

3. Drain off the broth, reserving for stock. Prepare a broiler pan or indoor grill with non-stick spray.

4. Brush the wings with barbecue sauce; grill until browned. Serve hot with extra sugar-free barbecue sauce and Tabasco sauce on the side.

Healthy Snacks

Snacks should be an integral part of a good diet. They should have nutritional value, look appealing, be suitable for children and adults, and satisfy the need for "a little something."

Broiled Baby-Chicken Drumsticks with Asian Flavors and Sesame

Yields: 24 drumsticks
Serving size: 2 drumsticks

stats **Per serving:**

Calories: 307.56
Protein: . . . . .32.14 g
Carbohydrates: . . . . . .4.33 g
Sugar: . . . . .0.20 g
Fat: . . . . .17.26 g

*2 ounces Toasted Sesame Seed Oil
(page 135)*
1 tablespoon fresh lime juice
3 ounces soy sauce
1 teaspoon cayenne pepper
2 tablespoons cider vinegar
1 teaspoon Splenda
1 clove garlic, minced
*1" fresh gingerroot, peeled and
minced*
24 very small chicken drumsticks

1. Whisk the oil, lime juice, soy sauce, cayenne pepper, vinegar, Splenda, garlic, and gingerroot together in a nonreactive bowl. Add the chicken legs; turn to coat. Marinate at least 60 minutes.

2. Preheat the broiler or grill to 500°F. Drain the chicken; discard the marinade.

3. Prepare a broiler pan with nonstick spray or heat your charcoal grill to very high and set the grill well up from the coals.

4. Broil or grill the drumsticks, turning frequently, about 4 minutes per side. When nicely browned, serve with mango salsa or other chutney.

Smoked Turkey with Sour Apples

Yields: 4 servings

Serving size: 2 pieces of turkey-wrapped apple

stats **Per serving:**

Calories: 44.13
Protein: . . . . .5.02 g
Carbohydrates: . . . . . .5.31 g
Sugar: . . . . .3.98 g
Fat: . . . . .0.60 g

*1 tart green apple, peeled, cored, and
    cut in eighths*
Juice of ½ lemon
*4 thick slices deli smoked turkey,
    halved*

Core the apple and slice it; sprinkle with lemon juice. Wrap each piece of apple in a smoked-turkey slice. Use toothpicks, if needed, and serve.

Snacks Versus Treats

A snack is a small part of a healthy diet, something you can eat every day to maintain well-being. Snacks include fruit, raw veggies, cheese and crackers, even a half-sandwich. A treat is something you have rarely on special occasions. Treats include cookies, cakes, candy, and ice cream.

Zucchini, Feta, and Ricotta Pizza

Serves: 10
Serving size: 2 (2" × 2") squares

stats **Per serving:**

Calories: 234.46
Protein: . . . . .7.87 g
Carbohydrates: . . . . . .26.92 g
Sugar: . . . . .3.84 g
Fat: . . . . .10.75 g

1 pound sugar-free pizza dough
2 tablespoons olive oil
1 tablespoon dried oregano
Salt and pepper to taste
1 cup low-fat ricotta cheese
¼ cup feta cheese, crumbled
20 Sicilian or Greek black olives,
  pitted and chopped
4 small zucchini, ends trimmed and
  thinly sliced
1 sweet red onion, cut into paper-
  thin rings
2 tablespoons additional olive oil,
  placed in plastic spray bottle

1. Preheat the oven to 475°F. Prepare 2 cookie sheets with nonstick spray. Divide the dough in half and roll the dough into 2 (20" × 10") rectangles; place on the cookie sheets. Turn over the edges to make a ½" rim around the pizzas. Brush with olive oil.

2. Bake 6–8 minutes. Remove from the oven; sprinkle lightly with salt and pepper.

3. Mix the oregano, pepper, ricotta, feta, and chopped olives; spread evenly over the dough. Layer the zucchini and onions evenly atop the cheese mixture, pressing it down; spray with additional olive oil.

4. Bake 10–12 minutes. Cut, serve, and enjoy.

Sugar-Free Pizza

Make sure you either prepare your own sugar-free pizza dough or scour your grocery store for sugar-free mixes or premade crusts.

Miniature Crab Cakes

Yields: 16 cakes
Serving size: 2 crab cakes

 Per serving:

Calories: 116.95
Protein: . . . . 7.28 g
Carbohydrates: . . . . . . 6.31 g
Sugar: . . . . 0.82 g
Fat: . . . . 6.89 g

8 ounces crabmeat
¼ cup Basic Mayonnaise (page 122)
Juice and zest of ½ lemon
1 egg
1 tablespoon Chili Sauce (below)
2 tablespoons sweet white onion,
    minced
1 teaspoon dried dill weed or 1
    tablespoon fresh dill, snipped
1 teaspoon dry Dijon-style mustard
    blended with 2 teaspoons water
½ cup panko bread crumbs

1. Preheat the oven to 450°F. Prepare a baking sheet with nonstick spray.

2. Mix the crabmeat, mayonnaise, lemon, egg, chili sauce, onion, dill, and mustard together in a bowl. Spread the panko bread crumbs on a piece of waxed paper.

3. Make little burgers using about 1 tablespoonful of the crab mixture; coat with panko.

4. Bake 5 minutes. Turn; bake another 5 minutes, or until very crisp. Serve on slices of cucumber, leaves of romaine lettuce, or small pieces of bread.

Chili Sauce

Mix 2 28-ounce cans sugar-free whole Italian plum tomatoes, drained, 1 6-ounce can sugar-free tomato paste, 1 tablespoon garlic powder, 1 tablespoon onion powder, 1 tablespoon chili powder, or to taste, 1 teaspoon ground cloves, ½ teaspoon ground cinnamon, 4 teaspoons Splenda, 4 teaspoon DiabetiSweet Brown, 1 teaspoon salt, 1 teaspoon freshly ground black pepper, or to taste in a large, heavy-bottomed pot. Bring to a boil. Reduce heat and simmer with the cover slightly cracked. Stirring occasionally, simmer for about 3 hours or until the sauce is reduced by one-half. Cool, jar for storage, and refrigerate. Chili sauce will keep for 3–4 weeks. The analysis is: Calories: 2.48, Protein: 0.12 g, Carbohydrates: 0.58 g, Sugar: 0.02 g. Yields: 1 quart; Serving size: 1 teaspoon.

Baked Cherry Tomatoes Stuffed with Three Cheeses

Yields: 12 tomatoes
Serving size: 3 tomatoes

 Per serving:

Calories: 26.78
Protein: . . . . .1.75 g
Carbohydrates: . . . . . .1.02 g
Sugar: . . . . .0.15 g
Fat: . . . . .1.82 g

12 cherry tomatoes
¼ cup ricotta cheese
2 tablespoons Parmesan cheese
Freshly ground black pepper to taste
1 tablespoon fresh chives, snipped
¼ cup grated aged Cheddar cheese

1. Preheat oven to 375°F.

2. Prepare a baking sheet with nonstick spray. Cut the tops off the tomatoes. Use a melon-ball scoop to scoop out the inside pulp and seeds.

3. Mix the ricotta, Parmesan, pepper, and chives; stuff the tomatoes. Sprinkle the tops with the Cheddar cheese. Bake 10–12 minutes. Serve hot or warm.

Crunchy Mini Panini with Tomato, Basil, and Provolone Cheese

Serves: 4
Serving size: ½ sandwich

stats **Per serving:**

Calories:............245.96
Protein:..............9.86 g
Carbohydrates: ......17.07 g
Sugar: ....2.30 g
Fat:.................11.96 g

4 slices sugar-free Italian bread
4 tablespoons oil-and-vinegar
    dressing
4 slices ripe tomato
8 medium basil leaves
4 thin slices Provolone
Sugar-free bacon or sugar-free
    prosciutto (optional)

1. Prepare the grill or pan with nonstick spray. Brush both sides of each piece of bread with dressing. Stack the ingredients with pieces of cheese to "glue" them together. Heat the pan to medium.

2. Grill the sandwiches until one side is brown. Turn and grill the other side. Cut and serve.

tip

If you don't have a panini maker, use an indoor grill or a frying pan. If you are using a frying pan, simply put another heavy pan on top of the sandwich with a weight in it.

Panini

These lovely Italian sandwiches enjoyed a recent surge in popularity in little restaurants all over the country. Some are like Philly cheese steaks, others filled with brie and roasted peppers. Be creative: They are wonderful either cut in small pieces as a snack or served whole for lunch. Vary the ingredients of the recipe based on what you have on hand.

Cucumber Slices Piled with Mascarpone Cheese, Shallots, and Prosciutto

Yields: 12 slices
Serving size: 2 slices

stats **Per serving:**

Calories:.............63.76
Protein:.............2.58 g
Carbohydrates:......1.26 g
Sugar: ....0.79 g
Fat:.................5.40 g

*4 tablespoons mascarpone cheese,
    room temperature*
2 shallots, minced
Freshly ground black pepper to taste
12 slices English cucumber
*3 paper-thin slices prosciutto, cut in
    thin strips*

1. Mix the cheese and shallots together; sprinkle with pepper. Place the cucumber slices on a plate.

2. Place a teaspoon of the cheese-shallot mixture on each cucumber slice; cross the strips of prosciutto on top.

You can substitute cream cheese for mascarpone and smoked sugar-free ham or smoked salmon for prosciutto.

Sweet-and-Spicy Toasted Nut Mix

Yields: 18 servings
Serving size: 8 nuts

stats **Per serving:**

Calories: 204.85
Protein:. . . . . .4.63 g
Carbohydrates: . . . . . .4.70 g
Sugar: . . . . .0.84 g
Fat:. . . . . .19.71 g

¼ cup Diabetes Sweet
½ cup unsalted butter, melted
2 teaspoons freshly ground black
   pepper
1 teaspoon coarse salt
½ pound blanched almonds
½ pound walnut halves

1. Preheat the oven to 400°F. Prepare a baking sheet with parchment paper or nonstick spray. Whisk the Diabetes Sweet, butter, pepper, and salt together in a large bowl.

2. Stir in the nuts; turn until all are covered. Spread on the baking sheet; bake 10–12 minutes, checking often.

3. Cool at room temperature, and store.

Nuts!

You can roast them, salt them, fry them, glaze them, and add them to all sorts of treats. Put them on desserts, add them to trail mix and salads, and even throw some toasted pine nuts into a salsa. Float them on top of soups or add them to cream cheese for some added crunch in your next sandwich.

Artichoke-and-Spinach Dip

Serves: 20–30

Serving size: 3 teaspoons on 3 crackers

 Per serving:

Calories: 51.61
Protein: . . . . .1.74 g
Carbohydrates: . . . . . .2.12 g
Sugar: . . . . .0.93 g
Fat: . . . . .4.18 g

10 ounces frozen chopped spinach, thawed
1 cup artichoke hearts, drained
8 ounces low-fat cream cheese at room temperature
½ cup sweet onion, minced
Juice of ½ lemon
¼ cup Basic Mayonnaise (page 122)
¼ cup low-fat sour cream
½ teaspoon cayenne pepper
⅛ teaspoon nutmeg
1 teaspoon Splenda
1 tablespoon Parmesan cheese

1. Preheat oven to 350°F. Squeeze the moisture out of the spinach and press the oil out of the artichokes. Puree all ingredients except the Parmesan cheese in a food processor.

2. Prepare a 1-quart baking dish with non-stick spray. Turn the spinach dip into the dish; sprinkle with Parmesan cheese. Bake 30 minutes.

Serve this dip in a hollowed round loaf of bread. Surround the dip with crackers or thinly sliced pieces of sugar-free sourdough baguette.

Dry Versus Prepared Mustard

Prepared mustards are generally mixed with sugar, vinegar, and sometimes spices. It's best to prepare your own mustard to make sure there is no sugar in it. You can also add all kinds of flavorings to it and make it very much your own invention.

Middle-Eastern Black-Bean Dip

Yields: 12 servings
Serving size: 1 ounce

 Per serving:

Calories:............112.15
Protein:.............6.91 g
Carbohydrates: ......26.66 g
Sugar: ....4.37 g
Fat:.................0.42 g

1 cup pineapple juice, no sugar
*   added*
1 tablespoon Splenda
1 tablespoon curry powder
1 teaspoon cayenne pepper
1 tablespoon almond paste
1 (15-ounce) can black beans,
*   drained and rinsed*
Salt and pepper to taste

1. In a small saucepan over high heat, whisk the pineapple juice, Splenda, curry, cayenne, and almond paste together. Bring to a boil; reduce heat to medium, and cook until reduced by half.

2. Let the sauce cool slightly. Place in the blender; add beans, and blend until pureed. Salt and pepper to taste

Eat Beans!

Beans are a great source of fiber and protein, and are very versatile. You can use beans in savory dishes and to complement onions and garlic. They also work well with sweet/hot concoctions such as this recipe. The best thing about beans is they are cheap. If you are on a tight budget, buy dry beans and soak them overnight before cooking.

Family Favorites

Kiwi Balls with Frosted Strawberries

Yields: 4 servings
Serving size: ¼ cup

 Per serving:

Calories:............40.22
Protein:.............0.73 g
Carbohydrates: ......10.06 g
Sugar: ....5.74 g
Fat:.................0.38 g

1 tablespoon Splenda
1 teaspoon cornstarch
½ teaspoon vanilla extract
1 teaspoon freshly squeezed lemon
    juice
1 tablespoon cold water
2 kiwi fruit, halved
12 medium-sized strawberries, hulled
    and halved

1. Whisk the Splenda, cornstarch, vanilla extract, lemon juice, and water together to make frosting. Set aside.

2. Use a melon-ball scoop to make balls of the kiwi fruit. Put kiwis and strawberries in a bowl.

3. Take a heavy-duty plastic bag; cut a tiny piece from the corner. Spoon the frosting mixture into the bag; drizzle over the fruit.

4. Chill and serve.

Favorite Tools

Every kitchen needs two tiny implements: a melon-ball scoop and a grapefruit spoon. The melon-ball scoop is great for more than melon balls; it scoops up tiny tastes of all sorts of goodies. The grapefruit spoon has a sharp point and is excellent for cutting out the insides of tomatoes, avocados, potatoes, and many other foods.

Frozen Grapes

Yields: 1 pound grapes
Serving size: 4 ounces

 Per serving:

Calories: 135.51
Protein: . . . . .4.75 g
Carbohydrates: . . . . . .29.65 g
Sugar: . . . . .26.52 g
Fat: . . . . .0.66 g

1 pound grapes, rinsed
2 teaspoons Splenda
lemon yogurt with no sugar added

1. Prepare a cookie sheet with nonstick spray. Place the damp grapes on the cookie sheet; sprinkle with Splenda, and freeze.

2. Use commercial lemon yogurt with no sugar as a dipping sauce for the frozen grapes.

Chocolate-Dipped Strawberries

Yields: 4 servings
Serving size: 4 strawberries

 stats **Per serving:**

Calories: 140.20
Protein: . . . . 2.94 g
Carbohydrates: . . . . . . 54.82 g
Sugar: . . . . 4.21 g
Fat: . . . . 12.03 g

3 ounces unsweetened chocolate
3 ounces Splenda
2 tablespoons strong decaffeinated
coffee
Pinch of salt
½ teaspoon vanilla
1 pint long-stemmed strawberries,
rinsed and chilled

1. Mix the chocolate, Splenda, coffee, salt, and vanilla; melt in a double boiler over simmering water. If you don't have a double boiler, melt in the microwave 10 seconds.

2. Dip the strawberries in the chocolate; lay on a piece of waxed paper. Refrigerate, and serve.

 tip

Try to find strawberries with nice long stems so you don't have to use a fork.

Involving the Kids

If children can help prepare a snack or a meal, they will be much more interested in eating it than if you merely set it in front of them. That is one of the secrets of establishing healthy eating habits.

Family Ice Cream

Yields: 16 ounces
Serving size: 4 ounces

 Per serving:

Calories: 281.00
Protein: . . . . 6.89 g
Carbohydrates: . . . . . . 52.72 g
Sugar: . . . . 8.94 g
Fat: . . . . 20.40 g

¾ cup half-n-half
6 tablespoons Splenda
½ cup fresh fruit sauce
1-pound coffee can with plastic lid
2-pound coffee can with plastic lid
Cracked ice
Kosher salt

1. Mix the half-and-half, Splenda, and Fresh Fruit Sauce together; place in the 1-pound can. Close the lid tightly; put it inside the 2-pound can.

2. Fill the sides of the 2-pound can with alternating layers of cracked ice and salt until you get to the top. Close the top lid tightly. Seat the children on the floor and have them "churn" the ice cream by rolling the tin around, back and forth. Soon the ice cream will thicken and stop moving in the coffee can, and—WOW! Fresh ice cream! Enjoy!

tip

To make this ice cream, you must have immaculately clean coffee cans. Remember, when the ice cream becomes aerated, it will expand, so be sure to leave room in the container.

Popcorn with Hot-Pepper Butter

Yields: ½ cup of pepper butter (for 4 cups of popcorn)
Serving size: 1 cup pepper-buttered popcorn

stats **Per serving:**

Calories:............223.78
Protein:.............0.73 g
Carbohydrates: ......4.18 g
Sugar: ....0.07 g
Fat:.................22.55 g

½ cup unsalted butter
½ teaspoon celery salt
1 teaspoon ground cayenne pepper
1 package plain or low-salt
   microwave popcorn

1. Mix the butter, celery salt, and cayenne pepper in a cup; heat them in the microwave just a few seconds.

2. Blend well. Then pop your corn, and toss it in a bowl with the butter sauce.

tip

You can substitute other seasoned salts, such as garlic, onion, or lemon-pepper seasoning.

If Variety Is the Spice of Life . . .

Seasoned salts and spicy peppers will help vary your flavorings. Try different combinations, such as a mixture of celery salt, ground coriander seeds, orange zest, and garlic powder.

Kids' Favorite Meatloaf

Yields: 16 (½") slices (Standard bread pan 4½" × 8½" × 2½")
Serving size: 1 (½") slice

 Per serving:

Calories: 105.80
Protein: . . . . 5.70 g
Carbohydrates: . . . . . . 6.35 g
Sugar: . . . . 1.89 g
Fat: . . . . 6.47 g

2 whole eggs
2½" thick slices Hot Corn Bread with
Cherry Peppers (page 61)
¼ cup Chili Sauce (page 365)
½ cup low-fat milk
½ teaspoon salt
¼ teaspoon pepper, or to taste
¼ cup grated Parmesan cheese
1 teaspoon dried oregano
1 pound ground meatloaf mix (beef, pork and veal) or beef
Optional: 1 slice sugar-free turkey bacon or regular bacon

1. Preheat the oven to 325°F. Whirl everything but the meat and bacon in your blender.

2. Prepare a bread pan with nonstick spray. Pour the ingredients in the blender into a large bowl. Add the meat; mix thoroughly. Pile into the bread pan without tamping it down.

3. Add bacon to the top, if that is your choice. Bake the meatloaf 60 minutes. Let cool slightly before cutting.

Mini Pizzas with Broccoli and Cheese

Yields: 4 (6") pizzas
Serving size: ½ pizza

stats **Per serving:**

Calories:............181.10
Protein:.............8.85 g
Carbohydrates: ......19.32 g
Sugar: ....2.86 g
Fat:.................7.45 g

½ pound broccoli florets, chopped
    and blanched
1-pound package sugar-free pizza
    dough or homemade pizza
    dough
2 teaspoons extra-virgin olive oil
1 teaspoon dried oregano
1 teaspoon cayenne pepper, or to
    taste
6 thin slices mozzarella cheese
¼ cup finely grated Parmesan cheese

1. Preheat oven to 450°F. Blanch the broccoli, drain it, and set it aside on paper towels.

2. Prepare a cookie sheet with nonstick spray, or use a pizza stone. Roll the dough out in a 12" × 12" square. Cut into 4 squares.

3. Turn the edges of the dough over by ½" to make a rim. Brush the dough with olive oil. Sprinkle with oregano and cayenne; spread broccoli and add the mozzarella, cutting the 2 extra pieces to fill in gaps.

4. Sprinkle with Parmesan; bake 15 minutes, or until the crust is nicely browned.

Endless Pizza Variations

You can make pizza with spinach, asparagus, peppers, or whatever you like. Try using oils infused with basil and/or garlic. Most kids will eat their veggies when they are incorporated into a pizza.

Marinated Chicken Tenders on Toothpicks

Serves 6–8: as a snack
Serving size: 2–3 tenders

 **Per serving:**

Calories: 166.36
Protein:. . . . . .11.23 g
Carbohydrates: . . . . . .15.77 g
Sugar: . . . . .3.25 g
Fat:. . . . . .6.57 g

*1 pound chicken tenders, cut in bite-
    sized pieces, on toothpicks*
*18 wooden toothpicks, soaked 20
    minutes in warm water*
*1 tablespoon Toasted Sesame Seed
    Oil (Page 135)*
½ cup orange juice, no sugar added
3 tablespoons tamari sauce
3 tablespoons Chili Sauce (page 365)
1 teaspoon Basic Mustard (page 98)

1. Cut the tenders into 1" pieces; put 1 or 2 on each presoaked toothpick. In a bowl, whisk the rest of the ingredients together; coat each piece of chicken.

2. Cover the bowl and marinate in the refrigerator at least 60 minutes, or up to 3 hours. Preheat broiler or grill to 400°F.

3. Grill or broil chicken about 5 minutes per side, depending on the thickness. Turn them often until nicely browned.

Turkey Meatballs

Yields: 32 tiny meatballs
(in standard-size bread pan)
Serving size: 3 meatballs

 Per serving:

Calories:............284.39
Protein:.............8.13 g
Carbohydrates: ......3.55 g
Sugar: ....0.34 g
Fat:.................26.73 g

2 cloves garlic, peeled
2 tablespoons chopped onion
2 slices sugar-free bread, such as
    Italian bread, cubed
1 egg
¼ teaspoon cinnamon
1 teaspoon oregano
Salt and pepper to taste
¼ cup grated Romano cheese
1 pound ground turkey
1 cup canola oil for frying

1. Put all of the ingredients but the meat and oil into your blender; whirl until well blended. Place the meat in a large bowl; pour the mixture from the blender over it.

2. Mix thoroughly; form into 32 meatballs. Heat the oil to 375°F in a frying pan; fry the meatballs until brown. Drain on paper towels.

Family Food

Good food must always be nutritious, and served with plenty of excellent baby veggies, such as grape tomatoes, little carrots, sticks of celery, rings of sweet peppers and/or raw broccoli and cauliflower florets. Peppers are delicious and have the most nutrients in red, orange, and yellow.

Cranberry-Walnut Spread

Yields: 2 cups
Serving size: 1 tablespoon

 Per serving:

Calories: 34.27
Protein: . . . . .0.79 g
Carbohydrates: . . . . . .1.05 g
Sugar: . . . . .0.41 g
Fat: . . . . .3.08 g

8 ounces cream cheese, softened to
    room temperature
¼ cup dried cranberries, no sugar
    added
¼ cup chopped walnuts, toasted
¼ cup celery, minced
1 teaspoon Splenda
Salt and freshly ground pepper to
    taste

Place all ingredients in a bowl; mix thoroughly. Use as a spread on sugar-free crackers or bread. This will keep in the refrigerator 4 days.

Chicken, Apple, and Celery Spread

Yields: 2¾ cups spread
Serving size: 2 tablespoons

stats **Per serving:**

Calories:............115.33
Protein:.............5.8 g
Carbohydrates:......2.1 g
Sugar: ....1.35 g
Fat:................9.37 g

1 cup Basic Mayonnaise (Page 122)
1 teaspoon sweet-and-sour mustard
Salt and pepper to taste
½ teaspoon Splenda
½ teaspoon freshly squeezed lime
    juice
½ teaspoon curry powder, or to taste
¾ pound cooked chicken (leftovers
    are fine), diced
½ cup fresh apple, cored and diced
¼ cup white onion, minced
¼ cup celery, diced small
¼ cup peanuts, chopped
Optional garnish: 1 cup green grapes
    or raisins

Whisk the mayonnaise, mustard, salt and pepper, Splenda, lime juice, and curry together in a bowl. When well mixed, stir in the rest of the items. Chill and serve later, or serve right away.

Skewered Shrimp with Bacon

Serves: 6

Serving size: 4 jumbo shrimp or 6 extra-large shrimp

 Per serving:

Calories: 314.84
Protein: . . . . .17.97 g
Carbohydrates: . . . . . . .0.72 g
Sugar: . . . . .0.03 g
Fat: . . . . .26.03 g

1 pound fresh or thawed frozen, raw
    shrimp (about 24 per pound)
¼ cup unsalted butter, melted
½ teaspoon garlic powder
Pepper to taste
8 strips of bacon, stretched, cut in
    thirds

1. Dip each shrimp in a combination of melted butter, garlic powder, and pepper.

2. Set broiler to 375°F. Wrap the shrimp with bacon; secure with presoaked wooden toothpicks.

3. Broil the shrimp until the bacon is cooked and the shrimp are pink, about 4–5 minutes per side.

Family-Style Hungarian Goulash

Serves: 6
Serving size: 1 cup

 Per serving:

Calories:............491.62
Protein:.............29.44 g
Carbohydrates: ......9.80 g
Sugar: ....3.20 g
Fat:.................36.78 g

2 tablespoons peanut oil
1 tablespoon unsalted butter
3 yellow onions, peeled, cut into
    coarse dice
2 pounds stewing veal, boneless
1 tablespoon whole-wheat flour
1 teaspoon salt
½ teaspoon freshly ground black
    pepper, or to taste
1 tablespoon paprika
1 teaspoon Splenda
1 teaspoon caraway seeds
1 teaspoon dried marjoram leaves
1 tablespoon red wine vinegar
1 cup beef broth
1 cup tomato juice, no sugar added
1 cup sour cream (optional)

1. Preheat the oven to 325°F. Prepare a 2-quart casserole with nonstick spray. In a large frying pan over medium heat, add one tablespoon of the oil and the butter. Add the onion; cook and stir until softened, but not browned.

2. Scrape the onions into the casserole. Add the second tablespoon of oil; stir in the beef. Brown the beef; add to the casserole with the onion.

3. Add all but the sour cream, one thing at a time, stirring to blend. Cover; set in the oven 2 hours, or until the veal is very tender. If the liquid dries out, add some more broth or tomato juice.

4. Just before serving, add the sour cream. Serve over noodles.

Deviled Eggs with Olives

Serves: 6
Serving size: 2 half-eggs

 Per serving:

Calories: 216.35
Protein:. . . . . .6.52 g
Carbohydrates: . . . . . .1.48 g
Sugar: . . . . .0.64 g
Fat:. . . . . .20.37 g

6 hardboiled eggs, shelled and cooled
½ cup Basic Mayonnaise (Page 122)
1 teaspoon sweet-and-sour mustard
½ teaspoon garlic salt
Freshly ground pepper to taste
12 small black or green pitted olives,
    chopped

1. Cut the peeled eggs in half. Arrange the whites on a plate, scooping the yolks into a bowl. Using an immersion blender or a fork, beat in the rest of the ingredients, one by one, until well blended.

2. Fill the eggs, and either serve immediately or refrigerate, covered.

387

Deviled Eggs with Smoked Salmon

Yields: 6 eggs
Serving size: ½ egg with ½ ounce smoked salmon on top

stats **Per serving:**

Calories:............68.12 g
Protein:.............4.54 g
Carbohydrates:......0.60 g
Sugar: ....0.36 g
Fat:................9.93 g

6 hardboiled eggs, peeled
½ cup Basic Mayonnaise (page 122)
2 tablespoons green onions, minced
½ teaspoon Basic Mustard (page 98)
½ teaspoon white wine vinegar
Salt and pepper to taste
½ teaspoon Splenda
2 ounces smoked salmon (lox), cut in small matchstick pieces

1. Arrange the egg halves on a platter. Blend everything but the salmon in a bowl, using an immersion blender or a fork.

2. Stuff the eggs with the yolk mixture. Decorate the tops with strips of smoked salmon.

Skewered Chicken Tenders with Sate

Serves 6: as a snack, 3 for lunch
Serving size: 3 tenders

 Per serving:

Calories: 171.04
Protein: . . . . .9.96 g
Carbohydrates: . . . . . .14.82 g
Sugar: . . . . .1.79 g
Fat: . . . . .8.63 g

½ pound chicken tenders, cut in thirds (about 18 pieces)
1 cup Barbecue Sauce (see below)

For the Sate:

¼ cup sugar-free peanut butter
Juice of ½ lime
½ teaspoon Splenda
2 tablespoons tamari

1. Preheat the broiler to 350°F. Dip the tenders in the Barbecue Sauce; broil 4 minutes per side.

2. Whisk all of the sate ingredients in a small bowl. Using toothpicks for the chicken, dip in the sauce.

Barbecue Sauce

Heat 2 tablespoons of oil in a 1-quart pot over medium heat. Add ¼ cup sweet white minced onions and 3 cloves minced garlic and sauté. Add 2 cups Chili Sauce (page 365), ½ cup sugar-free tomato juice, 1 teaspoon Basic Mustard (page 98), 1 teaspoon liquid smoke, 2 tablespoons cider vinegar, 1 tablespoon orange zest, 1 teaspoon lemon zest, 1/8 teaspoon cinnamon, 2 tablespoons DiabetiSweet Brown, 1 teaspoon soy sauce, cayenne pepper to taste, stir, cover, and reduce heat. Simmer for 45 minutes or until reduced to 2 cups of sauce. Cool and place in a jar. This will keep for two weeks when refrigerated. The analysis is: Calories: 28.89, Protein: 0.75 g, Carbohydrates: 4.07 g, Sugar: 2.48 g, Fat: 1.59 g. Yields: 16 ounces; Serving size: 1 ounce.

Cheese Soufflé with Artichokes and Spinach

Serves: 6
Serving size: 6 ounces

stats **Per serving:**

Calories:............215.11
Protein:..............9.12 g
Carbohydrates: ......8.42 g
Sugar: ....3.22 g
Fat:................16.27 g

1 tablespoon unsalted butter
1 tablespoon flour
½ cup marinated artichokes (from
    the jar is fine), drained and
    chopped
1 (10-ounce) package frozen chopped
    spinach, thawed and moisture
    squeezed out
1 tablespoon unsalted butter
1 tablespoon cornstarch
1 cup milk
½ cup grated Cheddar cheese
Salt and pepper to taste
6 eggs, separated

1. Preheat oven to 375°F. Spread a 2-quart soufflé dish or casserole with butter; sprinkle with flour to cover.

2. Put the well-drained vegetables in a bowl. In a saucepan, melt the butter; whisk in the cornstarch, let foam, and slowly whisk in the milk. When thickened, add the cheese, salt, pepper, and vegetables. Set aside.

3. Beat the egg yolks; add them to the vegetables and sauce. Using clean beaters and bowl, beat the egg whites until stiff.

4. Fold the egg whites into the vegetables and sauce. Bake in the middle of the oven 35 minutes. Serve instantly. Don't open the oven door too soon, or your soufflé will sou-flop.

Index

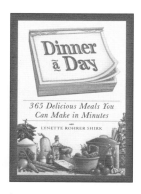